BRITAIN REVISITED

BRITAIN REVISITED

by

TOM HARRISSON

with
Leonard England
Celia Fremlin
Bill Naughton
John Sommerfield
Mollie Tarrant
Woodrow Wyatt

Illustrations by
Humphrey Spender
Julian Trevelyan
Michael Wickham

With a Postscript by
Professor Charles Madge

faber and faber

This edition first published in 2009
by Faber and Faber Ltd
Bloomsbury House, 74–77 Great Russell Street
London WC1B 3DA

Printed by CPI Antony Rowe, Eastbourne

All rights reserved
© Tom Harrisson, 1961

The right of Tom Harrisson to be identified as author of this work has been asserted in accordance with Section 77 of the Copyright, Designs and Patents Act 1988

This book is sold subject to the condition that it shall not, by way of trade or otherwise, be lent, resold, hired out or otherwise circulated without the publisher's prior consent in any form of binding or cover other than that in which it is published and without a similar condition including this condition being imposed on the subsequent purchaser

A CIP record for this book is available from the British Library

ISBN 978–0–571–25215–2

"Our words, our concepts, only name
A world of shadows; for the truth is plain"
Kathleen Raine,
"The Speech of Birds"

"I doubt if anything new or useful can be said or discovered at this stage in history about human conduct and motives. The sages and philosophers have been at it since the beginning of time. In pronouncing on your fellows you already have a wide range of choice."
George Schwartz,
Sunday Times
21 August 1960

FOR

Mary Adams
Penelope Barlow
Diana Brinton-Lee
Naomi Mitchison
Gay Taylor
Dr. Gertrud Wagner

and the late
Zita Crossman

Miss-Observers of the early days
T.H.

CONTENTS

1. Mass-Observation: a Brief Background — 15

A. WORKTOWN AND ELSEWHERE: OCCUPATIONS AND INSTITUTIONS

2. "Discovering" Worktown, 1936 — 25
3. Recovered: 1960 — 28
4. For God's Sake! — 46
5. To Vote or Not... — 85
6. Some Machinery of Democracy — 104
7. A Week-end to Worktown (with Voices in Character) — 107

B. FACES, PLACES: 1937–60

8. Photos and Pictures — 139

C. LEISURE PLEASURES ANYWHERE

9. Around the Tower — 143
10. The Pub and its People — 168
11. Up in Smoke — 196
12. The Telly—how Important? — 204
13. Totemism in our Time—with a spot of Spiritualism — 216

D. OPINIONS AND PROJECTS, NATION-WIDE

14. Royal Occasions — 229
15. Margins of Knowledge, Interest and Taste — 252
16. Who is/was Who? — 263
17. Panorama of Projects, 1937–60. — 267

Postscript — 275
Index — 281

LIST OF ILLUSTRATIONS

PART B

FACES, PLACES: 1937–60
following page 160

1. Worktown, 1960; a drawing by Humphrey Spender
2. The Christian Year preserves the pre-industrial life, *photo Humphrey Spender*
3. The Funeral, 1937, *photo Humphrey Spender*
4. Bethel Evangelical Sunbeam service: strict fundamentalist sect, *photo Humphrey Spender*
5. The act of voting, November 1937, *photo Humphrey Spender*
6. The late George Tomlinson M.P., successful candidate in the Farnworth Parliamentary Election (and later Minister of Education), *photo Humphrey Spender*
7. Listening to Clem Attlee, Worktown Labour Party, *photo Humphrey Spender*
8. Marking up the canvass, Worktown, 1937, *photo Humphrey Spender*
9. Party propaganda (Municipal election), *photo Humphrey Spender*
10. Dominoes in the Vault, *photo Humphrey Spender*
11. With the wife, Saloon Bar, *photo Humphrey Spender*
12. Corner of the bar—"a regular", *photo Humphrey Spender*
13. Closing time, *photo Humphrey Spender*

14. Steps of the Town Hall—a temperance speaker in full 1937 blast, *photo Humphrey Spender*

15. Children's playground 1937, *photo Humphrey Spender*

16. Operating the Lucky Grab on Blackpool promenade, *photo Humphrey Spender*

17. "Fruit Machines" 1937—illegal in 1960; the girl is a "decoy" bringing in the hicks, *photo Humphrey Spender*

18. Blackpool 1937: the Professor, *photo Humphrey Spender*

19. The Colonel, *photo Humphrey Spender*

20. "Win a Dolly," *photo Humphrey Spender*

21. The Golden Mile: strip-tease of 1960, *photo Michael Wickham*

22. At Gypsy Rosalee's 1960 booth, *photo Michael Wickham*

23. Looking up the Golden Mile, the Tower in the background, *photo Michael Wickham*

24. 83-87 Davenport Street, Worktown, August 1960, *photo Michael Wickham*

25. The latest in exterior decoration, next door to Davenport Street, *photo Michael Wickham*

26. Kids play in 1960 Davenport Street, *photo Michael Wickham*

27. "Keaw Yed"—a slight spot of totemism in Westhoughton, 27 August 1960, *photo Michael Wickham*

28. Relaxed in the "Red Lion" Lounge, *photo Michael Wickham*

29. Westhoughton Wakes' Funfair. The Baby Sputnik, the most modern attraction, *photo Michael Wickham*

LIST OF ILLUSTRATIONS

30. Worktown scene 1937. Collage by Julian Trevelyan

31. Worktown scene 1960. Ink drawing by Julian Trevelyan

Line drawings in the text are by Rayner Atkin (pages 141 and 195), Humphrey Spender (page 30) and Julian Trevelyan (all others). Graphs have been prepared by Mass-Observation.

The four-page inset after page 78 is a scale replica of one in a series of leaflets (described in Chapter 6) devised by T. H. for use in experimentally influencing voting in Worktown (and later other) elections. But the original in this case was in the same red colours and identical in size with those in use by the leading Football Pools firm of that time (1938)—which this leaflet superficially resembled exactly.

This is the hour of cock-crow and the men
Whose night was out of bounds clock in again,
(As innocent in sleep as plant or stone)
Wake to do wrong, grow old, and suffer pain.
                              Kathleen Raine
                              "Good Friday"

ONE

MASS-OBSERVATION: A BRIEF BACKGROUND

IN THE THIRTIES a situation developed in which a dangerous gap had widened between the ordinary and rather non-vocal masses of Britain and a highly specialised set of organs and organisations supposedly speaking for *all* through Parliament, Press, radio, etc. In circumstances to be described in the next chapter, the present writer was working towards an effort to tackle this situation by social research when he went to live and work in a Lancashire cotton town after returning from a then "cannibal island" in the South Seas. Quite separately, the poet Charles Madge—then a *Daily Mirror* reporter, now Professor of Sociology at Birmingham University—was approaching the same situation by a rather more literary method, aided by a lively group of friends, including the late Humphrey Jennings and Stuart Legge as documentary film makers; David Gascoyne, Ruthven Todd and Charles's wife Kathleen as poets, and William Empson.[1] From the industrial north, a more objective-aimed approach; from London in the south, a literary and documentary one, including the important idea of recruiting a nation-wide panel to report upon their own everyday lives and all that goes on around them (a source which has provided superb material, only touched on in the present account). We joined forces, north and south, as *Mass-Observation*.

★   ★   ★

Mass-Observation was first widely registered in a pamphlet of that name in 1937, after initial letters in the *New Statesman* of 2 January and 30 January 1937. The first full published M-O operation was a study of the Coronation, 12 May 1937, which was the subject of a large volume (by Faber and Faber) later that year.[2]

Now TV star and Labour M.P., then an undergraduate spending vacations from Oxford with M-O, Woodrow Wyatt specialised in analysing our public relations impacts. (He has written of this time amusingly in his book, *Into This Dangerous World*, Harrap, 1952.)

[1] Bill Empson, author of *Seven Types of Ambiguity*, also joined in the northern study and did some refined observing, unequivocally.

[2] A bibliography of M-O's published volumes is given at the end of the present book, Chapter 17.

Early in 1938 Woodrow Wyatt meticulously studied 62,000 words of outside writing covering the period of 4 June–15 December 1937. We were a bit solemn about some statistics in those days, and applied them to this mass of stuff on a set of classification criteria (described in some detail in our *First Year's Work* book, the following year). Rather over half of the early comment was (in this analysis) hostile, and some of it angry. Considered in relation to the general political character of the paper or journal, we got:

Slant of source	% of this slant with mainly unfavourable conclusions
Right wing	45
"Centre"	23
Left	50
General total	40

"Liberal" sources were kindest, leftists (including most intellectuals) meanest. There was a distinct difference between London and the provinces, however—well reflecting the then acute *centralisation* of "opinion-forming" mechanisms in W1, WC1 and SW1; and the consequent "provincial" feeling of a need for more reportage on "ordinary opinion".

Here are a few selected comments from long ago. Phrases are not unfairly out of their context; none of those quoted complained when we counter-attacked them with these quotations then:

1. a) "Subjective views"—*Tribune*, 26 November 1937
   b) "Fine objective reports"—*Daily Express* (Tom Driberg as Hickey), 5 June
   c) "Set down with admirable objectivity"—*Birmingham Evening Dispatch* (Maurice Wiggin), 27 September (see also p. 133)
2. a) "These boring reports"—*New Statesman* (G. W. Stonier), 9 October
   b) "Very great interest"—*Times Lit. Sup.* 2 October
3. a) "Truth so partial that it is scarcely truth"—*Sunday Times* (Dilys Powell), 10 October (see also p. 132)
   b) "No attempt to draw conclusions"—*Daily Worker*, 29 August
   c) "Mania for generalising and drawing conclusions on the flimsiest evidence"—*Daily Mail*, 23 August
   d) "Exhaustive, profound, unique and detailed"—*Lancashire Daily Post*, 1 June
   e) "Tends to stop at the collection of fact"—*Time and Tide*, 25 September
   f) "Facts simply multiply like maggots in a cheese and leave no shape"—*Listener*, 17 November
4. a) "Busybodies of the left . . . scientifically they are about as valuable as the chimpanzees' tea party at the Zoo"—*Spectator*, 19 November

b) "Some of the day surveys I have seen would put many orthodox scientists to shame"—Sir Julian Huxley, F.R.S. (then Secretary of the Zoo)
c) "This sociological research is of very real importance"—*Armchair Science*, 1 October
d) "A new sort of scientific investigation"—*Daily Herald*, 4 June
e) "A great deal of pseudo-scientific showmanship"—*Night and Day* (Evelyn Waugh), 14 October
5. a) "These apparently delight to stand and stare at those who delight to stand and stare"—*Observer* (Ivor Brown, Editor), 7 June
b) "If I catch anyone Mass-observing me, there's going to be trouble"—*News Chronicle* (F. Montague, Labour M.P.), 8 June

But Mr. Montague lived to have Mass-Observation study political problems in his constituency, the *Observer* to feature M-O results.

We had to fight quite a battle for acceptance of the idea that it was proper intimately to study ourselves. An advance was marked when Allen Lane published a fuller report as a Penguin Special, *Britain by Mass-Observation*, which sold hugely in 1938-9—in this, one of our theme studies was the St. Bartholomew's Day "Cow Head Festival" at Westhoughton, revisited (like much else of that volume) in what follows (Chaper 13). Today no one any longer seriously questions not only the right but the *need* to study such things in Britain.

★   ★   ★

In the nineteen-thirties, astonishingly little bridged the gulf between the organs of supposed power (Press, BBC, etc.) in Britain and the mass of relatively non-vociferous Britishers. In the nineteen-sixties there is much better linkage, mainly in one direction: that of the expression of popular views through statistical sampling for opinion polls (Press) and market research (consumer surveys and private client studies).

Mass-Observation helped trigger off this development on this side of the Atlantic; and in several respects was the first unit to draw wide attention to this type of research need. But what we principally set out to do then was to *observe*—to observe the *mass* and seek to have the mass observe itself: the first by field study (mainly our northern interest) of actual behaviour under normal living conditions; the second (mainly of interest to Charles Madge and his friends in London) through self-documentation and "subjective" reportage, including the network of voluntary, candid informants in all walks of life.

A good deal of what we then set out to do has not really been developed further since. It remains as a major gap not only in the science but in the common sense of our ever more complicated society. "*Public* opinion" is no longer so easily manipulated, or invented to suit editorial or advertiser policy. Much else outside public opinion still is so. In some ways, indeed, the advances in direct opinion-study methods by interview sampling have tended to obscure other research approaches, and other levels of human performance too.

* * *

So long as we continue to talk about "public opinion" as an all-embracing generality, we must have trouble in seeing some vital problems. First there are three main "levels" of behaviour: SAY–DO–THINK. What a person *says* (or writes) that he will do is often quite different from what he does actually do. What he thinks he will do, or thinks he will say, may also be very different from what he does do or say (or write). These distinctions are of fundamental *practical* importance to the understanding of social and political processes, in terms of actual field research. Their analysis and description in factual terms has barely yet been attempted in Britain. For the moment, consider only one aspect—what people *say*; within this we must distinguish:

What a person says to a stranger
„ „   „   „   „ an acquaintance (or writes to his M.P.)
„ „   „   „   „ a friend
„ „   „   „   „ his wife (and/or lover)
„ „   „   „   „ himself (or puts in his diary—different again)
„ „   „   „   „ in his sleep

It is often at the level of wife, self and dream that the most significant, as well as the most difficult, assessment of opinion can be made. This may be termed the level of private opinion—and can only be reached, ordinarily, by intimate self reportage. At the top level, the level of stranger (e.g. an interviewer) is public opinion. PUBLIC *opinion is what a person will say out loud to anyone*. It is an overt, and not *necessarily* candid, portion of "opinion" and attitudes. It is only when things have reached this level that they are *freely* discussed and gain a mass currency, perhaps an "upward impact" of influence. Many things which agitate many minds never reach this level at all.

A Mass-Observation Bulletin of December 1947 (New Series, no. 13) put it:

"In attempting to reduce expressions of opinion and outlook to simple tabular form, the social analyst is usually left with a handful of eccentric, curious and deviant comments, which does not even approximate to any of the mass trends he is primarily presenting in his statistics. For these he holds in reserve a *Miscellaneous* category, which always represents a tiny numerical minority, because any single type of outlook which begins to accumulate in it will probably be extracted and formed into a minority grouping of its own.

This *Misc.* 1% is a truly mixed bag. It includes at one extreme the advance guard of what may, years later, be an active majority. . . ."

★   ★   ★

But despite the complexity of verbal statement at different levels, the *whole* of verbal statement is only a fraction of the total subject matter of a living, realistic social science. Much of life has little or no speech pattern—the basic act of sex, for instance. And again much of speech may have *effects* different from those inferred in the uttered context. This vast area of human activity, to be studied by looking and listening, *only secondarily by* ASKING, remains excitingly—and rather terrifyingly—unexplored in our own society.

If the political scientist (for instance) were able to free himself of words, or to use them simply as subsidiary to actual observation of behaviour, he might at times be in a stronger position to reach sound conclusions in this complicated field. By and large, the more the subject matter of any study can explain itself, the less easy it is to study it objectively—that is, "free of prejudice". The nearer social anthropology gets to the anthropologist in life and the language of his own experience, the more difficult he finds it to achieve anything acceptable as social *science*.

The difficulty is an intellectual one. It is less when you are dealing with people whose language you have to learn and who have manifestly different sets of values and habits—Karens in Burma, Melanesians in the Western Pacific, or Kelabits in the middle of Borneo. But even in this environment the anthropologist who wants to go deep should try and spend long periods *not* so much listening to (let alone questioning in) words, but watching and recording exactly what he *sees*. Perhaps the most important—and as far as I know unexploited—piece of technical equipment for any sort of social scientist is the *ear plug*. Some of the best reporting done by mass-observers came during the long and bitter series of air blitzes which we analysed all over Britain (on behalf of the Naval Intelligence Division of the Admiralty and the Home Intelligence Division of the then Ministry of Information). For then the uproar and chaos of bomb-fall night made even such speech as was coherent largely inaudible.

By the same token, the record shows that some of the best mass-observers started life as ornithologists or painters. The present writer wrote his first book on birds and as a lad conducted the second National Bird Census, 1931. Two other well known ornithologists have helped run Mass-Observation during times of pressure—Richard Fitter and James Fisher. Others, life-long ornithologists, have given major help in field work and analysis—notably Stanley Cramp (see Chapter 5) and Humphrey Pease.

Richard Fitter, now Secretary of the Council for Nature and an officer of several key organisations (as well as Nature columnist on the *Observer*), immediately responded to a telephoned request at this point and put the following unprompted check note in the post:

"It was no accident that several of the early mass-observers were bird-watchers. There was a great similarity between the new methods that M-O was pioneering in social anthropology, and those with which Max Nicholson and others were revolutionising field ornithology.

"I passed from the laboratory research atmosphere of P.E.P., where reports were mainly based on written material supplemented by interviews and the verbal interplay of group meetings, to the field research atmosphere of M-O, where straight observation took first place.

"Of that period, August 1940 to July 1942, I remember most vividly my visits to the bombed East End, especially the vast, cavernous and fantastically unsafe warehouse in Stepney where hundreds of families lived in higgledy-piggledy squalor in defiance of the authorities. Tom emulating Churchill by giving out the day's instructions from his bath; an astounded temporary investigator asking 'Do you *really* want me just to go to Scarborough and report what I hear while I'm drinking beer in a pub?' And the fact that the Minister of Information *denied* in Parliament that his department was employing M-O at a time when to my certain knowledge it was doing so. My faith in Ministerial veracity has never recovered since that day!"

Painters also tend to be good at this sort of work. They, too, are trained to look without speaking. Three of them, Humphrey Spender, Julian Trevelyan and Michael Wickham, played an active part in M-O almost from the beginning. They have assisted in the present project by revisiting Worktown and making new observations with the same old freshness of eye after more than two decades. Other painters were attracted to the Worktown activity as a way of focussing their painting.

Painters and bird-watchers are used to observing unaided by words. A robin never answered Dr. David Lack back. Of course, some people

MASS-OBSERVATION: A BRIEF BACKGROUND

of all kinds make good observers. Many hundreds have done so, with M-O, since 1937 and found it fun.

★   ★   ★

M-O's fact and figure feedback (for the country generally as well as Worktown) has been maintained over the past fifteen years by Leonard England and Mollie Tarrant, the present executive directors of Mass-Observation, and both war-time observers.

The many other observers, past and present, who have specially helped with the *present* book have been acknowledged as occasion arises in the text. Special mention must here be made of Celia Fremlin, long-time mass-observer and now a writer of distinguished thrillers— one of which (*The Hours before Dawn*) lately won a major award in the U.S.A. She readily helped in organising and getting into shape Chapter 4, out of good nature and for old time's sake. Miss Grace Carter has acted as co-ordinator throughout.

This is also the place to record a lasting sense of obligation to H. D. Willcock, O.B.E., and John Ferraby, for years of deeply valued and generous help; to George Hutchinson (now a Beaverbrook man) for some of the best war-time observing; to Tom Driberg, who gave valued encouragement from the start; to Sidney Bernstein, who gave M-O its very first paid job, pre-war; to the great and patient kindness of the late Lord Simon of Wythenshawe (then Sir Ernest) who, untrammelled by any conditions, gave—not once but again and again— warming sums to keep our Worktown unit alive and kicking in those years of experiment and doubt; and to A. Everett Jones, J. R. Brumwell and Leonard Harris, over many years.

Sadly, too, we record our respect for four people at one time involved closely with M-O, but killed on active service in World War II: poet Brian Allwood, painter Graham Bell, student Richard Picton and dear Charles Pepper. All who knew them in those days will remember them with affection—and at this moment a sense of continuing loss.

On the way back from Britain to Borneo, this preface is finished in the lobby of the superb International House of Japan; sitting a yard away across this desk is lanky Dr. R. Oppenheimer of Hiroshima bomb fame. In a public lecture (reported in last night's *Asahi Evening News*) the great physicist made some remarks material to what follows, he said:

"One likes to call this a scientific age. There are two precautions. First, we have come to this age by a certain specific historical route, bringing with it much that is not logically required, of science or for science. And second, we have today many great sciences; but I am hopeful and convinced that many subjects *not* now part of science will become part of it. I think that the study of the human psyche will give rise not to one but to many sciences. In this sense we are not yet wholly a scientific age."

Tokyo
25 September 1960 TOM HARRISSON

Part A

WORKTOWN AND ELSEWHERE: OCCUPATIONS AND INSTITUTIONS

One of the "old" and first of the "new" style tombstones in Worktown's largest cemetery, 1960. (The names have been changed.)

And un-known all again
That face of man
Un-knows us now
        Kathleen Raine
       "The Holy Shroud"

TWO

"DISCOVERING" WORKTOWN: 1936

Worktown EQUALS BOLTON, Lancashire. There has never been any pretence about that. But we have from the start considered it as *Worktown*, because what counts is not only its particular characteristics as a place, but all its shares in common with other principal working-class and industrial work-places throughout Britain.

We were never under any misapprehension as to whether or not Worktown was a *typical* town: arguing about this sort of thing too often provides an alibi for avoiding basic social research.

Nevertheless it is relevant to ask why this particular place was chosen? Well, *chosen* is not quite the word. It was a deliberate act of choice, but in the beginning made on rather different grounds. The writer left his school to go on a scientific expedition and continued on a series of such enterprises in various parts of the world during the following years. This involved, among other things, living among and getting to know so-called primitive people in the middle of Borneo (1932), and eventually living among people who were still then eating each other on the island of Malekula in the New Hebrides (1934-5). The Big Nambas of Malekula proved as pleasant as and no more difficult to live with than the boys of a great public school (Harrow) or the society of an English county town (Winchester). What both extremes, geographically, had in common was much.

The inner question then arose: why are many people being generously financed to make prolonged studies of remote people, when little or no comparable research is being done among ourselves? That was the situation in 1935. And in some respects it is still the situation today.

It was—and is—intellectually very difficult indeed to look into one's own society, as has already been noted. It is relatively easy to look at a strange society, which you do not at once *think* you understand. Groping for a way to simplify and overcome this intellectual block it seemed best to follow up the rather crude contrast of "savage" and "civilised". What was there of Western civilisation which impacted into the tremendously independent and self-contained culture of those cannibal people on their Melanesian mountain? Only one thing, significantly, in the mid-thirties: the Unilever Combine.

Thus it happened that the trail led from the Western Pacific to the south of Lancashire. William Lever was born in Park Street, Worktown. In some ways a typical Worktowner, in other ways he was a supreme genius—perhaps the least recognised since his day—in interpreting and exploiting the new mood of twentieth century technology. From small Worktown beginnings, he became the first Viscount Leverhulme and built up one of the greatest industrial and technical commonwealths of the Western world; and the only one to have touched into almost every corner of it before the Second World War. So, from the incessant heat and sunlight of a Pacific island to the sounding cobbles and everlasting smog of the English north. More than a year was spent (1936-7) working in different sorts of organisation and unit in one way or another connected with the Lever origins and growth around Worktown.

It is difficult to remember (now) how in those far-off days, nearly everybody who was not born into the working-class regarded them as almost a race apart. Even good books like George Orwell's *Road to Wigan Pier*, which really tried to get under the surface, started out (1937) from this underlying and sociologically miserable premise. The biggest thrill which this lately initiated "cannibal" experienced was finding it no more difficult to be accepted as an equal in a cotton mill, as a lorry driver or ice-cream man. The fact that one had an accent very acceptable on the BBC of those days in no way led to suspicion that one was "slumming" or "spying". It was only necessary to claim to have come from another dialect area a few miles away. (For one thing, no workers in their right senses ever supposed that anyone came *to* work in Worktown for any other reason than dire necessity!)

It was at this moment that Charles Madge started up in London, and we joined forces. In the following three years the Worktown end of this Mass-Observation turned from one person, somewhat adrift, into sometimes over sixty observers at a time (especially during Oxford and Cambridge University vacations).

The same initial approach was continued. That is: penetrate, observe, be quiet yourself. For our first two years in Worktown we did not make a *direct* interview with anybody. At least three-quarters of the work was concentrated in *describing* what observers could *see* and hear without doing anything to alter the situation (or conversation). In this way we were able to penetrate into most of the corners of Worktown life, including all the forty-odd religious sects (see Chapter 4), every political party (Chapter 5), and scores of organisations, businesses and family situations ranging from the Royal and

Ancient Order of Buffaloes (since weakening) through to the Budgerigar Club (still thriving) or the tense Saturday night skirmishes of outlying Lovers' Lanes (Chapter 7).

Julian Trevelyan's book *Indigo Days* (MacGibbon and Kee, 1957) has much on those M-O days, including a description of how our continuous flow of voluntary and small nucleus of paid whole-time observers worked into and through the outbreak of the 1939 World War:

"Not for Tom the eighteenth-century house on Blackheath, but rather the working-class house in Worktown, anonymous, and like those on either side of it. He complained to me at this time that he could not really sleep unless he could feel through the wall the people next door going to bed; could not work unless the radio was turned on full blast. Tom went out for his material to the pubs, to the dogs, to the dance halls. He sent a band of willing workers flying round making reports on anything, from the contents of a chemist's shop to an account of a service in a spiritualist church. 'Bring back a list of the hymns and any other dope you can get hold of, and try and pinch a copy of the sermon,' he would say as he sent us out on our mission.

"What became of all this material that cluttered up the rooms of Davenport Street, the little house in Bolton that became our centre? How could it possibly be used? We liked to think that it was forming a museum for some future generation of social historians...."

What follows is a part answer to this last question: and Julian participated in using, this year, the reports he was sent out to make more than twenty years ago.

THREE

RECOVERED: 1960

IN 1960, AFTER FIFTEEN years spent back among the civilised Dayaks of Borneo, this some-time (even if short-time) Worktowner took a slice of leave from the Colonial Service to return to (among other things) Viscount Leverhulme's birth-place. The immediate effect was exciting. Some things had visibly changed. Others had visibly *unchanged*—including many that anyone reading newspapers and listening to the radio from abroad would expect to have changed almost beyond recognition.

Excited at this re-visit, we decided to go further, and see if our old, pre-war material was still intelligible so long after: then, assess if it looked possible to repeat some of those early observations without too much complication. With the help of Mrs. Rayner Atkin and Miss Diana Hirst, a major sorting and sifting operation began (June 1960). There was so much stuff to go through that Mass-Observation's own offices in South Kensington proved insufficient. Thanks to Mr. Larry Kirwan, C.M.G., Director and Secretary of the Royal Geographical Society at Kensington Gore, a spacious committee room was kindly loaned all through the summer exclusively for this purpose; piles of paper grew on tables, shelves and floor. This slowly proved tractable—since the original observations proved to have been comprehensive, properly recorded, dated and inter-related.

A few themes were presently selected, largely because on these there were good full reports for the months of July, August and September 1937-40 (primarily 1937-8) which could be repeated in the same places and times (and where possible by the same people) in 1960. We further, through M-O's present London organisation, extended some of the comparisons on to a nation-wide basis (Chapters 14-16, and elsewhere). This result is an experimental study, and essentially a *preliminary* one. It makes no claim to cover the whole field of change (or anything else). It is limited, selective.

Charles Madge and the Overcoat

The first thing mass-observers found on returning to Worktown was gratifying: *they* were welcome. In the intervening years, the original inconspicuous presence of the unit had, inevitably, been destroyed by publications which attracted a deal of local attention. But in 1960 we could find only one person (a local journalist) who resented anything we had done, written or left from the past. Indeed, the degree of co-operation received was now almost embarrassing—embarrassing because one object of the repeat operation must be to continue largely inconspicuous. Some strange memories of mass-observers had also weathered the years—like this one from a now leading Alderman on the Worktown Council, a young labour politician of our pre-war days, who tells it this way:

"One bitter winter day (in 1939) I met Tom in Victoria Square without an overcoat. I asked him what he was up to in this weather and he told me: 'Oh, it's Charles Madge's turn for the coat'."

Touches of Colour

85 Davenport Street, one in a continuous row of bug-ridden houses where we lived for years, looked very much the same in the smoke-filtered summer sunlight (Plate 24). But there was one vivid difference there at once: a handsome negro with a lively tie, leaning on the gate of the house next door, No. 87. And presently, out came another coloured gentleman, in bus conductor's uniform. None of us could remember seeing a coloured man in Worktown before. The nearest thing then was seeing a chimney-sweep—which was considered "lucky".

Closer inspection showed that there were many smaller differences in Davenport Street, though. Lots more bright colours, especially on the doors. Many of the old, standard, clumsy, brown, cracked wooden doors replaced with finer wood or ply, including Yale locks, letter slots and good quality chromium handles. The windows of many houses—subsequent counts gave over a third in some streets—have been decorated from the outside with do-it-yourself lead strips, sometimes in intricate patterns. Before the war, window leading was almost a monopoly of the better-off home where it was "built-in". Now it is becoming standard for all (Plate 25).

Continentalia

Down at the bottom of Davenport Street, what had once been an ordinary corner grocer's now had smart new wooden slat-panelling over the front and a big notice:

CONTINENTAL AND DELICATESSEN SHOP

This reflected what we soon found to be one of the more important lesser changes in Worktown outlook: a wider acceptance of the world beyond even Blackpool. Unthinkable in the thirties, successful now, were two Chinese, Spanish and Greek restaurants, an Indian one (often open after midnight). It used to be impossible to get anything except fish and chips after 7.30 p.m. The Nevada Skating Rink, first opened as such in 1909, cinema in the thirties, reverting to rink in 1955, currently boasts a "Dutch Bar" for snacks, a "Swiss Bar" for

Do-it-yourself window-leading, Worktown, 1960

soft drinks and sweets. Brand-new is the Ukrainian Society (with 100 members), the French Circle (founded 1950) and a thriving International Club (1956). Estimates give up to ten times as many Worktowners going abroad as pre-war. Cook's are currently opening large new premises beside the Town Hall. A travel agency in the main shopping street was window-plugging tours to Russia—July 1960.

The town's oldest established wine-merchants (we could seldom afford his good sherry in earlier days) told one of us:

"In Worktown people are *thinking* about wine nowadays. People are much more adventurous. We stock and sell *eleven* types of Vodka alone. The number of working class who travel abroad and get the taste is remarkable." (11 August 1960).

Building—Conurbal Fears

Only stray bombs fell here during the 1939-45 war and there has been no overall rebuilding programme. The population has indeed gone down slightly, to just over 160,000—and Worktown is well conscious of this loss. The look of the town as a whole seldom seems to have altered, with one exception. This exception: the rebuilding of an area near the Town Hall as a strictly "functional" new shopping centre. During the summer of 1960 there was a great deal of public comment on unsatisfactory, unattractive or unimaginative handling of this rebuilding. The local Press and many local people got quite angry about it. The first Viscount Leverhulme's ambitious scheme for re-planning the town centre back in the twenties was brought up and vigorously debated in public. Had his idea really been so visionary after all?

Some went on to regret—and this was a view more often heard in private conversations—that Worktown political interests were not keeping up with the times or recognising their responsibility to generations of the future. This ties up with a feeling of local consciousness and pride, which despite wider outlooks has in no way diminished in the last quarter-century. Worktown remains deeply conscious of being itself, regardless of its position virtually continuous with the vast conurbation of Manchester, or its general tradition, continuous and shared with that of other and similar adjacent towns which grew up round cotton and coal.

Worktown was hoping by now to have grown into a City instead of a County Borough, by absorbing some adjacent communities on its own account. That has not worked out. The result is some deep disappointment (not readily expressed in public). But one effect has been to make Worktown more than ever determined not itself to become absorbed and swamped by Manchester, Liverpool or 1970. To anyone familiar with what is going on in South-East Asia or Central Africa, there are quite often points of similarity in Lancashire attitude today. The desire to *accentuate* local and group characteristics often conflicts with wider pressures—and not infrequently with the actual self-interest in a narrower sense (e.g. immediate economics) of any group which feels itself threatened with the possible loss of a persisting and vital identity long cherished as "its own".

So it is that at the same time Worktown has grown both broader-minded and (in a different way) narrower. To document this process in detail must await a later opportunity. Rather, we will take (in following chapters) certain particular facets of continuing habit and developing trend from widely different angles—worship, voting, drink, holidays, and so on. But to give these some background, let us first glance at a broader range of aspects.

The Worktown Accent

No voice change can be detected between 1937 and 1960. Radio, television and other outside impacts orientated to a more standard English appear to have had little or no effect. A tiny minority have consciously altered their voices. But elocution and speech training are still not important here. An English master at one of the big local schools, a friend of 1937 and 1960, gave his considered opinion that if anything the standard of speaking what he called "King's English" had gone *down*.

Shawl and Clog, old Insignia

Some sorts of clothes have almost disappeared. For older women, the black shawl worn over the head was standard in the thirties (see the old lady going to vote—Plate 5). In 1960 only one was seen. An observer was detailed to pursue this matter to the bitter end, with this result:

I went to all the older shops, the Police, the Markets Superintendent, and asked numerous people, in my search for some information about any source of shawl supply. Had been told about a little old woman in U—— Street, who is reputed to be one of the last of the old Worktown characters, so finally tracked her down. Mrs. —— of U—— Street. Born in the house 64 years ago. She has a weakly husband, even though he's a bit younger, so she still works 4 hours a night at the Mill sweeping. 'I've worn shawl and clogs since I was 12, I've never had a pair of shoes on my feet. These black wool stockings, I have a place that they make them, they cost me 15/- a pair, and 5/- to have them refooted. But a pair will last about 4 or 5 years'. The shawl she wears now belonged to her mother, who died 12 years ago, but she doesn't know what she's going to do, because she's been to every shop in Worktown—'Nobody sells shawls any more—they try to get me to take one of them travelling rugs, but that's not a shawl. A shawl has four fringes.'

A stay-a-bed outsider of the thirties might be woken anywhere in Worktown by the sound of metal-shod wooden clogs upon the cobbled streets, going to the mills before daylight. Tonight the cobbles, millions of them, are the same as ever; but clogs are becoming a rarity. They have risen from as low as 1/6 a pair to a minimum of 15/11 (children) and up to 30/- for men. The main remaining clog-maker in town (business established in 1857) supplied his latest figures:

```
1930—still making 1,000 pairs a week
1940—   ,,      ,,   150–200 pairs a week
1960—just       ,,    60–70  ,,  ,,  ,, (some for export)
```

Clothes Colours

A more conspicuous change is among women. Counts, for instance, made at the same place and time and on the same dates as in those earlier summers give:

	% of all women	
	1940	1960
Women wearing mainly:	%	%
Brown	21	2
Grey	19	5
Blue	16	24
Green	12	14

Perhaps the largest single change, however, in summer 1960, is to one woman in three wearing a main dress scheme of definite patterns, usually floral, away from simple colour. 16% had strongly floral designs, often associated with hoop skirts; 10% had checks—of which there were none in 1940 counts (in those days checks were almost confined to upper middle-class women in Worktown, few of whom came through this street on a Saturday afternoon).

These figures do not adequately reflect the gaiety of 1960 dress as compared with 1940, nor the wide range of intricate detail (and often of mixed-up colour), as compared with the comparative *drabness* of 1940. In 1940 over half, but in 1960 one in twenty only, of all women's dresses could be called monotone.

This feeling of gaiety in colour is all through the town, on street doors and repainted house fronts, in women's shoes, men's ties and funeral robes for the deceased. Most outsiders would still call Worktown "drab". In many parts of the sprawling town-land the eye can see no tree, no growing thing. But out of this drabness now bud vivid gestures and blossom splashes of wide gaiety.

Jobs—out of 'Insecurity'

There were 13,855 *registered* unemployed in Worktown, when the present writer first went to work there in 1936. Through 1937 the figure seldom fell below 10,000. There were under 1,000 men unemployed in Worktown in the summer of 1960.

In 1936-7 it is fair to say that the whole *atmosphere* breathed insecurity and dread of unemployment. In 1960 we seldom felt such winds of fear, either among old-timers or younger folk. A nightwatchman, age 74 and still working, put it now:

"It seems brighter and healthier today, life's worth living in Worktown—I put it down as the best town in England."

Apart from the recognisable "affluence" of the time, local feelings of strength have grown from the weathering of secondary post-war recessions in 1952, 1955 and (markedly) 1958, all directly linked to textiles—Worktown's original speciality. Steadily the place has been working away from a 70% dependence, so that it is now much more diverse industrially (only 25% cotton and this still dwindling).

A romantic pilgrimage to the place he first worked in—as an unskilled, underpaid, sweating labourer in the "beaming" section—to see the old set-up, produced for this writer a come-down of this new kind: the great red cotton mill was now fragmented into a furniture maker, carpentry for boat hulls, an estate agency, engineering pattern makers, export packers, and floor space to let—and no trace anywhere of Old Ma Cotton. Another of the largest (and dirtiest) mills in town has been turned into a huge chicken battery factory (*The Times*, 9 August 1960, illustrating an article on this M-O revisit). Remaining mills are all on novel (to Worktown) shift systems; and largely modified for specialised forms of textile work, such as ring spinning, carpet making, and so on. Several of them prominently placard VACANCIES—a word inconceivable on any large Worktown building (except a church) in the thirties.

Savings, Pawning, Stealing

Nearly everyone managed to save a little—and tried to save more —in 1937; mainly for two purposes:

(i) Holidays (mostly then at Blackpool; Chapter 9)
(ii) Funerals, tombstones and cemetery space (see below)

Today they save on a much larger scale and for wider purposes, as well as making enormously increased Hire Purchase and other payments per family. Although the number of official saving groups has actually fallen over the past decade (except school groups, up 15%), individual saving continues to rise, the wish for organisation on this score declining with a growing level of security.

Saving per head of Worktown population per week (government channels):	Gross Saving	½ Year, as at date:
£1. 1.10	£4,555,276	March 1960
£0.16. 7	£3,700,786	March 1956
£0.11. 6	£2,495,580	March 1952

Compare Manchester 18/3, Bury 16/11, Liverpool 12/10; only Blackburn exceeds, 22/4 (March 1960).

Everywhere along the line, this new affluence is seen. Pawnshops, pre-war a great feature, have now shrunk to three, who do much more now than straight pawn. In adjoining Horwich, no pawnshops are left. At the other end of the scale, the Chief Constable's latest report shows a further rise in the value of property stolen:

Stolen	Recovered	Year
£2,944.15. 9¾	£806.10. 9¾	1937
£16,594.17. 5	£4,663.14. 3½	1958
£26,846.11. 7	£8,141.19. 9½	1959

The Corner Shop

The shop windows bulge with goods, many new, many as before, all more expensive. A bigger trade than ever is done by one of the town's oldest shops; but nowadays it stays open much later, caters for young as well as old:

YE OLDE PASTIE SHOPPE 1667 (says a new notice there)

The multiple stores have long played a big part in moulding local taste—notably Marks & Spencer, expansive and enterprising even in the drearier thirties. Their position has distinctly strengthened since. Some small shopkeepers complain. The operator of a small local newspaper remarked:

"The Multiple Stores are taking over, and the small man can't compete."

Smart small men can and do compete though—and, in the mild way of the place, boast of it. A milliner's shop we saw start in a little way back in 1937, run by a widow on her own with two girls, is now one of Worktowners' biggest and brightest, with hats from 25/11 to 7 guineas, latest fashions. She remembers:

"I can honestly say I've never looked back. My prices then ranged from 4/11 to a really smart hat for 25/-. Today ... you can take it from me, dear, Worktown ladies like a nice hat."

A fairly typical corner shop (with Off Licence) has stayed in the same hands, 1936-60. When the lady moved in, back in 1936, she found it in a bad way; as she told an observer then:

"There've been five different proprietors in two years and they'd all gone as they couldn't make it pay. I cleared it out and stocked it well and I soon made it pay. I never had a shop before."

Twenty years later there is the same notice over the door, but various new-style window cards for "Mother's Pride Bread" (she baked her own until 1938), "Winalot Dog Biscuits as seen on TV", and so on. Outside a new Ford Consul (bought 1959), inside a new deep-freeze and the smart son of the family, in charge since 1957, proffering:

"We've brought the place up to date and modernised it, but it's really the same family trade that Mum built up. She put a lot into it—when she started she hadn't got a bank book, and stocked it from her own cupboard. A lot of them are the same customers or their children. I've grown up with it myself."

He smiles as he talks—and we recall Mum's recorded words of over twenty years ago:

"The main thing to do if you want to attract custom and to keep your present trade is to have a smile and a word for them all and treat tham all *alike*. I've found that pays."

Shopping Centre

From the sprawling outliers of cobbled streets, move into the main shopping artery, tarmacked Bradshawgate. Here's a fur shop, one in a chain:

	1940	1960
Management	XY Coy.	As 1940
In shop windows	4 stoles and 7 coats	6 stoles and 2 coats
No. of notices displayed	5	6
Average no. of words per notice	26	6
Interior decor	Brown stained wood	Pale pink and blue (painted 1958)
Furniture	Simple (sofa, etc.)	Almost as 1940

These changes just about reflect the general trend. And whereas the pre-affluent message in the window read:

FURS' PRICES RISING
Be wise and buy now at old prices
while stocks last
Save £4 to £8 on purchase!

—in 1960 it goes:

SELECT YOUR FURS NOW
SAVE HALF SHOP PRICES!

In 1940 a Welshman ran one of the main Gents' Clothing shops in

Bradshawgate. Still going strong in 1960, he accurately summed up his shop's changes:

"More variety and more colour, and cutting. As far as we're concerned it's the younger element who are spending the money ... (stock) much heavier because of the variety ... (staff) exactly the same as in 1940—and the shop *has not altered either.*"

The prices have, though, as shown in the Sales:

	SALES PRICES	
	1940	*1960*
The best shirts offered	6/9 (+2 collars) to 7/9	24/9 to 27/6
"Wolsey" socks	1/10 to 1/11	3/11
Singlets and trunks	2/3 to 3/9	6/6
Caps	3/3 ("hand-made tweed, to clear")	9/9 ("Milano striped")

Down the same street was a shoe-shop manager, who summed up his lifetime of looking out on to Worktown's most crowded street:

"The Worktown folk never change, except that they're better dressed. They're more fashion conscious than they've ever been. Quality doesn't seem to matter so much as style. The price doesn't bother if the style is right."

Back in 1940, black boots were his best-sellers, at 16/9 to 18/9, marked down to 10/9 (sale). In 1960 these are hard to find; but black shoes were sale-priced £2. 5. 11 to £2. 14. 11 in August. Men's good brown shoes at 10/9 in 1940 ran at 49/11 (sale) in 1960.

Close by is a furniture shop ("At Your Service for Three Generations" reads the main 1960 advert), whose most expensive 1940-item was 28 guineas ("or 12/6 a month"); now:

TRADE THE PAST FOR THE FUTURE
Bedroom suite: £106. 9. 6.   Deposit £10. 3. 0.
104 weeks at 21/3

Participant Sport

Much has been written about the decline in participant sport in our time—sound radio, films, football pools, youth, T.V. and other factors being blamed at various phases over the quarter century. Some Worktown sports have stayed still, others increased in participation: none has significantly declined since 1937. Golf, for instance, remains so expensive—despite Worktown's pioneering of a Municipal Golf

Course (opened 1931)—that our pre-war year's 26,281 public rounds parallels 27,200 in 1959. Tennis is much cheaper and municipal court amenities have been improved. Bowls, on the other hand, remains rather a pastime for the elderly—some regard it as insufficiently "participant" anyway:

	Members paying fees to Corporation:	
Year	Tennis	Bowls
1938	26,243	101,983
1959	41,752	102,700

Only soccer has remained an exclusively masculine sport.

Out of Town

For many Worktowners, a difficulty pre-war was how to get out into interesting country—or anywhere. This is less so today:

Licences	1938	1950	1959
Private Cars	4,538	4,963	10,642
Motor Cycles	1,164	1,838	4,311
All types	7,545	10,307	19,337

Shared cars and car-hire are big new features; *mopeds* are coming up the biggest local garage reports "accident repairs are going up steadily 10% a year" (8 August 1960); the Ministry of Transport is three months behind with local driving tests.

A new phenomenon is the outbreak of skiffs, little sailing boats, crowding the surrounding moorland reservoirs wherever they are allowed—and even one veritable *pond*. Fishing (rods up to £9) has boomed too—very poor fishing usually. The Cactus Society started as a by-product of a Flower Show in 1946, soared to 200 members, but has since split owing to some spiny-mindedness. The local R.S.P.C.A. Inspector actually reported (conversation 5 August) that in this land of mounting crime:

"There are fewer people being prosecuted (locally) for cruelty to animals these days. We are certainly more animal conscious."

Organisations

There has been a decline in the support for some Worktown organisations once very powerful—such as religious groups (detailed in Chapter 4); most noticeably in the Trades Unions at the active participant (as contrasted with "just paying-up") membership. The elaborate Union structure remains virtually unchanged, with some forty units sending regular delegates to the Worktown Trades Council, and some sixty bodies "affiliated" thereto. But new observation confirmed what this Council's current Secretary mourned to us, a decline in attendance—at all levels of meeting—by 50% and even more in recent years.

The Co-operative Women's Guild cultural groups already showed decline pre-war. This has continued. The average age of active participants is now at least 50. A recent Men's Guild meeting was attended by five chaps (forty in 1937/40; compare Chapter 5, p. 101 below).

At a different level of communal obligation, most cultural organisations have, on the whole, prospered over the past two decades. As with corner shops or anything else, wide variations depend on personalities and upon procedures of intelligent adjustment. Thus amateur theatricals as a whole have enlarged, although the once strong Dramatic Society has totally perished—producing out of its ashes the virile "Phoenix Theatre", now performing in an outlying Anglican parish hall. The Little Theatre, pioneered by one of Worktown's true "intellectuals" (he is on the staff of the local *Evening News*) in the later thirties transformed an old Boxing Stadium; and since 1945 has regularly produced six plays a year, with a Guild Membership of 930, an "Acting Membership" of 210 and 60 Junior members (a new development). Recent productions: "Death of a Salesman" by Arthur Miller, Pinter's "The Birthday Party", "Othello" and "Measure for Measure". Thriving, too, are several Amateur Operatic Societies and the Art Circle (founded 1946).

Young People

Worktown children still play largely or wholly in the streets (see Plates 15 and 26). But today they often play with plastic ducks, expensive tricycles, balloons and rubber balls, seldom seen in the thirties.

Older young people still feel much the same lack of outlet as before, but eased by more money and more mobility. The Crowther Report (vol. II, 1960) gives a picture of rather vigorous if confused leisure outside the home. This certainly applies in Worktown today: more time is being spent outside the home or workplace than ever before, and on the whole with more purpose and positivity. This does not mean, of course, that there is any sudden wave of adolescent or sub-adult organised or "cultured" activity in Worktown. There is, in fact, no existing machinery to incite, let alone to take up and absorb, even a moderately big sudden move of that kind. A thoughtful survey by

Dr. Ralph Ruddock of Manchester University Extra-Mural Department, for the Worktown area (in part published as *After Work*, National Institute of Adult Education, 1959) concludes:

"Out of a hundred school-leavers in Worktown *thirty* will find their way into further education before the age of twenty; few will have joined voluntary cultural societies . . ." (p. 54)

Some elders in Worktown, however, readily make sweeping statements about modern youth, sometimes blaming them so readily for failures whose roots lie deeper if not elsewhere. M-O had much to do with the schools in 1937-40, and contacts were renewed in 1960. The overall impression was of an increased seriousness and intensity, though with it some new toughness—and a tiny faction very tough indeed. The greatly increased interest in technology—and with it some intolerance, loosely, of "old-fashioned" ideas—was pronounced enough. And it can be illustrated more specifically by just one example —the number of boys taking science subjects in the town's leading Boys' School:

	Aggregate Class Registrations	
5 year period:	Arts	Science
1935-9	29	31
1955-9	157	620

Other changes in Worktown education even since the war; data from Mr. W. T. Selley, Chief Education Officer:

	1945	1960
School population	19,202	23,373
Selective secondary school places	417	1,303
Students in Further Education	6,823	12,654

Rock'n' Rollishness

All who revisited Worktown in 1960 were surprised to find few— on some log-books, *no*—teddy boys and spivvy types. Most evenings moving about the town, you'd be unlikely to see three. Statistically they are under 0·1% (Misc.). They are not a topic of comment. No importance was attached to juveniles—other than in terms of general and usual complaint—by the very wide range of people (leaders and others) with whom we checked new impressions. Some local go-aheads even felt a little hurt when this deficiency in a modern community was mentioned. Thus the local paper:

"Jazz Clubs seem to die a sudden and unnatural death in Worktown. Don't ask why—they just do. They start with an explosive crash and end on the sleazy rasping whimper of the trombone." (12 July 1960)

The Worktown Jazz Club has opened (and closed) six separate times. Currently, the "Club Django" is trying again.

There were three large dance halls in Worktown before the war, and even in economically hard times they did fair business. Glance at the two largest now in 1960, as summarised from comparative observer reports:

(1) Same lady (now grey) at the paybox, greeting the kids by name as of old. Internal décor remains "old-world", plus a little strip lighting. 250 present (23 July). "We pride ourselves we haven't changed," she says.

(2) Taken over by a nation-wide organisation; staff of 40 and the place packed to capacity (23 July) with admission 4/6. No Rock'n' Roll on Saturdays and ordinary nights, but at special sessions (with records only).

Says the young, bright manager: "The lighting may look *fairgroundish*, but after drab hours it's what they're looking for. . . ."

Looking Closely

Worktown naturally serves a wider population than is registered within its civic boundaries. This is to its interest in terms of shopping centre or support of famed football club; but a source of irritation in that outliers, not after all absorbed into Worktown's sphere of paper influence and ratepaying, nevertheless benefit from the Museum and Art Gallery, etc. Several services in varying and sometimes complicated ways overlap surrounding places—such as some forms of licensing, transport, medical and fire services. Thus Worktown had, in 1959, 56,595 dwelling houses out of 81,137 in an area covered by Radio and T.V. licensing. Since T.V. got under way—local transmission on any scale began in 1951—the record reads:

Year	TV licences (approx.)	Sound only licences (incl. Car)
1952	12,500	57,500
1954	27,500	48,500
1956	41,500	38,000
1958	55,000	27,000
1959	62,000	23,000

Well over three-quarters of homes now have TV.

Among those who most widely "blame" TV for any changes felt to be detrimental to their own interests are librarians. Thus the Worktown Public Library, catering directly for a population of about

161,500 (cf. 172,900 in 1937) publicly considered TV responsible for a marked decrease in book-borrowing starting in 1954. In 1954-5, fiction borrowing fell by 48,000 volumes; in 1956-7 by 76,400 volumes. But in 1958-9 this decline was arrested and the fiction issue soared again—*increasing* by 76,890 volumes; and in 1959-60 an increase of 75,126 was registered. The "bare facts" of comparison may be simply stated now:

	1936-7	*1959-60*	+ or −
Possible "library population"	172,900	161,500	− 11,400
Total books issued in 12 months	1,525,116	1,604,629	+ 79,513
Reader tickets in force	72,904	103,890	+ 30,986
Average books on loan on any day	33,000	46,000	+ 11,000

The Worktown Public Library's results show an all-round if smallish increase in selective use; particularly this is so in the direction of more "serious" reading (non-fiction and classics) and younger users.

Areas of Unchange, also

The emphasis in this (necessarily rapid and partial) opening survey is on what *has* visibly and rather clearly changed, even if only in degree. It should become clearer—as we examine particular aspects in more detail later—that what has changed may not infrequently be less remarkable, in fact, than what has not. The areas of Unchange in Worktown life are indeed at times (in 1960) astonishing. For instance, in everyday gesture, pub behaviour, love life, kids' games, religious seasons. And this effect—both an impression of the eye and a documentation by the record—is only heightened when one steps across the Fylde to Blackpool (Chapter 9).

The difficulty is to separate out, coherently, "obvious" change (much of which may be mainly material and often *deliberately* conspicuous, e.g. for sales reasons) from the underlying *unchange* which is, after all, often the stuff both of human survival and all social science.

The point is often well taken by Worktowners themselves, such as these two, speaking at random this summer:

Time clerk, 44: "Worktown's improved into one of the finest towns there is, except that they *should have moved the Gas Works.*"
Labourer, 49: "Baccy's up. Beer's up. Oh, Worktown's all right—they've cleaned it up a bit, but it's *just the same.*"

Death, the Changer

Before World War II re-instituted mass slaughter of humans in 1939, one elaborate set of socio-economic interests in Worktown centred on the expectation (never quite certainty) of death, and with arrangements to associate the eventual departure with what then seemed proper circumstance. No other observance during an ordinary human life was so elaborate, expensive or emotionally surcharged. The treatment of birth often bordered on the off-hand.[1] A few marriages were large-scale, most small, some clandestine. Death was *never* without extensive display. The lowest income homes had money saved or "insured" to cater for this social compulsion. Only after death, too, might a lower status body hope to be upgraded to a better-than-life rating in the cemetery—the three huge municipal ones had and have a separate class-structure, based on grave-plot position (and price).

One of the first things we noticed in 1960, turning into Davenport Street from the main road, was a big black Rolls-Royce carriage which looked exactly like the old funeral friend of the thirties. So, on enquiry from the same old pal within, it proved to be. And he pleasedly showed in the back, eight more like it (including a fine 1930 vintage 45/50 class) which he bought up cheap during the war years to form the magnificent fleet of current coffin-bearers for his "Funeral Directors" firm. Funeral Directing has boomed in Worktown, and the several large parlours and "chapels" devoted to this branch of the economy are conspicuous. Yet changes at this end are relatively small when compared with those at the terminus, the last resting place; *not* that the handling changes are inconsiderable however. As another and larger Funeral Director put it (29 July 1960):

"The day of leaving the body at *home* before burial is completely over. More than 60% take place from a Chapel now, and it's increasing every month. I feel very proud of the fact that this is the best town supplied with Funeral Chapels.... People want *simpler* coffins now, it's natural wood instead of varnished. *The whole occasion is lightened.* And I would say only 5% have white (robes) now.... Another big difference is that they don't go in for having a meal now after a funeral, just *get it over nice and quietly*, and then all go home."

[1] There were 2,166 legitimate and 69 illegitimate births in Worktown in 1937; 2,243 and 75 in 1940. Both rose in the War Years (2,460 and 198 in 1945) and have remained rather higher since (*c.* 2,400 and *c.* 125, 1955-9). Infant mortality has steadily dropped, though—61 per 1,000 live births in 1937, 35 in 1950, *c.* 25 since 1955.

[2] That is, use a Funeral Parlour or Rest Home—commercially owned, not a chapel in the *religious* sectarian sense (see list in Chapter 4 below).

A third outfit nearby hands out a tasteful art-page pamphlet, which opens with the telling sentence:

"A *cordial* invitation is extended to the public to visit our FUNERAL HOME."

Seven pages of photographs illustrate the interior, including Chapel of Rest, Rest Room, "The Family Room", and a commodious "Selection Room"—coffins and vases of fresh flowers on them against a floral wall-paper.

The alert operator of this undertaking confirmed the trend:

"Twenty years ago a person was left at home after death. Now, 90% use a Chapel for the period between Death and Disposal. Coffins are not as flamboyant as they used to be, Worktowners don't want brass handles and fittings. White has gone out for gowns, no shrouds now. 50% choose pastel, 40% choose floral and 10% white (for robes: 100% white pre-war)."

This able exponent of his craft went on to underline two other changes which are indeed striking in present-day Worktown:

"In twenty years the increase in *Cremation* is terrific . . . *Embalming* is on the increase too, for *both* burial and cremation."

Another firm told us:

"It used to be 95% burial and 5% cremation. It's 55% burial and 45% cremation now."

The official returns support these views for the town's three main cemeteries:

Cemetery	No. of earth burials in 1939	1959
A	627	325
B	1003	579
C	273	209

The local Crematorium was opened 8 October 1954 and got off to a good start—273 before year's end:

```
1955—1,433
1956—1,786
1957—1,835
1958—1,932
1959—2,161 (and still increasing, 1960)
```

In 1960 cremations outnumbered earth burials by over two to one.

Someone familiar with this part of England twenty and more years ago, and out of contact in Borneo between, might find it difficult at first to recognise the depth of this quiet revolution. Cremation, in particular, has introduced a new idea of the departed—and one which would have seemed inconceivable in the Worktown thirties. Then, to have suggested to a decent Worktowner that he might have his mum burned to ashes and scattered to the winds—most have this done on the "Downs" beside the Crematorium, some further afield; only 1% *retained* in an urn—would have been to court an upper-cut.

Tombstone Terminal

This change goes further than the actual observances of death and departure. One of the things we noticed *at once* as different in the largest cemetery—overlooking the curious cobbled river-bed and the great sooted mills now no longer purely cotton—was a striking truncation and simplification of tombstones. The tall, curved, carved sandstone whose *mood* Humphrey Spender captured at a burial of those days (Plate 3) is gone; Julian Trevelyan, one of our three "resident artists" of both periods, deftly recorded the change in 1960 (p. 23). On the more strictly sociological side, the unit field report for cemeteries (9 July 1960) reads:

Outstanding differences to be noted in 1960:

1. *The treatment of the tombstone.* There are only two examples of the old cross, urn, or other elaborate tall tombstone to be located during an extensive search of the cemetery by two investigators. Practically every new tombstone is of a fairly standard form—and of a form rare in 1937, though it showed in the beginnings of the present pattern as a trend then.

2. The new *type of tombstone* is less than 3' high—as compared with the frequent 5' to 10' in the past; it is always broadly rectangular in shape, never curved and never with an out-jutting cross. The rectangle, which is usually of white marble, sometimes of black and very occasionally of brown, holds the name and other particulars on the top, and is often completely bare for the lower two-thirds or even more. In the thirties, the "modern" tombstone, breaking away from the elaborate earlier pattern, was considerably taller and decorated on the surface with more elaborate designs, such as scrolls of roses or chrysanthemums. The new trend is to severe simplicity.

3. *The treatment of the ground: chips.* Completely new is the placing of green glass chips instead of flowers or grass over grave surfaces. Before the war there were a few white marble chips. These have increased. But green chips now outnumber white by about two to one.[1]

On this synthetic marbled green chip note, let us now turn to broader themes, pre-death.

[1] See also drawing by Julian Trevelyan at p. 227.

FOUR

FOR GOD'S SAKE!
(Thirty-eight Variations on a Theme of Faith)

"Bright sunshine, and the ground is frozen underfoot. . . . No waiting, all turn sharply up the path to the door. The women, and especially the older ones, keep their eyes on the ground—it is very slippery owing to the frost. One woman of 50 makes a jerky movement, as though slipping, and a young man of 20 goes jerkily forward for three steps too. But the woman is still on her feet. She turns to smile at him, and says: 'I nearly went then!' He replies: 'It's slippy now, but it's nice out.' They go in together. . . ."

. . . into the great Parish Church of England, along with the Town Hall the tallest building in Worktown, upon a winter's day in 1937. On this particular Sunday, similar people—in this instance and that year distinguished by the proportion of bowler hats (see p. 146) among the men and furs among the women—similarly entered the porches of thirty-three other Anglican churches in Worktown. Most of these churches had (and have) a distinctive architecture of tracery window, arched portico, spire or tower, which distinguishes them entirely from their industrial surroundings. The same church, built by the same architect, in the same way, could by holy magic be wafted from a remote country village of the moors or a hamlet like Rivington on to one of the several empty lots around Worktown's centre, without causing any visual disturbance to the Worktown view.

These are the centres of Church of England worship in the Christian observance; for those who believe in, or ostensibly subscribe to the Established Church, around the status of which the citizens of these islands have shed more of each other's blood and broken more tens of thousands of commandments than around any other one idea in our later history. Yet the identification of these Churches of England with the other established formal institutions of Worktown life is today close. In the symbolism of civic affairs and living municipal foci, this comes second only to the Town Hall and its associated buildings (such as the Museum and the Employment Exchange). At least once a year, and sometimes more often, leading politicians, administrators and organisers attend the principal Anglican building, still called "Worktown Parish Church" despite all the others within

Worktown. Such occasions are, indeed, *the only ones in Worktown* where persons who do not "belong to" the Church of England and who quite often "belong to" other units of Christian observance distinctly *opposed* to the Church of England as a whole, nevertheless come together in common worship of the Lord God (whom all of them ostensibly believe in) and of Jesus Christ, whom nearly all at some point state they believe in (a few, like Unitarians, Spiritualists and Mazdaznan, in varying degrees dilute this actual Divinity).

In fact, with this single exception of the Parish Church affecting the upper hierarchy of Worktown's leadership, from birth to death it is improbable that a Worktowner will go into any religious building *other* than that of the sect into which he was initiated early in life—in the first decades of the century very powerfully, but by the late thirties decreasingly, through some form of Sunday School.

In 1960, as in 1937, this "above the issue of sect" significance remained intense in social implications, however tiny if measured in social statistics. Thus the Parish Magazine for July 1960 prints—after a four-line poem by the choirmaster and a list of recent legacies and gifts (total £155)—the following highly characteristic (and traditional) letter:

Mayor's Parlour,
Worktown.
31st May, 1960.

Dear Canon,
    The Mayoress and I wish to thank you very much for your sermon on Sunday morning last, and for your words of encouragement for my year of office as Mayor. . . .

I was very pleased that Mrs. X. and yourself were able to come and have a little refreshment with us after the Service, and I hope to see you both on many occasions during the next twelve months.

Kind regards,
Yours sincerely,
Mayor.

Important, in this way, as it firmly is, the huge and towering nave of the Parish Church often holds less than thirty persons at a main Sunday service; it could seat a thousand. Congregations at Worktown's Anglican churches together seldom grossed more than 2,500 at any one time in 1937; and, as we shall see, they would be glad to have that many—out of a population of some 100,000 adults—today.

Quite otherwise is the statistical picture for the only Christian group in the area which sometimes goes so far as to criticise one of its members (invariably, in this case, a Labour member of the Council) for attending one of the Civic Sundays under the auspices of the Anglican Canon. The Roman Catholics, who in past centuries so often killed or were killed by the ancestors of these Anglicans, have twelve places of public worship in Worktown, not one of which is central or conspicuous. But on any ordinary winter Sunday in 1937, regularly, over 5,000 attended the 10 o'clock Mass, one of a Sabbath series starting before daylight. Even then, some of their churches were filled to capacity; by 1960, these were bulging, with "standing room only" near the door.

The Variants

Variously poised between or around these two traditional giants with their pre-industrial roots, lie more than thirty other groups which distinguish themselves by separate names, have little or nothing to do with each other, and always have entirely separate officers, finances, and usually publications, centred round a specific meeting place which is kept for this purpose alone. Although in 1937 new groups had sometimes no distinct premises, by 1960, with more affluence (despite fewer active supporters in most cases) all of them had such premises—the Seventh Day Adventists catching up last with a conspicuous transfer to a suite in a new Insurance Building.

These are the identifiably distinct variants on the Christian theme in Worktown:

		No. of Premises
1.	Church of England	34
2.	Roman Catholic	12
3.	Congregationalists	11
4.	Methodists (West)	9 ⎫
	(East)	7 ⎬ 26
	("Wesley")	9 ⎪
	("Mission")	1 ⎭
5.	Independent Methodists	5
6.	Baptists	5
7.	Unitarian	3
8.	Presbyterian (Scottish)	2
9.	Welsh Tabernacle	1
10.	Holiness Tabernacle	1
11.	Beulah Hall	1
12.	Calvary Christian Mission	1
13.	Countess of Huntingdon's Persuasion	1
14.	First Church of Christ Scientist	1
15.	Friends (Quaker)	1
16.	Hebron Hall	1
17.	New Jerusalem	1

18.	Elim Four Square	1
19.	Queen Street Mission (Ind.)	1
20.	The Bible Christians	1
21.	Out and Out Mission	1
22.	Hebrew	1
23.	British Israel	1
24.	Advent Testimony	1
25.	Swedenborgian Church	1
26.	Bethel Evangelistic	1
27.	Salvation Army (Inter-denominational)	2
28.	National Spiritualists	1
29.	Spiritual Alliance	1
30.	Christadelphians	1
31.	Pentecostal League of Prayer	1
32.	Plymouth Brethren	1
33.	Exclusive Brethren	1
34.	Truth Centre } partly	1
35.	Theosophist Centre } "secular"	1
36.	Mazdaznah } partly	1
37.	Rosicrucians } "secular"	1
38.	Seventh Day Adventist	1
also (39.)	Ukrainian Catholics—looked after by Roman Catholics	1
(40.)	Small "Missions" of no defined denomination or remotely related to mother church	5
(41.)	Chapels in cemeteries, and Funeral Parlours, including non-denominational, etc.	12
	Total "units of worship":	147

Lines of Deviation

The organisation and observances of each of these 147 places was penetrated and studied by one or more mass-observers during the 1937-40 study or (if new) in 1960: and new information of a less detailed kind has been obtained for most of them up to date. The main features of actual worship have hardly anywhere changed except in small detail or for physical causes (decay, repairs, etc.). The tenets and principles, the particular version of faith in each case, has not appreciably altered in any single sect or unit studied. The earlier material on all this is just as "topical" today; we will look at some of it in a moment; and will hope to publish the fascinating whole of it in years to come.

There has, however, been one big, significant change on the

organisational side. The Methodists have now revised their machinery—which was indeed creaking in the thirties, when they were split into a number of semi-friendly sub-bodies within Worktown. The historical succession of powerful groupings in Worktown continues to exercise influence on the life of the community far beyond simply religious affairs and has broadly been:

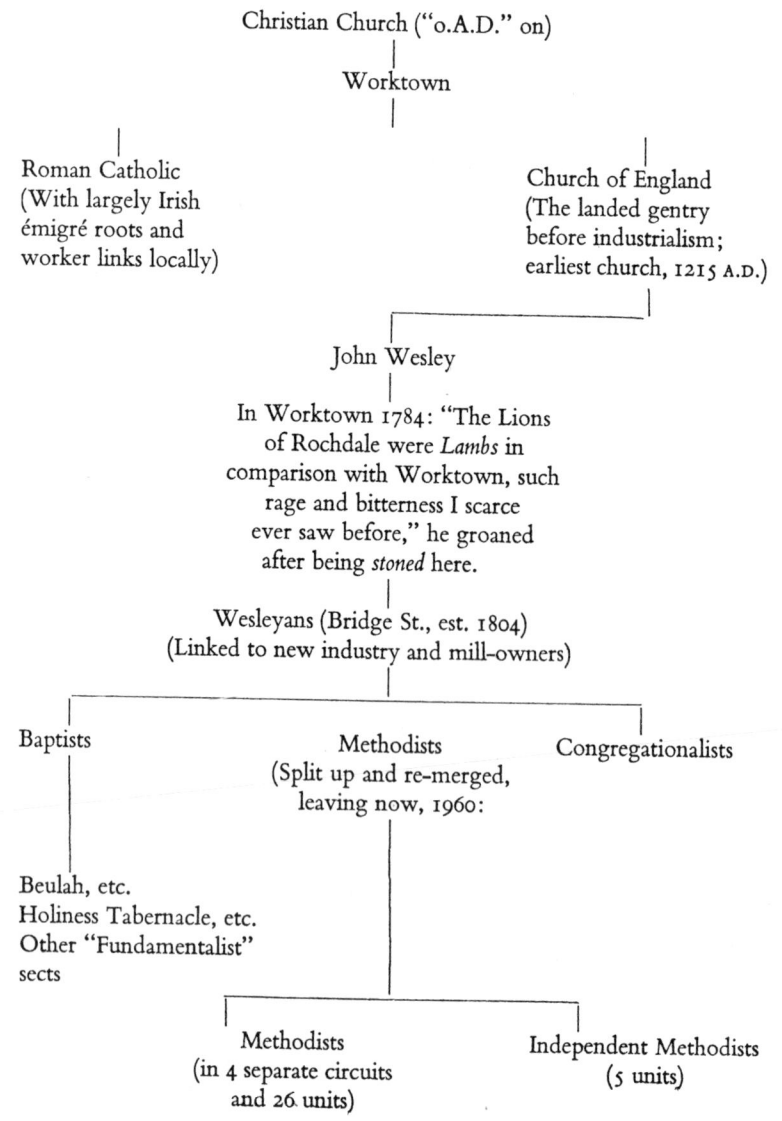

Christian Church ("0.A.D." on)
|
Worktown

Roman Catholic (With largely Irish émigré roots and worker links locally)

Church of England (The landed gentry before industrialism; earliest church, 1215 A.D.)

John Wesley

In Worktown 1784: "The Lions of Rochdale were *Lambs* in comparison with Worktown, such rage and bitterness I scarce ever saw before," he groaned after being *stoned* here.

Wesleyans (Bridge St., est. 1804)
(Linked to new industry and mill-owners)

Baptists

Methodists (Split up and re-merged, leaving now, 1960:

Congregationalists

Beulah, etc.
Holiness Tabernacle, etc.
Other "Fundamentalist" sects

Methodists (in 4 separate circuits and 26 units)

Independent Methodists (5 units)

In the present century several small sects have spread in from the U.S.A.: Christian Science, Elim Four Square (Aimee Semple Macpherson), Seventh Day Adventists, Mazdaznan Rosicrucian.

After many vicissitudes, the Methodists have reduced their places of worship from over forty in the early thirties, and are currently re-formed into "circuits" within the Worktown area. But no amount of persuasion or pressure from the logic (cash or economical) of the times has been able to bring the five surviving small Independent Methodist chapels into this fold—although to the unobservant eye the differences in religious observance that divide them may seem too small to be detectable at all. But that is a feature of very much in this Christian complex: the so far uninitiated observers of 1937 repeatedly expressed bewilderment along these lines on returning from an allocated duty:

"But *how* is this different from the one I reported *last* Sunday?"

And also, of course, "*Why?*". The experience was exactly repeated in 1960 by those who revisited Worktown then—several of them not having been in a place of worship in the interval!

Moreover, the visible variations *within* one sect or group can be as great—or greater than—the variation as between this group and another, depending largely on the size and style of church and congregation; and especially on the personality and prejudices of the current leader(s).

With the invisible, too (doctrine, prayer, the nexus of group belief itself) tremendous overlaps occur, as well as apparent contradictions. The Spiritualists, for example, though "split" in two groups, and adopting an attitude *outside* the Christian church in theory, in practice incorporate Methodist-type prayers into their séances, and now have a sermon.[1] The Seventh Day Adventists have (in Worktown) a certain amount in common with the Hebrew observance, though each would repudiate the suggestion. (There is a higher incidence of anti-semitism among the Seventh Day Adventists than anywhere else.)

Unitarians, though "ethical" and not strictly Christian in declared approach, in actual procedure at the unit level often accept the Trinity, and Christ's Divinity. In the fifties the leading local Unitarian church (established here in 1896) started Holy Communion as well as a link with the Moslem Mosque in Manchester (see below).

The established Anglican church itself has for the past twenty-five

[1] Further reference to Spiritualism is to be found in connection with Totemism, in Chapter 13.

years—and no doubt much longer—been divided on the basis of individual churches and congregations, into two major, plus some minor, divisions of opinion regarding the degree of "ritual" in services: Liberal Evangelical and "High Church" (or Anglo-Catholic) broadly representing these divisions; which are as deeply felt as, for instance, the current differences between Mr. Gaitskell and Mr. Cousins in the Labour Movement, and all that these both mean, in terms roughly of mind and body, within an established organisation.

The Congregationalists, who branched off within Methodist-type Nonconformity into a democratic, church-by-church system of "choosing" the minister (another abiding centre of dissatisfaction in most centrally organised sects), similarly show a notable range of internal variety, with tendencies both "high" and "low" within their eleven local units of worship.

What Places of Worship are . . .

To document this wonderful richness of variants in detail takes us outside the present limits of the study. But it must be constantly born in mind while considering the small part of the picture we are depicting here. It must also be emphasised that studies of this kind are made with all due respect. It is difficult to study religion anywhere without getting into hot water: it is impossible to study it anywhere without getting into deep water. But it is not the job of the sociologist to question the *reasons* for the existence of a state of affairs, however strange it may seem. It is his job to describe and analyse a state of affairs, free from subjective assumptions or the pressure of known prejudice—so far as it is humanly possible to do so.

In studying religion in Worktown we began our work with the centres of worship and units of sect, for reasons of effectiveness and simplicity in organising the observations and observers. At an early stage we had to face difficulties in deciding, for instance, what *was* a place of worship. Indeed, to the non-Worktown eye, it is by no means easy to distinguish some Nonconformist chapels from some cotton-mills. Several Methodist and Baptist chapels are very close replicas, on a smaller scale but in the same materials, of the great spinning factories whose enriched proprietors principally sponsored these chapels in opposition to pre-industrial sections of the Christian faith, whose older vested interests were often alien to the urban approach. Two chapels in particular have towers closely like the cooling towers on two cotton-mills.

The smaller sects may use sheds, shacks and barns in old sectors of the town or on allotment fringes. By 1960 the Welsh Tabernacle was approaching a state of ruin, painful to the eye, and incidentally also being used by another organisation's Classes for the Deaf.

Even by the least liberal definition, more than a hundred separate places primarily devoted to the worship of some kind of God have persisted in Worktown over the past twenty-five years; during that time a dozen have closed and only four new ones appeared. One of these latter is the only place of worship boasting "modernist" architecture—we observed the laying of the foundation stone on an outlying housing estate, by a local cotton baronet, in 1937.

This compares with the survival of only a dozen cinemas. There are more than three times as many pubs as there are places of worship; but the seating capacity of the Houses of God is at least three times that of the "Public Houses". A bigger difference is that on Saturday evening every seat—and every inch of standing room too—is occupied in the pubs, while on the following day, in the hours set aside for the purpose, only the Catholic *churches* are anywhere near full.

"Religion" as a Feeling

Before we go into these places of worship, established or otherwise, it must be realised that a great many Worktowners only enter them—if at all nowadays—to get married. Until 1950, virtually everybody also went in—or at least hovered near the porch—as a corpse. The introduction of a crematorium in 1954 diverted 147 local cadavers, and 126 non-local, from the direct church jurisdiction in that year. By 1960 the figure had risen to over 2,500. As one Anglican minister, who earlier mentioned that he had collected £10,000 in the past seven years, put it (July 1960):

"If we don't get the ashes or the funeral, not only is the link with the Church broken, but we are losing a lot of revenue. This also affects the Minister's stipend. We cannot turn ourselves into a business company to compete. Since Worktown Crematorium opened we have lost much."

At some point in their lives organised religion *touches* every family in Worktown. But apart from most Catholics, and a few individuals within some of the strongest tiny sects, organised religion plays no more part in the everyday thought and talk of Worktown than does organised democratic politics (as we shall see in the next chapter). This does not mean, though, that *Christianity as an idea* is unimportant —any more than not knowing the name of your local M.P. means that you don't care one vote for democracy. At a pinch, most

Worktowners, suitably directed, could be got to fight and die for the right of either to survive in their society; but approached another way "religion" might be abolished and many not bother much?

Listen to Worktowners, speaking at random in all sorts of circumstances, but with the topic of religion carefully (i.e. "naturally") brought into the conversations, during July and August, 1960:

Manager of Department Store, aged 50: "Religion is the basic and one fundamental thing in the world, without religion inside you, something unexplainable, I don't think the world would survive at all. I don't go to church, people who do go mostly for show."

This type of comment—"I approve of religion but don't go to church myself"—was by far the most common single reaction to the subject; more than a third responded in some such way:

Launderette assistant, 38: "I believe in it—I don't go to church except for weddings, funerals and christenings. We've had our bad times, and when things like that happen it makes you wonder if there's any truth in it, but it's there just the same. . . ."

This feeling that the mere *existence* of religion in the background gives a sense of security is echoed by a 50-year-old *hairdresser*—also a non-churchgoer:

"Unbiassed, that's me. I think if a person is born and brought up with a religion he will be faithful to it. I think that without a religious background you're like a ship without a rudder."

Only about a sixth of those interviewed claimed that they went to church at all regularly. Here are some of their responses:

Man of 37: "I think the church has a definite place. It's lost ground a bit. The H-bomb makes you wonder. I do go to church, and I feel better for it—well I suppose it's hope."

Paper shop manageress, 50: "I go to church, and I believe there's a God. I know right from wrong—mind you, I couldn't live without it in some little way."

Or this 30-year-old *wife of a slater*: "Well, I go to the church, I believe in God. I like to bring up my children the same. I think the Vicar makes a big difference. I only go to one, the eight o'clock Communion."

Practically no one expresses any kind of *hostility* towards religion. The "anti" comment runs:

Salesman, 25: "It's a pastime for people who like that type of thing. Religion itself—I have no real time for it, but that doesn't mean I don't believe there's a God. It can't all be good, there's so many different religions, and they're always fighting each other. I think some of them try to push you around too much."

Storeman, 22: "It (religion) seems to be dying out, I think it's old fashioned with everything advancing so rapidly. I never go to church—come to think of it, I *did* get married in church."

Window cleaner, 20: "I don't go to church since I was seven. Life goes on the same whether you go to church or not. Some of my pals go—I'd look a bit of a Charlie (if I did)."

Mild criticism was based on the feeling that some churchgoers are merely the unthinking victims of habit and upbringing, or of warring sects:

Salesgirl, 36: "I think a lot of people go because their mothers and fathers have brought them up to go, and *forced* them, and now they feel it's just a duty, and that's that."

Wife of worker at paint works, 35: "I'm not a religious person, I never had it drummed into me when I was a child."

Most critical comment comes from young people in their early twenties. But another large proportion of young people are quite strongly in favour of religion, and even of churchgoing:

Hairdresser's apprentice, M. 17: "Religion is something someone believes in strongly—it doesn't have to be the Christian faith, it's more a physical belief, it has to be deep, morally and mentally. I get satisfaction from it."

Shop assistant, F. 20: "I believe in it. It's like something strong that you can always go back to, you know it's there."

Another shop assistant, F. 21: "I don't go to church, but I believe in it. It gives you something to feel inside of you."

And this from a proudly 'teddy boy' (17), son of a bricklayer:

"I believe; I'm a Catholic. I think it makes you feel good when you've been to church. I'm a Teddy Boy."

No real scorn or dislike of religion is openly expressed, and very seldom privately. Neither in this series of conversations nor anywhere else did observers come across Worktowners dismissing the whole *concept* of religion as irrelevant bunk.[1]

---

[1] Compare these views on religion with those reported as what "any half-dozen working-class people" would "be likely to answer" according to Richard Hoggart's *The Uses of Literacy* (Pelican, 1959, p. 92). Most of the phrases he there puts in quotes as typical of northern workers do not occur in our real-life material. For other attitudes outside Worktown, and based on interviews (*public* opinion in the stricter sense), not observation or informal talk, see the important nation-wide data in Chapter 16, following below.

Going in or staying out

There are some, however, who say (nearly always in private), that they would quite like to go to church or chapel, but that they feel either absolutely bored or appreciably embarrassed by what goes on *inside*. Accompany to Matins, a person who has never been to the North of England before; nor before been to any kind of English religious observance. We are once more in the great Parish Church, at 10.30 a.m. on a damp Sunday summer morning in 1960. There are thirty-one other people in the body of the church (twenty-two of them women) most over 45. There are twenty-six more people in the choir and chancel, all of them male (fourteen boys), wearing white surplices or more elaborate uniform regalia. The new recruit reports:

Went into the church. One of the male helpers handed me a hymn and a prayer book, and said to me: "Nice to see you. Do you want these?" "Yes," I said, and took the books and went along. The hymn-book contained hymns that were first published in 1861, and the prayer-book contained prayers dated 1928. I have never been to an Anglican service before, and the division of time during the service struck me most. I felt that I was in a school where hymns were sung as a sort of exercise. I felt that at least three-quarters of the time was taken by singing hymns; there were 5 hymns altogether during the service and these had up to 6 verses.

The songs were mostly sung by the choir to the congregation. I could not understand much of what was being said by the priest, or what was going on. There was no time for concentration on prayer or any other religious activity because all the hymns were sung standing up, and if one was not standing up one was kneeling down or listening to the reading of the priest. At the very end of the service, after 45 minutes of hymns, readings and announcement, the priest went up to the pulpit and proceeded to deliver the sermon. He talked about three modern philosophers, politicians and writers. The first was a Labour Party man called R. H. S. Crossman, the second the French author, Camus, and the third Arnold Toynbee, and he quoted from their books, etc., in a way that implied that nothing was of any value unless you were protected by God, and that unless your thoughts and your vision were projected upwards anything you did was bound to fail. And he very strongly implied that every failure one had in one's life was due to not going with God, or under God's guidance. . . .

Then comes something which distinctly identifies the occasion as 1960; could not have happened in 1937—when one of the major features of any service was the taking of a collection, nearly always elaborately blessed by the operating parson or person, before the post-war growth of organised giving, weekly envelopes, monthly subscriptions, pledges and much else (to which we will return presently). This 1960 report thus continues:

> The *collection* did *not* take place inside the church during the service, but when I left it was being taken *outside*, and I was given at the same time a small pamphlet (on how to give on a regular basis) which I kept. The priest must have raced round, because he was there, when I came out, to greet the congregation and to say a few nice words; and one of the male helpers who had distributed the books came up to me asking if I was going to stay in Worktown....

The person just quoted was asked by the supervisor of this observer unit to record straight into a tape-machine the impact of this occasion immediately on her return from the service. Here is what she said:

> It was the first time I had attended an Anglican Service, and what most impressed me was the emptiness of the church and the number of the choir in comparison with the number of ordinary people in the church, so that one got the impression that the whole service was made up by the 14 small boys of the choir, and a few men singing the songs and attending on the priest.
>
> I also had the strong impression that the priest did not show himself at all to the audience in the church, being surrounded by these choir boys, and with the sermon taking place at the end of the service. There was no action at all at the *altar*, which was completely empty and felt practically non-existent, until at the very end the priest went up to the altar and prayed for a minute or two; he was praying in a very simple way for the Queen and Parliament, and the sick and all people to do with hospitals and so on. This form of prayer was the only *live* thing during the service. All the singing and announcements and reading were stereotyped and impressed me as doomed to failure, because there was no real connection between all that happened on the part of the choir boys and the priest *and* the people inside the church. It was more or less a routine taking place, which had lost the heart of the matter.

But it would be misleading to imply that this sort of impression in 1960 was peculiar to one individual, or that it was peculiar to 1960. Comparison with the 1937 reports often makes it difficult to be sure which year you are in—except for these points of detail in connection, like methods of collecting revenue. Here is an observer's report from this same Anglican church 22 years before:

> The congregation consists of 15 women, 4 men, 16 boys and 8 girls, the boys are in the charge of a young man of 22; they are coming from Sunday School class. They are laughing, and some of them are trying to slide on the cobblestones. When they get to the church door, the young man says "Sssssssh!" and opens the door to allow them to get in. They go down the centre aisle to seats in the front, on the left side under the pulpit. The young man goes round to the

front to take a seat on the end of the line of chairs, and bends to talk to the boys nearest. They begin to find places in their books.

The lads are now in position: next come the girls:

They are a mixed group of 8 girls aged 8-12 and 6 girls of 14-18. The youngest come down the aisle first, the older ones following. The youngest are looking round as they go forward, holding their books. They are all smiles, but none of them speak. They go to the front seats on the right side, the older girls sitting in the row behind them. All the girls bend down on their knees to pray. They all move back to their seats within 3 seconds of each other from the first to the last of them, then sit there looking at the chancel. . . .

The adults, however, far from entering in groups, rarely even come in pairs. The observer's 1937 report continues:

All the women, with the exception of two groups of two, come into the church alone. They are met by the churchwarden, who is at the back of the screen. He has a number of books of Common Prayer and hymn-books; smiling at the women, he hands them each one of each of the books. They walk down the centre aisle and find their own seats, all of them bending to pray, three of them on their knees. Two working-class women of 40 and 50 go down the centre aisle, find themselves a seat half way down on the right. The one of 40 kneels to pray, the one of 50 bends forward, not going on her knees. The latter finishes first, the other two seconds later. They sit back and whisper a little. The younger, on the inside, leans forward to catch what is being said. They sit very straight.

Two women, 50 and 40, very sallow, are wearing black coats with Astrakhan collars. The older has a round hat, flat on top, and made of Astrakhan fur. Both are greeted by the churchwarden. He smiles, and they smile back. He goes to get them some books, and they continue down the centre aisle, taking seats two-thirds of the way down on the left. They kneel in prayer, the younger getting up first. . . .

This is the 1937—and even more the 1960—Sunday morning scene in an Anglican church: a sparse congregation of elderly women, mainly solitary, with a small sprinkling of men and a little bunch of children (these last might be altogether missing at a 1960 service).

What of the other sects? Do any of them fare better in respect of "user statistics"? Here is an observer's account of a Roman Catholic church service one Sunday morning in July, 1937:

A sectional count suggested an approximate attendance of 500. The church was filled to capacity. A representative section of the congregation comprised 37 women, 17 men and 8 children. Of the women, 15 were around 50, and dressed in clothes which were worn, faded and shapeless.

To these facts the observer adds the "impression" he got of the behaviour of the congregation:

Responses were given loudly, in unison. Against the full body of sound could be heard the particular voices of those in close proximity, fully articulating the words of the prayer. For the majority of the time, while the priest was occupied at the altar the members of the congregation were reading prayers on their own, or using rosaries.

And on another July Sunday, exactly twenty-three years later, we get another report of the same Roman Catholic church, at the same time in the morning:

When the observer arrived at the church, the previous service was just over. There was a crowd of people in front of the church. The new people soon started going in, and the church filled up. Within 5 minutes there were about 300 people in the church, and nearly every seat was taken. There were about 4 women to every man. There was a slight accent on old women, but plenty of young people and middle-aged present. There were small children, tiny ones, and no attempt had been made to distinguish these into a separate service, as has been done in many other denominations in recent years in Worktown.

So far, the later report seems to follow indistinguishably closely the earlier one quoted; but now a new note is struck—something is described which could not have occurred before the war: namely, queueing up for Holy Communion:

At the end of the service there was queueing up for Holy Communion—something which the observer had never seen before in Catholic services in other countries, ranging from the Continent to South-East Asia. What impressed her was the actual fact of queueing, when at Communion no one would think of pushing or scrambling. But it was beautifully done, with self-discipline and in an exact queue, as if it had been for a bus in London—but better done than that.

The report concludes with the observer's personal impression of the service:

The whole atmosphere of the service and the congregation was one of devotion and concentration, but in a relaxed way, and without formalities. Nor was there any ceremonial going in or coming out—none of the shaking hands or stress on fellowship and friendship which characterised not only the Anglican but the Congregationalist, Methodist and Spiritualist services previously reported this week. The basis of the place was a large, local, completely adjusted congregation, knowing all about it and not worried in any way, from the priest down. This was further indicated by the fact that outside the church there was no notice or indication of any kind as to the times of services, or any other of the propaganda or information commonly found in Worktown churches.

This observation leads us on to a significant pointer of the 1960's, the fact that now, apart from the Catholics, all sects, even tiny ones, "advertise" in some way—and increasingly. Columns of the local papers are taken up by advertisements of services; and these are always headed by the advertisement of the leader of them all. All down one big side of the advertisement page of the *Worktown Evening News*, we find announcements like the following:

WORKTOWN PARISH CHURCH
Sunday July 10
Trinity IV
8 a.m.: Holy Communion
10.30 a.m.: Matins
2.15 p.m.: Children's Church
6.30 p.m.: Evensong

GOSPEL HALL
Sunday, 6.30 p.m.
Family Service
Speaker:
Mr. Harry Aspinall
"Be sure you hear the testimony of this young man who is a prospective Missionary"

CALVARY
Christian Mission
Full Gospel
Psalm 64
"O THOU THAT HEAREST PRAYER UNTO THEE SHALL ALL FLESH COME"
Jesus save. No Collection

And so on, down the page.

As well as this sort of advertisement, the many places of worship are themselves plastered with notices, some of them thirty feet long —e.g.:

IN A GROWING UNIVERSE A FIXED CREED
EXCLUDES MORE THAN IT INCLUDES

or:

> GOD'S POLICY FOR YOUR LIFE:
> THE BENEFIT OF OTHERS
> THE ONLY LIFE ASSURANCE POLICY THAT
> BENEFITS THIS LIFE *AND* THE LIFE TO COME!

Right in the middle of this industrial town there appear regularly in season, posters like this:

> At this Church
> THANKSGIVING FOR THE HARVEST

a specimen of which is beautifully illustrated in Humphrey Spender's photograph (Plate 2).

Nonconformist Observances

But let us look a little further into what goes on inside. An observer at an Independent Methodist Chapel in July 1937 reports:

There is a gallery over the entrance—not used now—and over this a stained-glass window. Doors are stained-glass, also all windows facing the road, while the side windows are painted a milky white. Pews are fixed, divided by two side-aisles. There are stairs up each side to preacher's desk, with small gates; below is the dish table within rails; on this table is a small dish.

The preacher, an oldish man with a small grey beard, opened the service with a short prayer, followed by a hymn—a children's hymn, he explained, and he was sorry there were so few children present; but he felt that in the eyes of God he himself was no more than a child. He then read the Lesson, which dealt with the sin of hypocrisy. Then came announcements of coming meetings, and the information that last Sunday's collection had amounted to 16/10. Today's offerings were collected; then followed Hymn 572—"This is my favourite hymn," says the preacher; "I love it, and often meditate on it. I like to suck it in like the sweet juice from the true vine."

After this came the sermon, the text of which was the whole of the Lord's Prayer. The sermon ran:

"What are the most important words of the Lord's Prayer? 'Our Father' and 'Amen'. We should think more about the 'Amen's' in prayers and hymns; they are part of the meaning.

"Why are there so many luke-warm Christians?" Quotes: " 'Why is it that thou art so lean, yet live in the King's house?' That is very true; there are many lads who grow up thin as rakes, and their friends ask: 'Aren't they getting their meals regular?' They aren't a credit to their cook. In the same way, people ought to worry about their spiritual state: are they a credit to God?

"You all know our text; I wonder how you'll describe it when you get home to Sunday dinner? The Lord's Prayer was not for everyone, Jesus taught it to the disciples only. It is for Christians, not for the whole world.

". . . The bounty of God: There are seagulls at the end of Southend Pier (joke about there being no fish in the sea at Southport any more) just as there are at Ramsey. A gentleman used to feed them—the birds would squawk and fly all round him. I thought how wonderful, and found my Bible: 'Thou givest them their meat in due season; Thou openest thy hand and satisfiest their desires'."

There followed a couple more bird-feeding anecdotes, the moral of which was "The Lord will provide", and the sermon ended in apologies for length, and was followed by a shortened hymn (two verses only). No one sang the "Amen".

It will be noticed that in this sermon no effort was made to tackle specifically modern problems; to "keep in touch" with the swirl of contemporary life. Vague goodness is felt to be enough, and will bring its own rewards. Similarly non-topical was the imagery of another sermon preached at about the same time at the biggest Methodist church in Worktown:

"How strange it is that some people see things differently from others. . . There was once a man who sprayed lupin seed through a railway carriage window 'Because he wanted to see them himself and let others too have the beauty.' But his companion only said: 'You might get prosecuted for it.'

Then again, two men looked through prison bars, and one saw mud, the other stars. Strange how some men see God in all things, others not."

This absence of topicality was a noticeable feature of most of the sermons heard during 1937–60. Rare was a reference to current affairs as specific as the following, by an Anglican parson on the track of the dictators:

". . . The Christian is terrified by what he sees in the surge of pleasure-hunting by the crowd. . . . The crowds of Christ's day were very little different from the crowds of today, only in dress. . . . The Pharisee is like Hitler or Mussolini, who want the letter of their law obeyed, and who will kill or imprison any who do not obey. They are like the Pharisees who would kill Christ, even; they hate him in their hearts, and would suppress him."

The "Logical" Approach of Ethics

A wide board outside the leading Unitarian Chapel in September 1960 reads:

RELIGION IN A SCIENTIFIC AGE—
THE BREAK WITH TRADITION

FOR GOD'S SAKE! 63

This poster indicates clearly enough the Unitarians' avowed intention to bring religion into harmony with reason and logic. We will now report two sermons heard in the main Unitarian Church of Worktown—one in July 1937, the second in July 1960: the comparison is illuminating. Here is the first one:

"My text is from 1st Kings, chapter 17, verse 7: 'And it came to pass after a while that the brook dried up because there had been no rain in the land'.

"No rain in the land—in Palestine that is no rare thing. . . . There is beauty and life and birds sing when there is rain . . . when there is none the brook dwindles, and that stream which a man could not ford, a little child could cross without wetting his feet.

"You are familiar with these facts. . . . It is the same in Nature as in life. This is what it means to lose boyhood and to grow old. . . . 'Heaven,' says Wordsworth, 'Lies about us in our infancy', but the

'Shades of the prison house begin to close
Upon the growing boy.'

"You see! Beautiful at first . . . the boy sees it a little more dimly; the youth a little more dimly still. Then, by and by, the heat of the sun, the dust of the road, make the vision 'Fade into the light of common day'.

"Perhaps, however, the fault is in ourselves, not in our stars (more quotes from Wordsworth). Wordsworth did not let the world grow poor and mean for him—it grew richer to his life's end.

"Just think—take any grass blade . . . and you find yourself face to face with an infinite miracle. . . . By and by the blossoms come, then the fruit—luscious juices packed within the rind. And out of what has all this come? Out of what we call dirty earth—raw, dead materials that to some of our moods have no wonder in them at all. . . . We are hardened to think the Universe is poor.

". . . There's another brook we mustn't let run dry. As life advances, we must do what some think there's no time for—cultivate our taste for books, for statuary, for music. . . . I have noticed that those men who have only time for newspapers have wasted so much time. . . . By merely using odd moments, we could really master the greatest books and works of art the world has ever known . . . Shakespeare, Michael Angelo. . . . We can make friends with them as no one who walked the streets with them could ever do. . . . I say to you, store up these treasures; then the world will not grow poorer as you grow older, it will grow richer."

Twenty-three years later an observer with a Unitarian type background—and whose church-shaking grandfather's portrait by John Collier is the most impressive thing in the Worktown art gallery (though T. H. Huxley had no local associations, and the existence of this splendid portrait was apparently overlooked during the Darwin celebrations)—went to this same Unitarian Church, in the same month of July, at the same time in the morning. He heard—to all intents and purposes—the same sermon. Although the 1937 minister has long departed, one cannot fail to be struck, on reading this second report, by its marked similarity to its counterpart of twenty-three years ago. There is the same careful philosophical approach; the same elegance of presentation. Even the theme is once again that of trying to recapture the joy and vision of youth by the deliberate cultivation of one's delight in beauty in nature and in art. This time, instead of quotations from Wordsworth's "Intimations of Immortality" we have quotations from Rupert Brooke's "The Great Lover." The minister introduced his 1960 sermon by reading part of this poem. The report of the sermon continues:

The Minister said his sermon was going to be about how to find joy in life. . . . Everyone would doubtless recollect the first joy they ever had, the exhilaration that came with adolescence, the flashes of insight. Now these things had left them, had all gone. How could we recapture that first, fine careless rapture? he asked. He made the point that memory was not the same thing as the rapture itself. . . . How is one to increase one's capacity for joy? One must think, perhaps, of Rupert Brooke's poem—"I have been so great a lover"—but not necessarily to think of *his* joys. You can think of your own joys, the joys that have come into *your* life. One must think, too, of one's own attitude to enjoyment—can it be reconciled with religious feeling? To enjoy a good meal, or a game—this is in no way contrary to religion, unless we allow enjoyment of such minor things to blind us to the higher things in life. . . . One should enjoy a visitor when he comes amongst us, whether he comes in the form of a tree, or a bird singing, a sunset, or a fire in the depths of the winter. But often there is the insatiable craving one has which interferes with enjoyment. It is as though we are going through a picture gallery, and are so intent on coming to the end that we look at none of the pictures.

At the end of the sermon, the Minister made the following announcements: If anyone was still without their calendars for the coming month, they would be printed shortly. There was going to be an annual summer flower communion service next Sunday, to which everyone should bring a flower, and would receive one from everyone else. It would be a "sort of midsummer festival". On Thursday, he went on, the Women's League would meet, and also the Forward Movement Committee, which was going to deal with the Moss Bank Open Air Service in two weeks' time. On Saturday the 23rd there would be a visit to the Islamic Central Mosque in Manchester, and eighty people of the three congregations in town would be going.

The Minister himself came and talked to me afterwards; he told me that he had no Communion service ever in the church except on Good Thursday, which was the only time when the people here would tolerate Communion. They didn't like it, as a rule, and on Good Thursday several people did come, but were certainly not pressed into it. He had himself gone to see a doctor of philosophy in Liverpool, who said that he had only been three times in his life, and it just happened that the one week when he (the minister) talked to him, he felt like it, and he felt that this was the best attitude to have towards Communion, since it had been so spoilt by Catholic insistence on dogma and the whole Eucharistic view of life.

Common to All Sects

To *explain* the strength and diversity of Christianity as a living entity in this modern industrial town would involve going far beyond our present bounds—and those of strict sociology. Nor is this the place to go even briefly into the multiple side-activities of religious organisations—a whole volume in itself. Let us, rather, attempt to sum up the impact of public religious observance in the churches as institutions today. It can be summed up, for present purposes, thus:

1) Every successful and continuing sect in Worktown possesses its own premises, used by members for some form of public worship. These vary widely in outward form, from conspicuous symbolic edifices with cruciform plan and the challenge of tower and spire, to the room over the Old Baths which the Bethel Evangelists rent from the Corporation; from the great Methodist Hall (on a circuit of its own) in Knowsley Street, which can hold 2,000, to the single room in Bradshawgate where the three members of the Christian Community meet once in eight weeks. In many sects there is a strong sense of collective ownership in the building, which is regarded as the House of God. An instance occurred at the end of a revivalist meeting of the relatively propertyless Bethel Evangelists. People were talking and laughing after an adult baptism service when suddenly the preacher rose and chastised them, calling out:

"Be silent! Remember where you are!"

Of the thirty-eight sects known to us in Worktown, twenty-one own at least one building exempt from rates; four of the remainder rent premises from "rival" religious organisations; and the others rent from secular owners.

2) *Religious Service*. Public observance is common to every sect, and is closely bound up with the church building. It consists of certain things said or sung (usually both), and it is almost always conducted by a specially appointed leader or priest. At some point in

the service this leader, or the worshippers, or both, address remarks directly to God.

3) In almost every sect, the religious life is centred around *a special service* in which bread (or a substitute) is actually eaten by the worshippers or by their leader; sometimes this symbolises the partaking of the body of Christ; sometimes the meaning is much vaguer. Different sects attribute very different significance to this act; but always the crux of the ceremony must be conducted by a person who stands (either temporarily or permanently) in some special intermediary relationship between the worshippers and their God. This service had its origin in a sacrifice, and the outward sacrificial forms are always present in some degree, some form of altar or "holy place" being used in every case. There are four Christian sects in Worktown which do not regularly celebrate this sacrament. Two of these, the Christian Spiritualists and the Christian Scientists, are far removed from the central traditions of Christianity; another, the Salvation Army, is organised on an explicitly inter-denominational secular model, not excluding its members from other sects; and the fourth, the Society of Friends (Quakers), is grounded on the absolute equality of all its members before God, and does not distinguish between priests and laymen.

4) *All* sects assume that a number of people worshipping together at the same place at the same time have a special religious value, and play an essential part in religious life. This assumption is not shared (as we have seen) by the great mass of part-time religious persons who may never attend an organised service, yet profoundly respect religion and God.

5) Common to every Christian organisation also is an *initiation ceremony*. There are two types of entry into most of the sects. One is Christian Baptism, a ritual ceremony by means of which, through blessed water, people are admitted into the sphere of influence of Christ. The other is the secular method of admittance by verbal or written agreement after an *examination* at the hands of a committee of members. The emphasis laid on one or other of these varies very widely amongst the sects, but is always there.

The Three Christian Cycles

Baptism is crucial in most of Christianity, and is one of the things that has helped to cause the proliferation of sects. Today, 2,000 years after the baptism of Jesus Christ by St. John, we have in Worktown over 100 churches run by the thirty-eight Christian organisations there. Baptism is trigger-mechanism in the life-cycle of Worktown Christians' public observances. In the rich tapestry of these observances, three cycles can be followed in the study of the Christian Churches—and were so followed, in detail, by M-O:

I. The Cycle of Life (and After-Life)
II. The Cycle of the Year: Easter to Christmas
III. The Cycle of the Week (built round the Sabbath, usually Sunday).

These basic cycles are shared by everybody, even the non-churchgoers and "irreligious" folk who are not *consciously* involved. Seventh-day Adventists, who insist on Saturday for their Sabbath, still can't go to the Worktown museum on Sunday (neither can the Atheists); and they must watch the local football match on their Sabbath, or not at all.

Let us now examine, in some detail, a few samples of the kind of ceremonies which make, for believers, the crucial points of these cycles.

Baptism: A Beginning, or an End in Itself?

Anglicans baptise soon after birth, often in a rapid ceremony attended by six persons or less (including the baby). The "Churching" of the mother may even be done at the same time, at the font, immediately after the baptism. An observer attended one such double occasion at the Parish Church, and got into talk with the mother concerned, who told him that she was far from an enthusiastic Christian, entirely unconvinced of the value of what was to be done, and in fact against it:

"But Mother and the rest insisted—I just *had* to give way."

One of the criticisms most commonly voiced by the other school of thought about this "Sacrament of Dedication to God" is that infant baptism is not so much *wrong* as cynical; it implies that the state of mind of the chief participant is utterly unimportant—a curious attitude to take about so solemn a ceremony, (they agree).

However this may be, there is no doubt that Infant Baptism can be an impressive ceremony, as many observer reports have shown—including the latest one, that of the baptism of the Minister's own baby at a large Presbyterian Church in July 1960.

Even more impressive, however, are the adult baptisms—ceremonies in which only those who "know what they are doing" can be baptised and admitted fully into the church. A very striking service of this sort was reported in June 1938 at the headquarters of the Bethel

Evangelists, a hired room over the baths. The ceremony had been well publicised, and more than 300 people—a big turn-out for anything religious at Worktown—turned up in the rain at 7.0 p.m. Two-thirds of this crowd were women; the big, ordinarily drab room was packed out, tense with life and colour (Plate 4):

Observer arrived during the singing of the first hymn; they are repeating the chorus 4 times, the Pastor on the platform swinging his arms to get the rhythm, and to induce them to sing louder and quicker:
> "Someone has suffered, someone has died,
> Someone for you has been crucified!"

On the platform with the Pastor are five rows of people, the women wearing white blouses with a 4-inch black bow at the collar, and black berets. Eight of the women in the front are in white dresses; these are the women to be baptised.

A marathon service ensues, which includes a number of detailed, personal prayers:
> "Let us pray for Jimmy with a bad cold" or—
> "Let us pray for Mrs. Jones' children in their trouble, and for their grandmother."

A vigorous collection is made and taken up to the Pastor, who says that last week's £10. 10. 7 was "Just above the red line—don't forget the Lord's work." In conducting the service, he veers between violent exhortation and chatty homeliness. He interrupts a hymn to correct the singers:
> "*Whom*; not *Whome*."

He beats times with a swinging arm:
> "The need of the world is Jesus
> To soothe its longing soul."

The sermon is very long, and delivered with all possible force, interspersed with asides like:
> "Sometimes I have heart-searching. God forbid we should just preach sermons. We want to be sure our message comes from God."

Or (to the children on the left):
> "Be quiet! They distract me. I know it is difficult for children."

and then, suddenly, to all present:
> "I feel inclined to turn this (baptism) meeting into a testimony meeting. How many of you here will say God's answer to prayer?"

(Nearly every hand goes up: no waiting, straight up. He smiles widely....)

As the sermon at last draws to an end, the eight women who are to be baptised, young and middle-aged, are taking off their coats, leaving them with the white frocks underneath. They are helped by the other women. The Pastor says:
> "May those going through the water realise what they are doing."

and now begins the actual ceremony:

The women are taking off their shoes now, and the Pastor has gone down to a chair behind the tank, 8 feet by 4 feet, and 3 feet deep in water. There are 6 steps down into this from the platform, and behind this is the Pastor, in a black robe ruffled at the sleeves.

One of the women comes right down into the tank, and he says:

"We do not believe in baptismal regeneration, but to give evidence before all. The only Baptism in the Bible is by immersion, and is in the case of believers. Remember this, if there are any in the room who have been sprinkled, this is not Baptism."

The woman faces the right, standing waist-deep in water. The Pastor, on the side, puts his right hand on her chest, his left hand on her back, and says:

"On your confession of faith, I baptise you in the name of the Father and of the Son and of the Holy Ghost. Amen."

With this, he swishes the woman backwards, completely immersing her; then swings her up into a standing position again.

Soon all the 8 women are dripping with water. On the platform, 2 middle-aged women are waiting, one with a towel, another with a black robe; each baptised woman in turn has her face wiped and is given a black robe; then she passes through a door on the right.

The second woman nearly faints, but they steady her.

The ninth is a man of 40, partly bald. He is in tennis shirt and grey flannels; he wipes himself, and so away. Throughout the ceremony, everybody strains to see it all, particularly the ducking; each person in turn gets no gentle swish of water, but a real dose of it; he or she goes back with a flop, and the sound of hitting the water carries to the back of the hall.

As the last Baptism is completed, the Pastor asks all to pray:

"We praise Thee who hast caused these Thy children to have witnessed and been blessed today. As He can save, so He can keep. Amen."

Another of our steady observers covered the same high-pressure adult baptism from another part of the church, and was most impressed by the hymn-singing. Always the politician as well as the observer, Walter Hood (who has since become a T.U.C. Scholar and Union boss), ended this report in his clear round writing (which few observers have) on a personal note:

Let's hope that some political party can get some sturdy tunes like these! Now I know why A. J. Cook (the Miners' leader) was always late for his meetings, and advised singing to be done.

Cycle of the Year

Christianity remains the determinant of most of the key ritual points; but this situation of strength, based on nearly 2,000 years of tradition, is being nibbled at by new influences, such as non-denominational cremation, marriage in Registry offices, and so on. As a determinant in the fundamental cycle of the year, however, Christianity remains unchangingly dominant, even though its rituals were built up on a rural economy superficially many millions of cotton-twists removed from a Northern industrial town. There are many homes in Worktown from which you cannot see a single tree or growing thing (see Plates 5, 15).

Nevertheless, the modern calendar is derived from the systems of moon- and sun-worshippers, and is therefore in its origins religious. The secular year begins and ends with the rites of the Christmas season, religious at least in name. The Christian year does not coincide with the January to December unit, but extends over little more than half that time, namely, from Advent in November to somewhere about May: Sundays after Trinity fill the gap.

The main Christian festivals—Christmas and Easter—are observed by the majority as times of less work and more good cheer; while the chief work holiday, coming in the summer, has no religious background at all. Other popular days of ritual, such as Guy Fawkes' Day and St. Valentine's Day, have indeed a very ancient traditional origin, but certainly not a Christian one.

Thus there remains now a fragmentary religious year, ruins of a fine pagan edifice; a year partially observed by a bigger-than-Christian population. And there is the Christian year, observed consciously by Christians.

What one recognises as the important events of the year depends a great deal on one's job. The farmer is ruled by the seasons, and must plough, sow, reap and harvest; only the harvesting is associated today with a religious rite—the Harvest Festival. The clerk's special times, however, are the ends of the quarters, when accounts have to be made up, and these peaks have so far not been recognised by religion in any form. Yearly times of effort and glory at school are speech and sports days, to which may be added a few prayers or hymns. The non-Christian year has now so much variety, on account of the variety of jobs in the modern world, that it would be exceedingly difficult to link the peak points of all these different occupations to some kind of religious observance. True, occupations' services are held annually by some parsons, but the modern industrial and clerical year, its shape so varied, is on the whole not dedicated to religion, nor linked at all closely with religion, Christian or other.

But the Christian year reflects the life of Christ. There is a period of preparation before he comes, and besides the two main festivals of Christmas and Easter, which recall his birth and death, there are others corresponding to incidents in his life. Ascension Day and Whitsun reflect his appearance after death, and his departure. To model his life on Christ's is the earnest Christian's endeavour, and as he follows the Christian calendar through the year he has many opportunities of familiarising himself with Christ's life in detail, and of meditating upon its excellences. Many of the ceremonies in the Christian calendar, of course, of pre-Christian, pagan significance, remain and have been remoulded by Christian sects. In just the same way, in the political field, the pagan May Day has been remoulded by the Labour Party into a day of Left-Wing demonstration.

By 1937 (and no doubt much earlier) ministers of many denominations were uneasily aware that their churches were in danger of becoming less and less relevant to the fast-moving, technological society in which they found themselves operating. Dwindling congregations of mainly elderly women were a warning sign—since all attach importance to statistics of attendance. The nature of the problem was clear enough to any thoughtful cleric. Religion had lost its material supremacy in the scientific age—for whatever may be the efficacy of prayer in, for example, making the crops grow, anyone (short of a religious maniac) can see that it is less than the efficacy of scientific fertilising. And, anyway, what do crops and harvests mean to a society that lives mainly on tinned and packaged goods, and seldom sees a field of wheat? What sort of visual significance can a Harvest Festival have for these?

But there are other holds over people besides prayers and services; and in Worktown in particular there existed a wealth of popular customs and ceremonies over which the church was still able to maintain an apparent dominance. Foremost among these were, and still are, the Processions. Before discussing the significance of these, let us describe one such occasion in detail—the Civic Procession to the Parish Church from the Town Hall on 12th May, 1937.

The procession was led by the Chief Constable, who walked in front of the Salvation Army Band. They were followed by two policemen, and two men in bowler hats with staves, on each of which was a ball with cross keys on top. Then came, in order: four Salvation Army officers; one beadle, dressed in black edged with red, gold collar, and topper band; three parsons of various denominations; then some dignitaries—the Mayor, in scarlet cloak, cock-hat, chain; the Town Clerk in wig, gown and proctorial tie. Next an Equerry in black tails, gold edges, gold topper band; then the Aldermen and

Councillors; the Boys' Brigade, the Masons, the British Legion, and finally a little bunch of policemen. The observer's description of the scene continues:

Along the side goes a scout with a most peculiar green dragon, about 9 feet long and 4 feet high, green with black spots and a jagged mane, a great dragon mouth which waggles, and in its side a knob which, manipulated frequently by the boy, produces quite an absurd and sudden whirring noise. Passing Woolworth's, he is up to the Alderman and Councillors, who are all solemn, nearly all with umbrellas. It was remarked of their passing:
"The chief thing I notice is the strong smell of cigars."
Nearly all wear gloves; only the young are in light coats and hatless. A policeman comes up and orders the boy, rather uncertainly, back. A scoutmaster rushes up and says:
"He can't understand you. He's deaf and dumb."
The lad happily makes the dragon's belly defy the P.C. The dragon is delayed, its mouth wagging hungrily at Aldermanic backsides. It bears, inset on its flank, the notice:

REMEMBER ST. GEORGE

Outside the chip shop and the Grand Theatre, a bodyguard lines the gutter on each side. This is composed of Guides, Church Lads, one fireman, St. John's Ambulance, scouts, etc. They are in bad order, and not properly stood either at attention or at ease.

After the procession had passed into the church, the Church Lads form up in the street, in a very unsoldierly way, the band in front, and march off up to Silverwell Street and away.

Seven police are now at each side of the gate, leaving a wide avenue to go through, but no one goes. Plenty of people wait about, but there is no big crowd.

This, of course, was a civic occasion as much as a religious one; but the majority of sects and individual places of worship in Worktown stage, at least once a year, a similar major procession within or about their constituency. This originates most clearly in the old, and tribally functional, "Beating of the Bounds". Whereas people in the south of England tend to think of sermons as things which a minister preaches, in Lancashire, when you talk about sermons, you mean these ceremonies, which are the outdoor climax of the Christian year, just as Christmas is the indoor one. During the thirties, this was the time when anyone even vaguely associated with the church community made the mild public gesture of walking in procession, or at least looking on and applauding from the pavement. In the unaffluent thirties a good deal of the economic cycle of saving money was to do with buying new clothes, including sometimes exotic ones, "for Sermons time" (usually July or August—the pre-Harvest period). With recent increased spending power this is less true, but observer reports of July and August 1960 show changes only in detail. If there is a conspicuous change in 1960, it is an added emphasis on finance. Thus the Rose Queen Procession and Festival of July 1960 was announced by a two-inch headline in the local paper:

>   FESTIVAL AIMS HIGH
>   FOR £1,000 TARGET

No such cash aim would have been so blatantly proclaimed in 1937. This difference, as we shall see, is in line with a general change in the church's financial policy over the past twenty years.

In addition to these processions and festivals, the more enterprising churches get up to all sorts of schemes for enlivening Christianity, and perhaps extending its influence beyond the usual, very limited, Sabbatarian population. Thus, in the lull period of spring, a group of Methodists float a Football Sunday. Such a gathering was described by one of our observers on 4 May 1937; here are some short extracts from his report:

Football Sunday is a feature of Worktown's church and chapel life. Every church and chapel who run a football team (the R.C.'s excepted) try to get a prominent footballer or referee to speak to the men of the class; and the classes are usually well attended.

The observer describes the speaker at this meeting as "looking like a cotton-factory worker", and gives a brief summary of his address, which consisted of an attempt to relate Christianity convincingly to the world of sport:

"If Christ came back to this world," the speaker declared "I know he would be doing many things we are doing. We should find him on the football field . . . and I know he would be thinking of the unemployed. . . ."

He then tried to show that Christianity was a part of the spirit of sportsmanship, and not antagonistic to it, as some people supposed:

"I was asked once if I show my religion on the football field when I am refereeing a match; I had sent off the field a goalkeeper, and I was asked: is *that* what you call Christian charity? I answered that we are all bound by the laws of life, like we are in a game, and we must observe them."

The Cycle of the Week

It is hardly necessary to labour, and impossible to document in the short available space, the extent to which the Christian cycle of the week has been built into modern civilisation. Moreover, in some important respects, the Christian Sunday, with its associated Saturday build-up, has become much more important in the last two decades of increased leisure. The churches have not directly benefited from this; on the other hand, they have not lost anything like as much as they vociferously protested twenty-five years ago. It could even be argued that the strengthening of the day of rest (as a holiday) actually increases the chances of statistical improvement in future congregations.

Statistical Change, 1960

The decline in the numbers of people attending places of worship throughout Worktown is very general; the only exceptions are the Roman Catholics, and some of the special occasions of individual small sects. During this summer, we talked with twenty-one widely-representative Worktown ministers, and many more related people in various organisations. The evidence of these ministers is irrefutable on the main issue; only on the question of youth did some difference of opinion arise, some ministers claiming an actual *increase* in youth attendance. This seemed to be connected more with the personality of some leader figure than with any particular sect or policy.

Trustworthy reports of this kind come from Anglican, Catholic, Presbyterian, Unitarian, Baptist, Congregationalist and Methodist sources. These do not support the sweeping generalisations we often hear about the younger generation. Let some of the ministers speak:

Superintendent of Worktown Wesley Circuit, age 63: "I notice an awakening among youth. Their parents may have neglected their spiritual education, but, although they may not be fully aware of it, the young people are beginning to come back into the Church. . . . We hold a Circuit Youth Fellowship once a month, after the Sunday service. The average attendance is 70, between the ages of 15 and 20."

The forty-year-old Minister of a larger Methodist Church also speaks encouragingly of the outlook for the younger generation on the housing estate in his area. He is getting over the problem of lethargic parents who don't send their children to church by arranging for the children to be collected by car. This by-passing of parent-inertia he claims to have been very successful:

"Thirty children are brought in this way, but if we had the transport, it could be 300. The car is an inducement, but it has been proved that the children are responding."

While the Minister of an old Anglican Church has noticed that any new members who join his congregation tend to be in their twenties or early thirties. He adds:

"Our Young Wives' Groups are popular, and that means we should get the youngsters into the Church."

Naturally, the other point of view also appears, several Ministers experiencing the reverse of the above. The Minister of one Parish Church, age 55, reports:

"Two youth clubs have been formed, but youth work has been found to be more difficult than it was.... What I have learned of discipline is not effective with the young of today. For example, a child sucking a sweet in class was asked to stop; she didn't, and when questioned she said she had not had breakfast. The class of girls of 11 to 13 was questioned, and it was found that 5 had not eaten since tea the previous evening. This is because they sit up late at night watching TV, and can't get up in the morning, and so don't have time to eat."

While the Minister of an Independent Mission said:

"Youth? We're not getting them. We don't have dances and things, the Trust Deeds don't allow it. We have Scouts and Cubs, and Girls' Fellowships, all are well attended, but young people are not coming to the Mission for its own sake."

Elaborate statistical analysis of so local a character might be tiresome here. Instead, consider M-O's latest collection of statistics for two of the larger sects, as supplied by their ministers and accepted as satisfactory:

CONGREGATIONAL CHURCHES

		1939	1960
A	1. Church Members	77	27
	2. Sunday School	106	50
	3. Teachers	18	10
B	1. Church Members	213	167
	2. Sunday School	319	141
	3. Teachers	67	24
C	1. Church Members	46	27
	2. Sunday School	130	78
	3. Teachers	14	13

CONGREGATIONAL CHURCHES—cont.

			1939	1960
D	1.	Church Members	156	126
	2.	Sunday School	254	175
	3.	Teachers	31	29
E	1.	Church Members	258	178
	2.	Sunday School	139	140
	3.	Teachers	31	29
F	1.	Church Members	80	66
	2.	Sunday School	180	53
	3.	Teachers	30	8
G	1.	Church Members	232	105
	2.	Sunday School	77	17
	3.	Teachers	21	5
H	1.	Church Members	133	72
	2.	Sunday School	110	110
	3.	Teachers	15	11
I	1.	Church Members	177	158
	2.	Sunday School	390	190
	3.	Teachers	52	21
J	1.	Church Members	509	412
	2.	Sunday School	211	75
	3.	Teachers	39	20

Calculating the totals for these figures, we find that the membership of these ten Congregationalist churches has dropped from 1,881 in 1939 to 1,338 in 1960—a drop of nearly 30%; while the drop in Sunday School lists has been even greater, from 1,804 in 1939 to 929 in 1960—a drop of nearly half. If Sunday School pupils are to be regarded as the potential church members of the future, these figures would suggest that the process of the decline is an accelerating one.

BAPTIST CHAPELS

	Church	Membership	Sunday School Teachers	Scholars
1940	A	213	28	91
	B	36	10	53
	C	101	27	148
	D	20	4	25
	E	58	5	36
1945	A	219	17	70
	B	41	14	120
	C	121	27	148

BAPTIST CHAPELS—cont.

	Church	Membership	Sunday School Teachers	Scholars
	D	18	2	15
	E	58	5	36
1950	A	215	23	122
	B	45	15	125
	C	101	27	148
	D	10	—	—
	E	53	7	65
1955	A	192	21	112
	B	37	11	90
	C	58	21	84
	D	(Closed down on the last Sunday of 1952)		
	E	28	8	69
1960	A	190	12	44
	B	38	14	90
	C	58	12	50
	E	28	6	59

These figures give a similar picture to that of the Congregationalist churches—a total membership of 428 in 1940 has dropped to 314 in 1960; and a total Sunday School list of 353 in 1940 has dropped to 243 in 1960—again, a slightly larger proportional drop.

Church of England membership theoretically involves putting your name on an Electoral Roll. There are all sorts of inconsistencies and variations in the degree of registration, and the extent to which the rolls are kept up to date—or even kept at all. But the following Anglican churches, after careful scrutiny, seem to provide accurate comparable data between our 1937, very detailed, records and the so far less intimate recent study:

	Church	1937	1950	1960
A	Parish Church	500+	414	421
	B	743	—	170
	C	510	(500)	200+
	D	432	385	355
	E	400	309+	350
	F	296	—	205
	G	192	—	220[1]
	H	318	520	574

[1] The vicar of this church told our checking observer that this roll has not been corrected for loss by death during the past fifteen years. (Some churches leave their rolls unchecked for much longer.)

Church H is one of the only two out of thirty-four which on any criterion have been able to report an increase since the war. Both these increases have been in upper middle-class parishes. As the verger put it (August 1960):

"The increase in numbers is entirely due to the present, and previous, vicar. They each in their turn have appealed and got results. The vicar does not leave the parishioners alone until he has made them realise it is their duty to be on the roll.

"This is a wealthy, residential parish, and its popularity is increasing."

It must be remembered that none of the above figures necessarily represent any actual acts of worship: they represent only a willingness to be associated with a particular place of worship. Often, the drop in actual worshippers on a Worktown Sunday has been less than the drop of those on the rolls. It seems that the "Faithful Few" are becoming only slowly fewer, and certainly not less faithful. Some spot counts of actual congregations will illustrate: all are taken from directly comparable services in the same church:

Church	1937–8	1960
Church of England	48	45
(Medium size)	67	53
Roman Catholic		
(Medium size)	262	300+
Congregationalist		
(Large, "Upper-class";		
"J" on previous list)	82	84
Methodist	91	67
(Large)		
Methodist	32	31
(Small)		
Total	582	580

Affluent Christianity?

A few places of worship have been forced to close down for financial reasons (e.g. "D" Baptist Chapel in the table above). The great majority, including some of those with the sharpest numerical drops in congregation, not only receive more gross cash, but *feel* more comfortable financially than they did in 1937. The reasons for this are twofold:

See Chapter VI

£1,483,057

(One million, four hundred and eighty-three thousand and fifty-seven)

POUNDS

Poll-Pools

NO ENTRANCE FEE

Home Matches to be Played on

Monday, Nov. 1st, 1937

HOME MATCH ON MONDAY NOV. 1			WIN or LOSE NO DRAW	
Cleansing & Sewerage	U			X
Clothing & Stationery		O rt		X
Electricity	2			X
Education		V	OTE	X
Finance		O		X
Gas		T		X
General Purposes		E		X
Housing	U			X
Libraries		O rt		X
Local Pensions	2			X
Markets		V	OTE	X
Parks		O		X
Public Assistance		T		X
Public Health		E		X
Rating & Valuation	U			X
Small Holdings		O rt		X
Streets	2			X
Transport		V	OTE	X
Watch Committee		O		X
Waterworks		T		X
STAKE 👉		VO	T E	X

All these Committees must be filled up from the Councillors you elect

POLL-PO

VO
in the Bolton
VO
on Nov
VO
for the be
VO
for the p
will hav
to spen
more tha
£1,000,0
of your
money

DIVID

More t
Vote for
the peopl
you think
best:
VOTE
Novembe
ALL

THE POPULAR
17 RESULTS POOL
17 Wards:- Candidates and Entries in Every Ward

MUNICIPAL ELECTION
YOUR WARD

YOU VOTE AT
(the place mentioned on your poll card)
ON MONDAY, NOV. 1st., 1937
Poll doors open from 8 a.m. to 8 p.m.

CANDIDATE 1	
CANDIDATE 2	
CANDIDATE 3	
CANDIDATE 4	

There are Candidates for each of the parties
They are all sensible adult BOLTONIANS

When you go to the Polling Station take one of the cards left by a Party Canvasser, but if you have lost it you can go without.
(A Card is desirable but not necessary)

17 MATCH POOL POOL Must be won

For Matches Played 1st NOV., 1937

CREDIT YOUR VOTE The minimum amount accepted

a MILLION POUNDS to be paid out by the New Council.

A L L   Y O U   H A V E   T O   D O
I S   T O   P U T   X   A G A I N S T
T H E   N A M E S   O F   T H E   2
C A N D I D A T E S   T H A T   U
T H I N K   B E S T

RIES MUST BE IN BY 8 P.M. MONDAY, NOVEMBER 1st.

£1,483,057 was spent by the Council last year. The new Council, that will be elected on Monday, Nov. 1st, is almost certain to be spending even more. There are 25 committees that allot the expenditure of this money; last year they met 932 times.

There are 96 members of the Council, and 17 wards in the town for them to be elected from. Each Councillor is elected for a term of 3 years at a time. You have the right to vote in their election. But not everyone in Bolton who has that right uses it. They say they aren't interested.

But whether you are interested or not, you still have to pay your rates; you still have to pay money over to the Council when you take a tram or a bus; when you switch on the light, turn a tap, or light your gas, you are using services run by the Council, for which you have to pay money to the Council.

Other people say it's all the same whoever gets in. But the town's concerns are everybody's concerns, and there are many things in the town's affairs that are nothing to do with politics. A town has no foreign policy, armaments programme, trade barriers, control of national law. So there is not so much room for disagreement on policy between parties in local politics as THERE IS in national politics. But that doesn't make local politics any less important. In fact they are more important in the day-to-day lives of most people. It cannot be a healthy sign of a great town's progress or alertness if a large number of its citizens long continue to ignore there right to elect their councillors, who are really the town's business and welfare managers for the time being.

Every British subject over 21 has a Parliamentary vote. But to have a municipal vote he or she must must be a RATEPAYER, or must occupy, as owner or tenant, land or premises in the area; or be the husband or wife of someone who does. These qualifications give you the privilege of voting for the Council. But more and more Boltonians are neglecting that right. During the last ten years the number of people voting in the Municipal Elections has steadily gone down. For example, in 1926 over sixty per cent. (nearly two-thirds) of the West Ward electors voted. While in the by-election this year LESS THAN A THIRD of the electors went to the polls. In other words, two people out of every three did not trouble to vote.

ARE YOU GOING TO LET THAT SMALL MINORITY WHO ARE INTERESTED IN POLITICS DECIDE ON MONDAY, NOV. 1, WHO IS GOING TO GOVERN—NOT ONLY THEM, BUT *YOU*, for another three years? DON'T YOU THINK YOU OUGHT TO LOOK TO YOUR OWN INTERESTS, SPEAK FOR YOURSELVES, CAST YOUR VOTE.

If this argument is true and sensible then VOTE TO-DAY. VOTE FOR ANYONE IN YOUR WARD CONTEST, BUT VOTE.

Published by CIVIC RESPONSIBILITIES, 95, Princess St., Manchester.
Printed by James Collins & Co. Limited, Royal Works, Elsinore Road, Old Trafford, Manchester.

1) A few people are giving very considerably more—see previous remarks on the growth of the Church élite.
2) Some churches—notably the Church of England—have developed better techniques for collecting money: in many 1960 services the cash collections, statutory in 1937, have now been completely dropped.

The Church of England has even been employing an American Market Research organisation to advise on techniques of money-raising. These post-war off-shoots of Davenport Street have analysed Worktown, and flustered some of the more conservative clergy and choristers. Outside our old friend the Parish Church a large new hoarding exhorts parishioners:

> A DIRECT GIVING SCHEME
> (Planned Giving)
> IS NOW IN OPERATION
> Please support your Parish Church

The Parish Church is not the only one to have adopted the new methods of collecting money on a basis of regular weekly and monthly subscriptions, instead of the haphazard collections during the actual services. The minister of a small Congregational church on the outskirts of Worktown describes a big rise in income from the new system:

"The income of the church has gone up since the introduction of the Voluntary Offering Envelope scheme:

                1940   £240 per year
                1960   £600 per year

"People are no longer interested in things like bazaars."

And a Scottish Presbyterian Minister said of his Worktown flock:

"The congregation is increasing, but we cater for the 'adopted sons' of Worktown, people who come here because of their professions. This is a very wealthy church. A large proportion of the members are doctors and specialists. . . . People are very generous—£2,000 a year in offerings. No endowments, all the money is raised by the people themselves."

In addition to the increased revenue from organised schemes of giving, it sometimes happens that the actual Sunday collections (where they still exist) are increasing, irrespective of increase or decrease of congregation. A big Methodist church in the town centre, with little status change, gave figures for its Sunday collections, over and above the organised giving:

1937   £5. 1. 9 average week
1950   £6. 4. 0 average week
1960   £7. 0. 0 or over per week

The conclusion we must draw from all this is that in the past two decades—and particularly in the last one—religious organisations in Worktown have tended to become more independent, economically, of the *numbers* publicly using their facilities for worship. The old and traditional insistence on giving *at* church, during the service, as part of the act of worship, is over and done with in many places, for the time being at least. We say "for the time being" because it is clear that any sect which continues to develop these systems of regular "extra-worship" payments to their logical conclusion is liable to find itself at last in a novel—and rather disconcerting—position, from which it may wish to withdraw. For such methods may in the end bring about a situation not far removed from the almost Orwell-seeming fantasy of empty churches with piped services and sermons from selected suitable sect-centres to each empty establishment.

This is one way of looking at it. The other is to feel that all these variations on the theme of giving—all the regularising and systematising—are not really new; in spirit, they represent a return to the simplest premise of early Christian obligation:

"Give a tithe to the Lord's Service."

Which of these two interpretations is nearest to the socio-truth only time (and study) will show.

FIVE

TO VOTE OR NOT . . .

MOST OF THE Christian Churches, basic "religious" institutions, have lately decreased *statistically*, measured in terms of *visible behaviour response* in Worktown. There's some reason to believe that this is so in Britain widely. At the same time, as we have seen, while weakening quantitatively in some respects they have strengthened qualitatively in others. A striking example (expressable in figures) is the increase in money given to many churches today: more income from less people. In part a product of the affluent society; in part a *deepening* sense of responsibility towards religious institutions by those who remain concerned. This sort of change is difficult to measure, sometimes can only be analysed by insight at the individual level. It is not the *sort* of feeling that can be expressed by an ordinary Briton holding it—sometimes only vaguely and far down in private opinion—when asked by a stranger, however subtly questioning.

Christianity certainly requires no sanction of *popularity*. In this it differs from the other main expression of traditional "ideology" in democratic society, also grown slowly out of our past: *party politics*.

Party politics depends on the statistical index of the Vote. As things are in twentieth-century Britain no other measure is so "relevant". Yet on a snap check in Worktown, August 1960, informally asked who the local M.P.s were:

—34% did not know any;
—Only 24% knew the names of *both* (Worktown has been divided into two constituencies since 1950, see below)

This is a little better than the 1960 national average of M.P. don't know (41%; see Chapter 15). But at the time local M.P.s were much in the news, since one was resigning to become a High Court Judge and cause a by-election. The picture barely differs from 1937-8.

Twentieth-Century Trend

Even the political leaders of Worktown today are largely those of the thirties. Seventeen of the Aldermen and Councillors on the Municipal authority have served as such for more than twenty-two years; five for over thirty years. The *influential* places of Worktown's local politics are nearly all held by old friends of pre-war days.

Worktown has a strong Liberal tradition, kept alive by the active local evening newspaper, owned by relations of the first Viscount Leverhulme, Worktowner. It has one of the few Liberal M.P.s in Parliament; by virtue of a local pact between Conservative and Liberal against Labour—which also enables them together to out-vote Labour on the Council when they co-operate. This pact is being broken by the Liberals (in finality) at the Parliamentary by-election late in 1960. Thus the set-up reverts to an open three-party system, as before. The Deputy Mayor contests the seat for Labour; another local for Conservative; and a national figure, ex-M.P. Frank Byers, for Liberal.[1]

In 1950 Worktown was split from one double-seat constituency into two singles, East and West. In 1959 the electorate voting in East was 81·1%, in West 79·9%. The national 1959 voting figure was 78·7%.[1]

During the sixteen *general* elections of this century, sometimes more than a quarter, and always more than one-seventh of the total British electorate have *not* recorded their vote:

Year of General election	% of total U.K. electorate voting
1895	78·0
1900	74·4
1906	83·3
1910 (Jan.)	85·6
1910 (Dec.)	81·0
1918 ("Khaki election")	57·6
1922	71·3
1923	70·8
1924	76·6
1929	76·1

[1] The Worktown record of parliamentary elections may be briefly summed up:
  1929 (General Election): 2 Labour M.P.s returned with small margins; Liberal bottom of 5 candidates.
  1931 (General): 2 Conservatives by large majority over 2 Labour (the previous sitting Members); no Liberal candidate.
  1935 (General): Same 2 Conservatives returned; decreased majorities.
  1940 (By-election): On death of one local M.P. another Conservative returned unopposed.
  1945 (General): 2 Labour M.P.s (new men) in with 10,000 margins over 2 Conservative; this time 2 Liberals (with a fifth of total poll).
  1950 (General): 2 Labour, with fair margins over 2 Conservative; 2 Liberal (again score a fifth).
  1951 (General): 1 Conservative; 1 Liberal by pact; defeating 2 Labour by small margins.
  1955 (General): As 1951, but *decreased* vote for all candidates.
  1959 (General): As 1955 (still same 2 Conservative M.P.'s) with further decrease.
  1960 (By-election): Conservative returned, small margin over Labour. Liberal gained substantial vote.

Year of General election	% of total electorate voting
1931	79·8
1935	74·4
1945	76·1
1950	84·0
1951	82·6
1955	76·8
1959	78·7

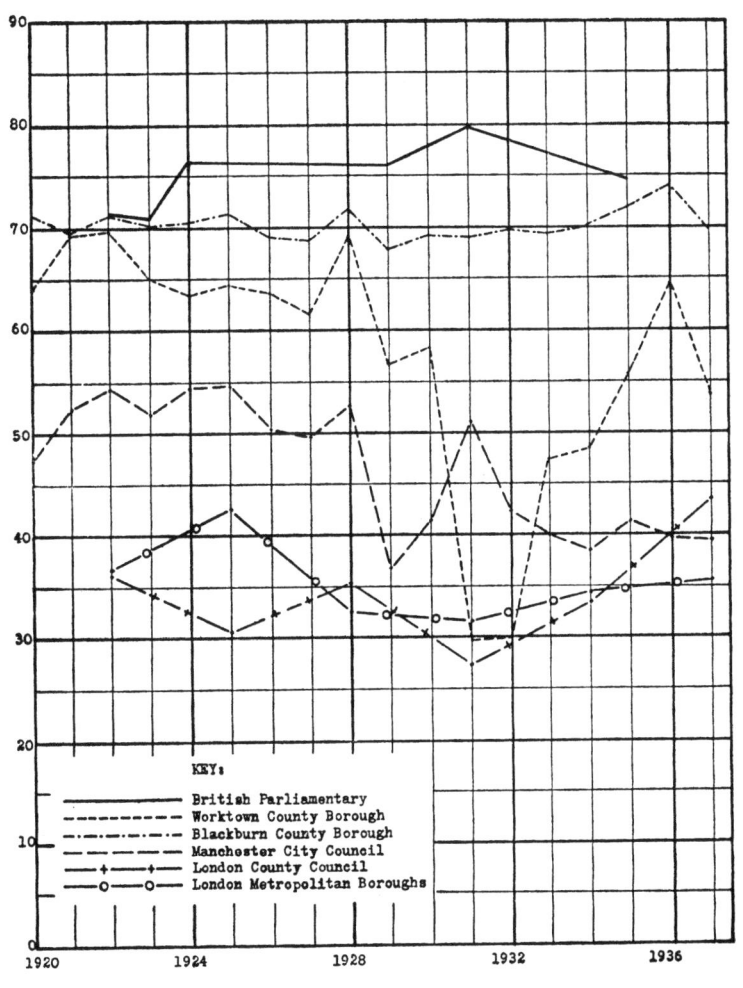

Voting percentages in some pre-war British Elections.

Assumptions about Vote-Use

The complicated system of government in Great Britain, both central and local, is based upon the popular vote—and the belief that it is decisive. The individual citizen does not, as sometimes in ancient Greece or modern Switzerland, vote directly upon specific measures; but he can influence the nature of such measures by electing selected representatives to the various legislative bodies. It is normally only at election times that the "average citizen" can definitely affect the course of the nation's political destiny.

Although in the past the right to vote has been considered—and in some ways still is—the central tenet of human rights as a whole, the experience of recent years has indicated how little value may be attached to it in countries where it has no tradition and is not a part of the accepted landscape. Some of the sadness of the sixties derives from the failure of democracy to attract where it has no traditional roots and inbred rites.

In social fact, the act of voting within Britain in general and Worktown in particular may be a very tiny, can indeed be quite a *trivial*, incident in the total activity of a free man's (and particularly a free woman's) contemporary living and thinking. A great many Britons, rather than starting off with assumptions about the importance of politics and the meaning of party or policy, do not feel these to be necessarily implicit in the process of living and daily thought.

Political scientists themselves are among those who attach to the subject matter of their studies values which are not necessarily shared by large sections of their subject matter, the studied. As Professor G. K. Galbraith, the American originator of the conception of the Affluent Society (through his book of that name) has well said, regarding general political and other attitudes:

"Intellectuals in politics are always deeply concerned with these things for themselves. It is their invariable conviction that the tastes and interests of the people at large are far behind. This I doubt." (*Observer*, 7 August 1960.)

After some years of intensive study, first in Worktown and then more widely, those engaged on this side of Mass-Observation would probably go beyond Professor Galbraith's doubt. It is even possible, at this level, that many ordinary people with votes are showing (e.g. in *not* using these votes) more discernment. It remains remarkable that little work has been done on this crucial problem of democracy. In the latest of the valuable volumes sponsored by Nuffield College,

TO VOTE OR NOT . . . 89

The British General Election of 1959 by D. E. Butler and Richard Rose (Macmillan, 1960), for instance, the only substantial reference to non-voting comes in the chapter of conclusions, in which the following appears:

"Non-voters *seem* to have been pro-Labour."

The word "seem" (our italics) is fairly used, for the closest scrutiny of this fact-packed, 290-page volume fails to reveal any adequate evidence to *prove* that this is so.

Evidence from Voter Research in Worktown

We started out, in our Worktown study, partly on the basis of this huge group of non-voters in parliamentary elections: and not only these, but the much larger number—often nearly half the electorate—who do not vote in any form of provincial election. How did these people differ, if at all, from those who did vote?

The greater part of the original Worktown studies was necessarily done during municipal elections. These have the advantage of occurring rather frequently. And it so happened that there was no General (Parliamentary) Election after 1935, when our studies began, until the end of the war in 1945.

Fortunately, though, an important (then) parliamentary by-election occurred in 1938 at Farnworth, which abuts on and is in many senses part of Worktown, wherein the late George Tomlinson (subsequently Minister of Education) won the seat for Labour (see Plate 16). Many other parliamentary by-elections were studied, as the Worktown results incited political interest widely. In some of these M-O was able to test some of its northern conclusions in detail (Chapter 6). In the initial instance, at Farnworth, we concentrated (for the statistical part of the study, involving as it did much concentration of effort) on suitable wards within the constituency, after general study of them all.[1]

---

[1] The fieldwork on politics was directed by Walter Hood, assisted by Frank Cawson, Herbert Howarth and others under my supervision. Boxes of fascinating data which have resulted must await repetition and full analysis at a later date. In the non-voter part of the work, we received major assistance from a civil servant, Stanley Cramp, who spent much of his spare time over several years doing the statistical analyses of our voluminous voter returns—and, by deduction, non-voting results. In the years since, he has turned from men back to birds and has since written many original papers on ornithological problems, as well as being Chairman of the Scientific Advisory Committee of the British Trust for Ornithology and one of the editors of the world's best bird scientific journal *British Birds*. Like many others on this occasion, Stanley Cramp readily spent some of 1960's bird-rich summer turning his eyes back to scan again those old but not out-dated voting figures. The brief extracts from the voting material that follow have been compiled with his generous and able help.

"Number-Snatching"

The (usually) young people who stand, note-book in hand, outside the polling booths and ask for the election numbers of voters going in and out are *"number-snatchers"*, employed by the various political parties to help them bring (in theory) every available supporter to the polls. In the hands of amateurs this method may or may not give reliable information as to the people who *vote*; often it is more ritual than function—as so often in politics. But using trained observers it can be very valuable, despite two main weaknesses. Firstly, some of the voters may be missed. Secondly, the voter himself may give the *wrong* number to the "snatcher".

The extent to which people give wrong numbers is difficult to estimate with any great accuracy; but errors from this source tend to be haphazard and the incentive is for people to give correct numbers in order to avoid being further disturbed by people wishing to transport them to the polls.[1] An essential part of any such operation, aimed at obtaining accurate, objective, statistical information, is of course to have your "number snatchers" at every polling booth. There must be more than one for each candidate at busy periods, for the "snatcher" is a party man and can only snatch for his "side". It follows that observation of this kind can only be made when competent observers are trusted personally on behalf of all candidates concerned.

Votes and Sex

The initial studies covered occasions between 1937 and 1938, when electors in the Worktown area had an opportunity—candidates nearly always called it an obligation—to use their vote. The table opposite shows how they reacted.

In six of these elections the men voted proportionately better than the women, though the differences were not large, ranging from 0·5% to 5·8%; in the remaining ward women voted proportionately *better* than men by a small margin of 0·7%.

[1] The official electoral registers contain the names of all parliamentary and local government electors, each with an official number. As approximately one-fifth of these electors possess only a parliamentary vote, it is easier to detect *wrong* numbers in the municipal than in the parliamentary elections; for in the latter case this can only be detected where two people give in the same number, but in the former there is the possibility of their hitting on a number which refers to a person with only a parliamentary vote. Instances where an elector was recorded as having voted twice or as having returned a number which belonged to a person with no municipal vote were rare—averaging about 0·5% of our whole. The total proportion of wrong numbers was probably never in excess of 2% in this study.

	Ward or Constituency	MEN Registered electors studied	% Non-Voter	WOMEN Registered electors studied	% Non-Voter
1.	West (Municipal and General)	1,795	54·9	2,166	59·0
2.	West (By-Munic.)	1,795	73·4	2,166	76·3
3.	Great Lever (By-Munic.)	3,338	51·6	3,791	57·4
4.	Tonge (By-Munic.)	3,808	64·9	4,259	68·1
5.	Astley Bridge (By-Munic.)	909	55·7	1,079	55·0
6.	Farnworth (Parliamentary: study ward)	1,577	30·8	1,880	31·1
7.	Farnworth (Munic; study ward)	1,270	60·2	1,516	61·3

No official records are kept in this country of the numbers of each sex who actually vote in either parliamentary or municipal elections; and one of the few results available for comparison comes from the American Professor Gosnell.[1] He found, in an unofficial check in three typical English polling districts (not wards) by means of "snatcher" sheets that 10% less of the women electors voted than the men (1924 parliamentary election). Professor Tingsten separately concluded that in other countries "the difference in voting frequency between the sexes in recent years seems to have amounted to about 10%"; Worktown women would appear to have been above the average in their use of the vote over this period.[2]

Mr. and Mrs. Voter

It will be noticed (from the sex-vote table) that in every Worktown case women electors considerably outnumbered the men. So that,

[1] Gosnell, H. F., *Why Europe Votes*, p. 18. Chicago University, 1930.
[2] Tingsten. H., *Political Behaviour*, p. 222. This work has summarised many earlier investigations into non-voting in Europe and elsewhere, otherwise scattered in often inaccessible publications.
The following references covering Britain and America are of value also:
American
Lipset et al. (1954), *The Psychology of Voting*. In Lindsey (Ed.) *Handbook of Social Psychology*. Vol. II. Addison-Wesley.
Lazarsfeld, Berenson, McPhee (1954), *The Voter Decides*. Row, Petersen and Co.
Converse, P. E. (1958), *The Shifting Role of Class in Political Attitudes and Behaviour*. In Maccoby, Newcomb and Hartlet (Eds.) "Readings in Social Psychology", 3rd. edition. Henry Holt. (London, Methuen, 1959.)
Kronhauser, W. (1959), *The Politics of Mass Society*. Free Press.
British
Rhodes, E. (1938), *Voting in Municipal Elections* in "Political Quarterly", June 1938.
Benney, Pear and Gray (1956), *How People Vote*. Routledge and Kegan Paul.
Milne, R. S. and Mackenzie, H. C. (1958), *Marginal Seat 1955*. The Hansard Society for Parliamentary Government,—an original and continuing study in Bristol.
Butler, D. E. and Rose, R. (1960), *The British General Election of 1959*, Macmillan.

although in the majority of these elections the percentage of women polling was lower than that of the men, the actual *number* of women voting was greater than the number of men; in the above seven elections nearly 600 more women than men. So that, although their political "interest" (as measured by electoral participation) was slightly less than that of the men, owing to their greater numbers they formed a greater part of the actual *voters*. Yet the propaganda of the political parties was in every case aimed (unconsciously?) at the male voter; and every candidate was male. An enquiry in Great Lever ward showed that 52·2% of the women interviewed had *not* read the ordinary election leaflets; only 36·7% of the men had shown similar disinterest.

The greater part of the municipal electorate consists of *married people*—in a typical ward analysed they formed 85·9% of the whole electorate (1938). How far is the strength of the *married* couple as a sociological unit reflected in electoral behaviour?

Type ward	Number	%
Both voted	1,015	33·2
Husband only voted	465	15·2
Wife only voted	280	9·1
Neither voted	1,301	42·5

In other words, 2,316 out of 3,061 couples (75·7%) acted *in the same way* and only 745 (24·3%) acted differently. The tendency towards similarity of action was shown even more strikingly when, in the same ward, party canvassers asked a sample of married couples whether both spouses allegedly voted for the same candidate—85·8% said that they did. In Farnworth, where married couples formed 80·1% of the municipal electorate and 64·5% of the parliamentary, similar results were obtained. Thus at the parliamentary election 71·6% of the couples (in a sample of 1,115) acted in the same way and 28·4% differently, whilst in the same municipal elections the figures were 71·7% and 28·3% respectively.

Age and Vote Interest

As successive Registrar-Generals have pointed out, many people, and especially women, are extremely reluctant to give accurate information as to their age. When a State enquiry meets with such hesitancy, it is clearly difficult for an unofficial one to discover such details by direct questioning.

Age analysis was first tried in a municipal ward election where the ages of 331 people (mostly women) were estimated in a special canvass *before* the election, their actual voting record obtained subsequently.

The interviewers (as canvassers) spent, on an average, at least five minutes at each house and so had opportunity to make a fairly accurate estimate.

Age	% Non-voters Male %	Female %
30 and under	80	59
31–45	36	44
46–60	41	49
Over 60	36	50

The general trend for the two sexes is similar and the results in harmony with some European figures (Tingsten, p. 229, etc.). To get larger checks, a slightly different method was employed in further enquiries. The ages of the actual voters were guessed by observers while "snatching" at the polling booths. These ages are probably less accurate; but the samples obtained were much larger—64·8% of the voters in Tonge municipal, 46·2% in Farnworth parliamentary and 41·8% in Farnworth municipal. Before these figures could be used it was necessary to estimate, on the Census figures, the actual age distribution of electors in the two areas. After this, the non-voting percentages for the various age groups could be computed. The results obtained, which are necessarily only approximate:

Age	Total Numbers Voting	Estimated Non-Voting % Total %	Men %	Women %
TONGE				
21–25	(30)	86	81	89
26–40	638	64	65	64
41–55	731	59	58	60
56–70	305	75	72	77
Over 70	(19)	87	77	93
FARNWORTH (Municipal)				
21–25	(9)	(81)	(89)	(77)
26–40	134	67	67	68
41–55	224	43	46	41
56–70	84	69	66	72
Over 70	(5)	86	69	93
FARNWORTH (Parliamentary)				
21–25	(64)	69	71	68
26–40	396	31	27	34
41–55	432	4	6	3
56–70	191	34	38	31
Over 70	(17)	78	70	82

The estimates for the middle three age groups are likely to be substantially accurate; but the numbers voting amongst the youngest and oldest are so small that margins of error in these calculations are very considerable. Although the non-voting percentages varied to a great extent in the three elections, in all electoral participation was strongest in the 41–55 group, followed by the 26–40 and the 56–70 groups, with the youngest and oldest groups easily the weakest in those pre-war years (as now?). In the three largest groups there is little difference *between* the figures for the two sexes, though the women *actually voted better than the men* in the 41–55 group in both Farnworth elections, as on some other occasions.

These results were further supported by a different analysis of the Farnworth results. In the parliamentary election it was found that those electors with municipal votes showed better voting records than those with *only* a parliamentary vote:

	Parliamentary and Municipal Vote		Parliamentary Vote only	
	Electors	% N.V. %	Electors	% N.V. %
Men	1,270	28·6	307	39·7
Women	1,516	31·0	364	32·6
Total	2,777	29·9	671	35·9

As the electors with only a parliamentary vote are for the most part young unmarried people, these differences are in broad agreement with age analysis. Again, in the first group men voted relatively better than the women (difference 2·4%), whereas in the second women showed a greater superiority (difference 7·1%)—lending further strength to the suspicion that non-voting tends normally to be higher among young men than among young women?[1]

Though a very much higher poll occurred at the Farnworth parliamentary by-election than at any of the municipal elections, the greater increases in parliamentary voting were found in just *those groups which had the best voting records in the municipal elections*. The higher poll was not achieved by greatly increased participation amongst the age groups with the poorest municipal record. If the Tonge voting figures, which are (with one exception) the lowest in each case, are compared with the Farnworth parliamentary results, the notable fact emerges

---

[1] In general there are few signs that the 1960 youth of Worktown are any more "irresponsible", etc., than they were in 1937-40, apart from a 0·1% *Misc.* Group, see also Chapter 12 and p. 19.

that *not only do the three most active groups show the biggest net increase in voting, but in two of them (41-45 and 56-70) the percentage increase is greater than in either of the two most apathetic groups.*

In all the Worktown-Farnworth areas studied the same tendency for electoral participation to increase with age was found, except for the increasing decline after 55, which may be assumed for the present to be due more to increasing infirmity and sickness than to a fall in "political interest".

Mobility of Votes

The wards are usually divided into two or more polling districts, each with their own polling station. The majority of urban electors live within half a mile of the polling station. Yet even these small distances may act as a deterrent to voting, particularly in those working-class areas where over half of the electors vote after finishing their day's work. The political parties of course realise this and try to overcome the difficulty by providing motor-cars, but there were rarely sufficient of these for the purpose, not only in 1938 Worktown but all over Britain in the 1959 elections. The following results, from one large ward, indicate the effects of distance:

	Electors	% Non-Voters Total %	Male %	Female %
Less ⅛ mile	1,301	47·7	42·2	52·7
⅛ to ¼ mile	1,840	51·9	48·8	54·7
¼ to ⅜ mile	1,674	55·9	51·6	59·7
⅜ to ½ mile	1,247	58·7	56·5	60·5
½ to ⅝ mile	514	61·0	59·8	62·3
Over ⅝ mile	455	62·4	64·0	61·1

The amount of non-voting increased steadily with the distance from the polling station. Also, male non-voting percentages rise more rapidly than female, so that in the most distant group the women (with more "leisure") have actually a better voting record than the men. One explanation for this is that the political parties normally send (or try to plan to send) available cars to the more distant voters. The women, who vote more evenly throughout the day than the men, are thus able to make more use of them. This was supported in 1938-9 by information obtained from the Labour party *canvass* in two selected polling districts. In the following table are shown the voting records of the electors who consistently *said they would vote*

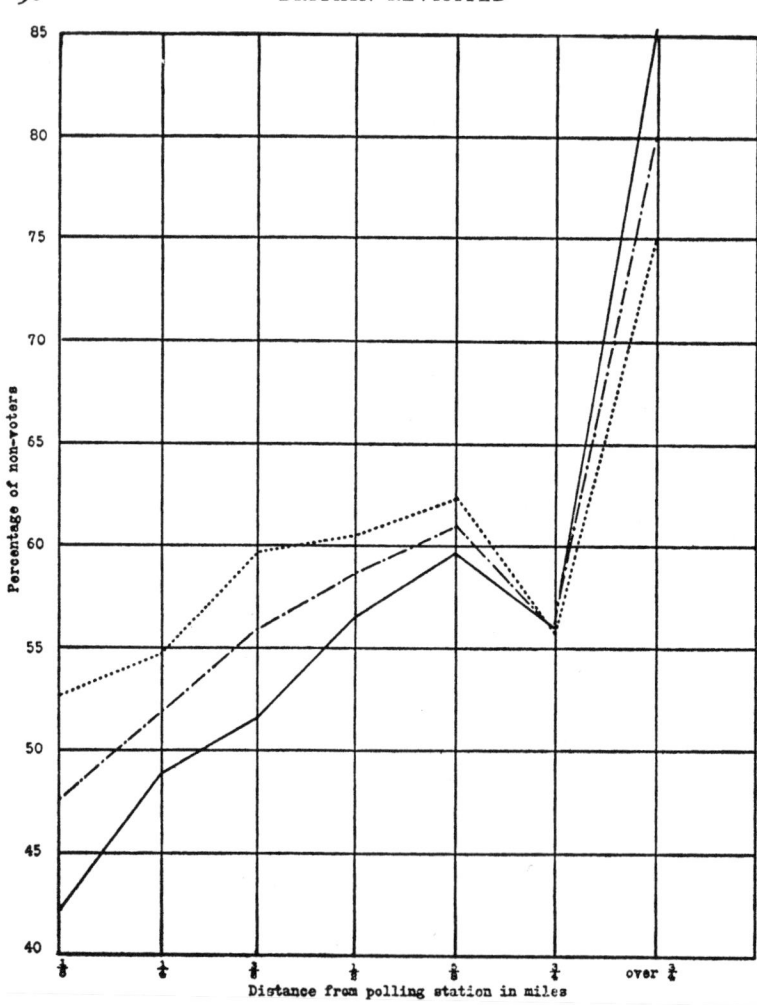

Effect of distance on non-voting, municipal ward, Worktown.

Labour or Conservative to the canvassers, according to distance from polling station:

	LABOUR % Non-Voters		CONSERVATIVE % Non-Voters	
Distance	Men %	Women %	Men %	Women %
Less ¼ mile	45	49	32	45
¼ to ½ mile	53	58	40	49
Over ½ mile	54	57	36	39

Here, the distance had a much greater effect on the voting of Labour supporters than on the Conservatives—the differences between the voting percentages for the two parties being 7·9%, 11·8% and 17·4% as the distance increased. In this particular election the Conservatives had more than four times as many cars at their disposal as Labour.

The Farnworth ward is small and fairly compact, with one polling station in a central position, so that the average distance the voter must travel is much less than the urban average; even so, the effect of distance was marked in both elections.

Distance	PARLIAMENTARY % Non-Voters Men %	Women %	MUNICIPAL % Non-Voters Men %	Women %
Less ⅛ mile	25·4	23·8	56·3	53·4
⅛ to ¼ mile	35·2	28·9	57·1	60·5
¼ to ⅜ mile	32·1	34·8	62·7	64·4
⅜ to ½ mile	28·9	35·3	57·1	56·9

Social Status and Voter Intensity

Social status can be measured more or less accurately in a number of different ways. Most accepted indices present practical difficulties in the case of voting behaviour, where a great deal of information must often be obtained *quickly* and *simply* in order to get results at all. We used two principal sets of criteria for status—Job and Home:

Type of Home	% Non-Voters Total %	Male %	Female %
"Good" (£20 rates)	53·8	50·5	56·7
Medium (small gardens)	54·7	51·8	57·1
"Poor" (no garden— under £10 rates)	56·2	54·6	57·5
Housing estates	59·5	60·4	58·7

The tendency is still more noticeable when the *distances* from the polling booths are taken into account. The streets in the "Good" sample were situated, on the average, half a mile from the various polling stations, whereas those in the "Medium" and "Poor" samples were situated at an average distance of less than three-eights of a mile.

A further opportunity was found to study the housing estate question in Tonge ward, which contained two large new estates, the northern one situated in one polling district (A), the southern estate divided between two (A and B).

	Electorate Number	% Non-Voters Total %	Male %	Female %
Polling district A				
North housing estate	1,092	82·0	81·7	82·4
South ,, ,, (part)	645	72·7	72·3	73·0
Non-estate	930	68·3	66·4	69·9
Polling district B				
South housing estate (part)	457	66·7	67·3	66·2
Non-estate	3,134	62·1	59·8	64·7

Again some allowance must be made for distance. The northern estate averages about one-eighth of a mile more distant than the remainder; but the southern estate is hardly affected by this factor. So that, when full allowance has been made, the voting record of the housing estate residents is still much lower than the remainder. The other polling district, with no housing estate, had the best voting percentage in the ward.

There was no very great status difference in the Farnworth ward, a largely industrial zone. Here, therefore, we made a simple comparison between those houses *with* a garden and those *without*.

	Electorate	% Non-Voters Both Sexes %	% Non-Voters Men %	Women %
Parliamentary				
With gardens	1,120	31·8	29·1	33·9
Without gardens	2,179	30·8	31·7	30·1
Municipal				
With gardens	906	60·8	58·5	62·8
Without gardens	1,770	60·5	61·1	60·0

In both elections the women voted relatively less than the men in the better social areas, and relatively more in the poorer district, thus supporting the tendency, shown previously in Worktown proper, for voting *discrepancy between the sexes to increase with the rise in the social scale*.

Social status was also measured by job in these studies. Three broad groups were fixed, based on our detailed local knowledge and only initially defined by average weekly income: A=over £6; B= £6—£2. 15.; C=under £2. 15. (1938 rates).

Three sets of results were then obtained by ticket-snatching and subsequent analysis on these criteria, on samples covering under 2,000 main income-earners (women and dependants ignored).

PERCENTAGE OF EACH STATUS GROUP NON-VOTING

Status	Worktown Municipal %	Farnworth Municipal %	Farnworth Parliamentary %
A	38	33	(10)
B	42	55	26
C	48	60	26

There is a steady consistency in these status results, including a Farnworth parliamentary contest almost bound to be won by Labour.

Local Roots: New Resident, Owner, Tenant

A new resident in a ward is not immediately eligible to vote in municipal elections; for the registers are made up annually and the elector must have been living there for at least six months before the date of compilation of the registers in order to be included. Even when eligible to vote, many people do *not feel sufficiently interested* in the affairs of their new neighbourhood to do so, as the following results from Great Lever (363 electors) imply:

Length of Residence	% Non-Voters Total %	Men %	Women %
Under 3 years	56	53	59
3–10 years	44	40	48
Over 10 years	45	45	45

In Tonge at the 1938 election the 1,213 *new* electors (i.e. electors who had changed their residence since the compilation of the previous register) had a higher non-voting percentage than the older electors, 70·2% as compared with 61·4%. These figures held for both sexes. In a part of Worktown's West ward in 1938 the differences were still more striking: new electors, total non-voting 80·5%; old electors, total 64·8%.

Those who *own* their houses not only have an interest in the particular area, but feel the impact of the local *rates* more directly than tenants (who often pay an inclusive rent). A special canvass in Great Lever gave limited information on this point:

Electors	% Non-Voters %
Owners 203	46·3
Tenants 210	50·5

Other Local Associations

Again, non-voters may be correlated with institutions to which they belong, e.g. churches, trade unions, co-operative societies, etc. For example, in one ward the names of all those electors who appeared on the Church of England registers of three important Anglican churches were collated with their voting record in a municipal by-election:

	% Non-Voters %
Church A	37
Church B	36
Church C	32
All Churches	37
Whole Ward (all electorate)	55

In another ward, the 134 electors on the register of an Anglican church had a non-voting record of 38·8% (men 35·7%, women 41·0%), whereas the figures for the whole ward were 66·6% (men 64.9% and women 68·1%). In both wards the Anglicans had a much higher voting record than the rest of the electors. But other influences (too complex for this brief discussion) of course played a part in producing these effects.

In a third ward 203 people who normally gave financial support to various Church of England functions voted above the average:

	% Non-Voters %
Church	47
Whole ward	61

In a fourth case the names of electors who were connected with the Methodist Sunday School—as teachers, senior men or women, on the parochial list or as parents of children attending the school—were obtained. For all these the voting record was superior to those of the ward as a whole. Anglican and Baptist church lists in another ward showed the same tendencies (1,836 persons):

	% Non-Voters %
Anglican	42·5
Baptist	41·0
Remainder of ward	56·4

The voting records of 720 members (and their husbands or wives) of one of the principal *Co-operative Societies* differed little from the general average:

	% Non-Voters		
	Total %	Men %	Women %
Co-operative members	53	50	56
Whole ward	55	52	57

Although the Co-operative movement as a whole plays a part in politics, it is often contended (in Lancashire) that its members are not greatly interested in the political aspects; these figures indicate that members in this ward at this time displayed little heightened interest —and it has certainly not risen since (see Chapter 3).

It was not possible to obtain the voting records of all *trade-unionists* in any ward, but observers were intimately acquainted with nearly a hundred electors belonging to various trade unions. Their non-voting percentage was proved considerably lower than that of the other male electors in two polling districts studied from this angle—48·7% and 66·6% respectively. Their *wives* also voted above average.

"Chronic Non-Voting"?

Regardless of theories on *why* people vote or don't, it was almost invariably assumed by politicians in the thirties—and is still largely so assumed in the sixties—that electors can be separated into two distinct classes, *voters and non-voters*. And that, except at elections where unusual feeling is aroused and the "apathetic" ones are hustled to the poll, the two groups largely include the same people from year to year.

Some clues on this were given from three wards where *more than one election* was covered. In West ward results were presently obtained for three municipal elections—1937 by-election and November 1937 and November 1938 general:

	% of whole	
	Men %	Women %
Voted at *all three* elections	14·4	10·8
Voted at two elections	22·3	20·8
Voted at one election	29·2	24·7
Voted in *none*	34·1	43·7

In no case was the poll in this area a high one, the respective total votings being 25·0%, 46·8% and 35·2%. Yet *over 60% of the electorate used their vote at least once.* There was a tendency for the core of non-voters to be reduced at each succeeding election, though at diminishing rate. In November 1938, when only 35·2% of these electors polled, *nearly one-third of these were people who had failed to use their vote at either of the preceding elections.*

In Farnworth a comparison of the record in successive parliamentary and municipal elections of some 2,800 electors entitled to vote at both gave us:

	% of whole Men %	Women %
Voted at *both* elections	32·3	29·0
Voted at parliamentary only	39·1	39·9
Voted at municipal only	7·0	9·6
Voted at neither	21·6	21·5

Thus over a quarter who did *not* vote in the keenly contested parliamentary election *did* vote in the municipal. Many people who failed to vote in the parliamentary (with a 68·9% poll) thus voted in the municipal—which aroused much less effort aimed at the electors as a whole (poll 39·2%).

Similar checks were later made in another Worktown ward for two successive municipal and general elections covering 12,303 vote opportunities:

	% of whole Men %	Women %
Vote at first election only	18·0	15·5
Vote at second election only	19·3	19·6
Vote at *both*	19·7	18·6
Vote at neither	43·0	46·3

Similar researches carried on over a longer period would probably confirm that the proportion of electors who *consistently* fail to make use of their vote *is very much smaller* than has generally been supposed.

Meanwhile, if it is even tentatively agreed that the *sort* of result indicated by consecutive electoral incidents in the Worktown area may have some wider validity, it follows that exact understanding of the factors causing people, both deliberately and casually, *not* to use their vote in any election, become of wide importance—irrespective of "party" propaganda in the ordinary sense. Along this line it could be argued that a party concentrating a large part of its social and economic effort, and even more of its inside thinking, on to voting *as a physical act* (or accident)—at the expense, if necessary, of election issues and party differences—might "win" many more votes that way.

One may not like the implications; but they are implicit in the existence of political science as well as of party politics.

Chalk drawing on wall; Worktown 1960.

SIX

SOME MACHINERY OF DEMOCRACY

THE NORMAL PERSONAL approach in politics is that by a "canvasser", advancing the cause of a particular party or candidate. Canvassing was considered indispensable in the thirties. In every election studied, both in Worktown and elsewhere, parties made major efforts to get a maximum canvass. This canvass was partly in order to encourage voting for a candidate, but also (where "properly" done) recorded the stated *"promise"* (or otherwise) of each person canvassed. Those who promised to vote for the relevant candidate were then further incited to so vote on election day. "Knockers-up" were employed to bring out these votes. Transport was provided, as possible, supposedly on this canvass basis.

Failure of Contact: the Canvass

There is nothing in the canvass system itself—any more than in any other "stranger interview" contact—to ensure that the person approached will publicly proclaim his private intentions. On the contrary, there is much in healthy democracy as well as in British character to favour misleading on such an electoral occasion. The ballot is theoretically secret, after all.

Now, in the sixties, the canvass method is not in such high repute as before—partly as a temporary result of an overestimated value attached to the TV approach. But the trouble about undervaluing this is that no substitute has yet been devised.

How ineffective modern party machines prove in this direction is illustrated by a *Daily Telegraph* survey during the 1959 General Election (*D.T.* 7 October 1959), showing that in marginal seats where there was a great concentration of party effort:

—23% of voters said, just before the poll, they had been visited by Conservatives during the previous month;
—22% ditto by Labour;
—60% said *no* Labour canvasser has been near them at any time;
—57% ditto no Conservative.

Discussing this and other results, Butler and Rose (*The British General Election 1959*, Chapter 11) properly conclude:

"Even allowing for faulty memories these figures could induce some scepticism about party claims based on canvass returns."

It is certainly true that party "claims" intended to sway the outcome of an election based on such canvasses are liable to be ludicrous —largely because influenced by wishful-thinking. But this does *not* mean that the canvass itself is useless. On purely observational grounds it can be strongly suggested that a 100% canvass, linked with *permanent* canvassing records, is one pre-condition to effective party organisation at the constituency level within the existing machinery of British democracy.

Canvassing Contradictions

Early on in the Worktown studies, the unreliability of a crudely interpreted canvass was borne in heavily upon us. It will be remembered that we had the advantage of people working together, at the research level, from different political "sides".

To take one early example: in the Farnworth by-election (which duly returned a future Minister of Education), partly through our influence *over 95%* of the electorate were "properly" canvassed by the Labour Party and just under 62% by the Conservatives. Subsequent "number snatching" showed that those electors who gave *consistent* answers to our canvassers on both sides had the lowest non-voting figures. Those who were canvassed by both parties but gave *contradictory* replies came next. Those who were only canvassed once had the lowest voting record. There are inevitably a number of complicating factors which make that picture much less simple than it sounds.[1]

A more significant result, in terms of the canvass itself, was the degree to which people were "*untruthful*" when canvassed. Nearly as many people told the Labour man they would vote Conservative, and *vice versa* (i.e. promised "Yes" to both sides) as gave consistent answers, among the thousands of cases where the record is undoubtedly accurate and complete on our books. And this was reflected in actual voting conduct too:

	% Non-Voters Men %	Women %
Same reply	26·8	29·4
Contradictory	29·9	29·8
Canvassed once only	35·0	34·0

[1] Detailed analyses of these and other returns must await publication at a later date.

These provisional canvassing returns incited us to make a series of experiments to test the hypotheses which naturally followed from what were then—and as far as we know remain—rather novel researches.

Special Canvass Experiments

In one Worktown ward in 1938, we concentrated a special effort on all the registered voters at two polling stations where we could be certain of maximum observer efficiency. We divided the register into two exactly equal, unselected samples, evenly balanced. One half, as "control group", was left to the ordinary processes of canvassing by the political parties—very mild in this municipal election. The other half was given a special and intensive canvass by our observers prior to the election. This canvass was done on non-party lines and *no reference to any particular candidate was even implied*. The canvassers, in this instance, had a set "ploy", urging that household to use its votes for one side or another in the election.

Effect of Special Canvass on Non-voting

	NOT SPECIALLY CANVASSED N.V. %	SPECIALLY CANVASSED N.V. %
Polling Station I		
Men	62·0	43·5
Women	66·8	51·8
Total	64·5	47·9
Polling Station II		
Men	48·0	37·0
Women	55·5	46·3
Total	52·1	42·0

In every case a considerable decrease in non-voting followed the special canvass; and the result is still more striking if the actual increase in *votes* is considered.

We then carried out an experiment of a more "topical" nature, in another Worktown ward. Instead of the usual sort of election address or other preliminary literature, we printed (outside Worktown) three special leaflets. One of these presented local politics on a football-pool coupon (then only in its mass infancy)[1]; another, aimed especially at younger people, was in comic strip form; a third, especially for women, in a dance-hall and music-hall style. Each of these

[1] See inset between pp. 78 and 83.

dealt with municipal elections and the responsibility of the electorate. None of them mentioned or implied support for any specific candidate or party. Random samples of electors were taken from a register, in groups of 3,000; with a further "control group" of 3,000, who received no special literature or any other attention of this kind over and above the ordinary electioneering activities of the parties.

In every case those who received these hitherto unprecedented documents, polled between 11% and 19% higher than those who received nothing special—their immediate neighbours and statistical equals.

Fortified by this limited success, M-O sought a larger outlet for this type of experiment. The Labour Party, being then out of power, provided a special opportunity to do more technical experiments, through the good offices of Mr. Hindley Atkinson (then Chief Labour Party Agent for the London area), Mr. Herbert (now Lord) Morrison, and locally Dr. Edith Summerskill (who first became an M.P. under circumstances to be described . . .).

The "Vote Killer": a London Experiment

The 1938 West Fulham by-election was one of the more important tests of "democratic choice" in the shattering period of world and local power shifts following the General Election of 1935, with Stanley Baldwin subsequently handing over the reins to Neville Chamberlain (who was never *elected* Prime Minister at the public level) before the World War of 1939. A few key constituencies not themselves of special relevance, became crucial in judging, from above, the wind of political mood. M-O studied each in turn.

In the West Fulham by-election, by getting the canvasses of both parties, we were able to define Conservative and Labour "supporters" fairly accurately—nearly half the electors said different things to the two canvassers, a common local practice being to promise Conservative to Labour and Labour to Conservative.

Papers all over the world treated the result as representing British public opinion, what "the country" was thinking about our foreign policy. In fact, what did those few hundred votes more for the lady doctor actually add up to in terms of human *choice*, down at the concrete-edge of Cockney ideology (or idle curiosity)?

Well, it is probably fair to say that in the course of undertaking a "controlled experiment" to test non-voting hypotheses developed from the Worktown studies already described, M-O incidentally influenced the election sufficiently to *help* decide that margin of victory.

It did so without recourse to any attempt to influence anyone to vote *for* anyone. What we were then interested in testing could be boiled down to just this:

If (as we suspect) the act of voting—taken regardless of who is voted for—is often decided by quite trivial circumstances (which with a large minority of electors leads to the vote not being used) it should be possible to demonstrate that as well as increasing voting by controlled influence, non-voting can equally be increased by similar methods.

Any experiment devised to this end had to be undertaken with great care and conducted with caution. No body of men is more conservative than Labour electioneering operatives. In this they only echo—or rather emphasise—the innate character of political executives in every established democracy, bound by a set of standards crystallised into ritual almost as fully as that of Independent Methodism or the Royal and Ancient Order of Buffaloes. Anyway, elections are governed by very proper and elaborate laws.

We eventually came up with three workable and legal approaches. The third was so simple in application and so positive in reaction that it deserves to be put on record briefly here.

We printed a leaflet tastefully composed of statements by leading "National" or local Conservative politicians in the recent past or present, regarding matters of state, policy, possible war, Air Raid Precautions, conscription, and other issues. This was in Conservative blue, on a simple format similar to current election leaflets. The statements, each of a phrase or two, were juxtaposed to give a somewhat chaotic and even contradictory effect. The impact was intended to be bewildering! The only *message* of this unusual propaganda product was: if the recipient *felt* bewildered, uncertain or suspicious about these policies or personalities, he or she had much better *not vote* at all.

The leaflet was only concerned with Conservatism. To be effective, however, it was essential to direct its message at those more likely to be affected, rather than those many who had probably "made up their minds" anyway. On the other hand, since we were not asking anyone to add to or alter extant opinion—only to ignore (negatively)—it was clearly efficient to direct it at those we felt less attached to the urgency or responsibility of their vote in this instance.

At this stage, our earlier developed system of *double canvassing* came in. By this means it was possible to pin-point one section of the West Fulham electorate who at that time (1939) might be most susceptible to the impact of a rather striking message suggesting that the Conservatives were for the time being in a muddle (and, by inference, "politics" generally also); and that, therefore, there was less point than usual in voting for them. Every voter for whom two mass-observers had reliably recorded *inconsistent* promises, but with "Conservative" bias, was marked off on our register. As this sample proved too large to be workable, it was reduced by specific polling areas where we could be certain of having adequate "number-snatching" coverage throughout the hours of the actual poll.

The organisation, supervision and individual care involved in completing this operation was large (over fifty observers). But to make the results significant it was also necessary to prepare an exactly equal, parallel, sample *not* subject to this special pressure, for "control"—by splitting the original sample. Every household which received the special leaflet had another "control" next door or very close, which got nothing special.

The experiment produced an unmistakably *positive* result. *Over a quarter more of those selected to receive the leaflet did not vote*—as compared with the other half giving the same "promise" pattern and otherwise electorally "identical", but receiving nothing special.

An Open Question?
On this querulous but questing note, the discussion of voting, non-voting and political responsibility or otherwise must be left for the time being: with an open question mark? We hope to carry on this field work in the sixties for comparison, independently.

Next let us try and approach patterns of change during the last quarter of a century, with particular reference to Worktown, from an entirely different, strictly *qualitative* documentary angle—the opposite of vote observation.

Among the hundreds of people who became friendly with mass-observers in Worktown, and who in varying ways got integrated with our non-Worktown personnel scattered through all the arteries of industrial living, one was the driver of a coal lorry for the Co-op. Bill Naughton had to do with us for several years. During this time he developed his capacity for writing about real people, the people of his own life; yet giving a magic of his own Worktown insight. To encourage such literary documentation was very much a part of Mass-Observation's programme from the start; and particularly of interest to Charles Madge and Humphrey Jennings back there in 1937. Now, in 1960, a leading television playwright, short-story writer and novelist, some of Bill Naughton's best work in recent years has been done from and on a Worktown background. It seems suitable, therefore, for him to contribute here some of his own documentation of how Worktown people talk and think. No brief was given to him. He chose to start from London and revisit (as we also in 1960)—recapturing upon the way the authentic sounds and tastes of a living texture in which Vicars, M.P.s, Non-voters and all else operate equally (or not).

Over to Bill Naughton, Worktown observer born. . . .

SEVEN

A WEEK-END TO WORKTOWN (WITH VOICES IN CHARACTER)

THURSDAY: *Harry Crow, Spinner*

I WAS ON MY way to Westminster Central Reference Library in St. Martin's Street, opposite the Pastoria, to meet Harry Crow, a fellow Worktowner. There was a standing arrangement between Harry and myself to meet on the first floor (philosophy, religion, art, etc.) at three o'clock every Thursday. If either one failed to turn up by half-past three the other would know something had stopped him, and it was on for the week after. I always looked forward to this meeting, because after an opening chat of what had happened during the week we would stroll round London, Piccadilly, Lower Regent Street, St. James's Park, the Mall, talking away about Worktown. Worktown as it was in the old days, and of the things we did and the way we lived, and of any changes we had heard about since.

Harry is a short podgy man, approaching fifty, with a round face, bright brown eyes, and a spinner's walk. He has lived in an L.C.C. lodging house since just after the end of the war, when he left Worktown. He said he didn't fancy going back to work in the spinning mill. Now he earns his living selling football programmes, touting tickets at any of the gatherings in London from boxing to ballet, and going around the country in search of Cup Final tickets and all that sort of thing. He loses his money betting—at the dogs, on horse racing or in the billiard hall. He is very fond of a glass of port and he likes reading. Shelley is one of his favourite authors and he can quote at length from him. He often says he would love to spend hours reading in the library, but, as he remarks, "When you're doing nowt you never have no time, it's all eaten up doing nowt."

It was by his spinner's walk that I first spotted Harry in London. I can't describe the walk exactly, except it is one that most spinners develop from walking up and down the wheelgate watching the mules. It has a sort of lordly air to it. Anyway, one very hot day in the summer of 1947, I was just coming out of the Serpentine after a swim when I recognised the walk in a dumpy, white-skinned figure strolling amongst the masses of brown-skinned bodies on the edge of the Lido. When I saw the face I knew at once I was right. Worktown faces seem to change but very little. In early life most faces take on a certain set look, that of the comic, the honest man, the rogue, or a dozen other expressions to do with the man himself, his upbringing and his job. Once you've known that face, you will probably recognise it quite easily for the rest of its life. I think one of the reasons for this is that one's life there has a simple continuous pattern, and there are relatively few acute changes to be assimilated.

I went up to him and gave him a shove. "Harry Crow!" I said. "What the hell are you doing amongst this lot?"

He stared at me. First there was what seemed a momentary uneasiness in his look, then a matey but unsure smile.

"Don't say you don't know me!" I said.

"I know the voice," he said. "but I can't just place your face. But I know them eyes. Hold on a minute." He kept staring at me, grinning, but very puzzled, and not at ease. I didn't tell him who I was.

"How's your Bill?" I said.

"Not bad," he said.

"Are you still as good at snooker?" I said.

"Oh, I can still handle a cue," he said.

The water was dripping off me, and I rubbed my face with my hands. Harry kept staring at me. I felt the meeting was spoiling, so I said: "Don't you know me?—I'm Bill Naughton."

He still kept staring at me.

"Not Bill Naughton fru' Bolton!" he said.

"Course I am," I said, "who else? How are you, Harry?"

I shook his hand very warmly, and slowly he began to see that I was who I was. I was happy to see him, and longing for a chat, and I got away from the people I was with to have a cup of tea with Harry and tell him what I was doing and hear about his doings.

"I can't get over the change in you," he kept saying. "In your face. You used to have a real bulldog look about you—" he laughed, "—bloody stubborn you were but now you look different, you look brainy, this great big 'ead on you! I can't get over the transformation from when you were a coalbagger. I read your book yu' know. You put me in—me an' Bishop Berkeley's philosophy applied to snooker. Eeh, but I can't get over the change in your face from what it was like in the old days."

In those days—the thirties—I was driving a coal lorry. It was an old Halley, with a short gear stick, gate change gears, solid tyres and oil lamps for headlights. (I remember one driver going to the boss and asking him for some "dimming wick".) Your approach to your job had to be wholly determined and stubborn, from start to finish. There was a little starting handle on the Halley, and unless you went to it full of determination, you could never turn it. The slightest doubt in your mind as you were cranking it up and it would kick back and you were lucky if you got going at all. Once out on the road, the four solid tyres vibrated so much, especially over cobblestones, that if you gave way at all to your feelings you'd be sick. You got into the habit of setting your face and it seemed to set. At the sidings you had to delve into the coal with huge spades. You would climb on top of a wagon and start grafting. On the sole of your clog were two irons, heel and front, and for coal filling you had a third iron known as a "grafting" iron, which was placed between these two, and which protected the wooden clog sole from the iron of the spade as you forced it through the thick cobs of coal with the sole of your foot. Never a day passed at work without knocks and bruises and cuts. Some customers wanted their coal put through little holes at the top of a shed, others wanted it carried to the back of low sheds. The only way you could get the job done was to ignore all the knocks you got and keep going. Some days it rained all day long and you got soaked through. I remember working one such day with a chap we called Blucher. Next morning he said to me, "Wife opened door for me last neet. Wut dust think silly sod said: 'Are you wet?' So I took me cap off and I sloshed her across face wi' it. 'Is that bloody weet?' I said. I were sorry once I'd done it, but she hat pay for t'lot. But wut a bloody daft question t'ask."

You got a lot of rain. I worked with one carrier-off called Tommy, who hobbled from rheumatism. I never knew him to complain or to take anything for it. "If rheumatism plagues thee," he used to say in a loud hoarse voice, "*plague it back!* Don't let it fricken thee. It gives me some gyp, but the more it gives me the more I give it back. At the end o' the day there's nowt in it 'atween us."

I imagine this sort of life tends to give the face a set look. But when it came to writing for a living I did find a certain help from my training. Writing was something that had to be done, and no matter how much you sweated and made mistakes, you had to keep going.

"If writing plagues thee—plague it back." In all other respects the transition was painful. You had been used to handling things, hard stubborn things, and now you had to learn to take hold of ideas and images, and yet do it in such a way that you did not change them.

Now to get back to Harry Crow. Harry Crow was a bachelor.

And he was the type of bachelor very common in Worktown before the war, but now becoming rare. Such men as Harry made up an important element of the male social life in Bolton in those days; at the street corner, at football matches, in billiard halls and, most of all, in pubs and especially in the taprooms and public bars. They had their own form of humour, their own way of seeing things, and you could *always rely on them to turn up*, a thing you could never be sure of with a married man. The bachelor always had more time and money, less domestic interference, was more regular in his habits, and could usually supply more than his share of humour to the talk. For whatever marriage does to a man, it rarely sharpens his wits or his tongue—although, oddly enough, it often does for a woman.

Most working men of guts and character would not—before the war—have taken their wives out to the pub of a Saturday evening. They might have taken them to the Market Hall or perhaps to the first house pictures, and then sent them home whilst they had an hour with their mates in the public bar, playing dominoes or darts and arguing. Other wives, more forceful and fond of a drink themselves (Worktown women didn't drink much in those days), might force their way into the pub and sit in the snug, parlour or kitchen, order their drinks, and get the waiter-on to collect from the husband. True, there were men who sat in the "best room" of a pub with their wives on a Saturday evening, and talked to other married couples of the same outlook; but such men were not likely to add much to the taproom character. They were too much under the wife's thumb. Today, *all the new pubs* cater for the husband and wife trade.

Now I shall say what I think to be the reasons for the prevalence of such bachelors in Worktown in my day. And I'll use Harry Crow as an example of what I mean. I know his life very well, and we were brought up in very similar streets.

In the street where Harry lived—as in my own—the boys never mixed with "the wenches". There were never any such events as children's birthday parties or gatherings where boys and girls got together. It was only in the better-off homes that this could happen, a few streets from ours, where they weren't ashamed of strange children coming into their homes. We all had something to hide in our homes, something worn that needed replacing, some little domestic idiosyncrasy that we wished to keep to ourselves. I was madly in love with a girl when I was twelve, but we had to meet miles away from our street. And when the news of the affair leaked out—she told her best friend—I had to suffer endless leg-pulling from my mates.

To attract girls lads would stand at the street corner and let out screeches and catcalls as they went by—or start whistling in time to their walk, and, as they changed step, they changed the whistle.

At fourteen (in 1924) Harry went to work full time in the spinning mill as a little piecer. The pay was good, about nineteen shillings a week compared with ten or twelve shillings as an apprentice, but he wouldn't get a rise until he became a cross-piecer or side-piecer, and that might be a long time.

He wasn't brought in contact with girls as he might have been in the cardroom or weaving shed, and there was no way of meeting any. For a couple of years he mixed with the street corner life of the lads. They would sit there and talk and squeeze each other's *grubs* (blackheads) which abounded on little piecer's legs; and then they would go off for walks with a gang and a melodeon. In this way you reached a fairly intimate understanding of your mates, for you spent so much time with them. If they came across courting couples they always let out yells of laughter, and the usual old call: "Cum outa that meadow an' put that worm back!"

At sixteen Harry became a cross-piecer, and now, all togged up in plum-coloured "whipcord" suit, a cap with a big neb and brown "high-up" shoes, he began to visit the "monkey runs" with one or two better-off and more venturesome mates.

These "parades" as they were called ("I saw thee paradin' at Four Lone Een last neet!") were the recognised places for youths and girls to get to know each other.

There were a number of parades all around Worktown at the time, but there were three that were the most popular. Smithills Dean (or Halliwell Dean as it was often called) was for the younger teenagers. One part was unlighted and those who ventured there could expect some horseplay. Also, there was a considerable risk in the fact that you couldn't see what the girl looked like in the dark. I've had one or two shocks myself when I've arrived at the tram terminus with a mate and the two girls we were "taking off". And no doubt on occasion they've had shocks too. There was a great deal of grabbing of hair-ties and handkerchiefs and that sort of thing.

Four Lane Ends was another parade where you paraded all evening. They had a "posh" side and a "cheap" side at Four Lane Ends, and so strict was the social demarcation that no one who belonged to the cheap side would have the nerve to walk on the posh side.

The greetings (on the cheap side) were of the following kind: "How's your mother for soap?" to which the girl would reply (if at all): "Up t'neck in lather." The words counted much less than the way they were said and the timing. On the posh side many of the youths wore pots or trilby hats and they would raise these and get into conversation.

I remember every girl carried a handbag that seemed to be packed with snapshots of all her relatives and friends and once you got under a lamp-post all these would come out.

Bradshawgate in the town centre was the most popular parade of all; on Saturday nights, Sunday afternoons and Sunday nights. ("Let's see if can pick owt up ont' Gate".) There were two sides, a "bob" and a "tanner" side. These parades served a very useful purpose in that you had a good chance of meeting a girl again, perhaps one you had quarrelled with. When you wanted to stop a couple of girls you arranged with your pal to watch for the next time they came and then blocked their path. This needed some nerve and skill and very often you'd miss them altogether.

On Saturday nights there were parades round the side and back aisles of two cinemas. The Olympia (The 'Lymp) and the Runworth ("Rummy"). These were for the "younger end" between the ages of 14 and 17. They were boisterous affairs, especially the one at the 'Lymp, and you never got a chance of taking home the kind of girl you wanted. It seemed that the noisy lads had all the fun but they got the girls in such a mood that they wouldn't go home with anybody.

Harry Crow and I had gone through all this in search of a girl. And we each went home on Saturday and Sunday nights full of misery and frustration. Then I began to go dancing. (It was at the Girls' Club, 1927. A committee of two women and one man watched the dancing from a platform. If you held your partner too closely—there was supposed to be not less than six inches between you all the time —a whistle was blown and you were warned. Yet after all the parading around it seemed wonderful.) Harry was too shy to go dancing. He took up physical culture. If you couldn't get a girl to fall in love with you, you could fall in love with yourself. Actually, it did bring about enormous changes in one's physique. Harry and his mates rented a cellar for sixpence a week and whacked together pennies and halfpennies to raise this sum.

They whitewashed it and put their body-building gear in—weight-lifting appliances made from old mangles and other stuff from the scrapyard. They had a pal with a melodeon and they skipped to his music. Harry was fond of reading and his favourite author—a real favourite—was Jack London. Later he started visiting the billiard hall.

Then he began to go drinking, although he was never a boozer.

Over the years he became set in his bachelor ways. The early part of the evening was all right—setting up the drinks, playing darts and dominoes, swopping tales, and enjoying a certain camaraderie. But getting towards ten o'clock, closing time, the male company began to wear thin, and you'd keep hearing those waves of high-pitched laughter from women in the other rooms.

The Chief Constable had banned singing in Worktown pubs, and every weekend Worktowners went in large numbers to pubs in Farnworth and Walkden. Harry was one who went outside town in search of gaiety. You sat there in the big room with the piano going and the singer roaring out "Thora" or "Song of Songs" and you looked about for women.

"There's two in yon corner, Ned, keep lookin' o'er here. Across theer—a big fat'un with a red hat an' the little 'un with the frizzy hair."

"Don't be daft—they're wi' two chaps. Them two over t'other side there. They've been sendin' 'um drinks across. Just watch."

It was always a very chancy business getting off with two women in a crowded singing room of a pub. The atmosphere was always respectable and there would never be any prostitutes there. The women you saw in couples were mostly married women having an evening out—they probably worked at the mill during the day. Their husbands might even be in the public bar. Another danger was that one or both women might be "separated"—in which case there was a danger of a husband and his mates trailing you both when you got outside. But the most common risk of all was that the women would accept your drinks, winks and signs, and then at closing time, pretend to go out to the back, and would slip off, leaving you and your mate standing shivering in the cold, regretting the money you had spent on them, without exchanging more than a word.

If all went well and the women were waiting, and you all went off together, there was a certain way these things went. If it was a Sunday evening nothing was much use because there was always the thought of having to get up early on Monday morning. In the bright warmth of the pub the women may have looked attractive, but now, out in the cold, you wondered why you'd been so daft as to buy them drinks.

Saturday evenings were better. You usually went off and bought fish and chips. The main thing was to try out all your jokes and make the women laugh. They would very often insist on paying their share towards the fish and chips. You'd go along the street eating them (you weren't in your own town) and joking away. It was most exceptional if all this led up to the sexual act. The main thing was the company, the fun, perhaps a cuddle round the back street, and above all, the nice sense of intimacy between men and women. It was the situation itself that was most enjoyed. The women enjoyed the feeling of being courted, and the men enjoyed the feeling of courting.

So this was Harry Crow's bachelor life in Worktown. I've written about it at length, not so much to tell of a Worktown background, but rather because it's the sort of thing I enjoy writing about. He went into the army for a brief spell towards the end of the war. He couldn't bear the thought of going back to the spinning mill, and so, with a mate, he left Worktown and came to London. His pal, Joe, became a vegetable cook and he and Harry quarrelled over something and then Harry was alone.

* * *

Harry was at the far corner table when I went into the library. His hand was up against the side of his face, elbow on the table, as he read with a quiet, respectful air. I could see he was engrossed and I left him alone for a minute or two. Then he looked up and saw me and closed the book. We put our thumbs up to each other in silent greeting and left the reading room together.

As we walked down the library steps he gave me a nudge and recited:

"O let me in this ae night,
This ae, ae, ae, night!
O let me in this ae night,
And rise and let me in."

"You've turned to Robbie Burns," I said. Harry nodded and went on:

"O lassie, are ye sleepin yet,
Or are ye waukin I wad wit,
For love has bound me hand an' fit,
And I would fain be in, jo."

Harry detained me with his hand as he recited the last two lines. Then his round face and piggy eyes flushed into a big smile and he exclaimed "He's bloody champion!" Then as we walked through Leicester Square garden he went on:

"O this is no my ain lassie
Fair tho' the lassie be,
Weel I ken my own lassie,
Kind love is in her e'e."

He grinned again, repeated, "Kind love is in her e'e", and said. "How're yu' going' on, Bill?"

He told me he couldn't see Shelley on the shelf and he had taken Burns.

"Dun't he make love sound sweet," he said. "My memory's goin'. Once I'd have been able to memorise them lines forever—now I can feel 'um slipping away. They'll be gone by tonight, when I need 'um most."

As we walked along he told me that for the first time in his life he had been sleeping badly.

"I seem to lie there wide awake with my mind full of thoughts. Somehow it keeps goin' back to Worktown—to dozens of different things I used to do, an' folk I used to know. D'you remember Billy Topping?"

"Dark lad," I said, "good looking, hair parted in the middle."

"That was him," said Harry. "Every Saturday night when we were little piecers we used to go to the Rummy looking for girls. Now Billy always made straight for Radcliffe's florist shop in Derby Street. He had to have his rose. Mostly they were a penny each, sometimes tuppence. But he'd always have one. 'You can't go out of a Saturday night 'about your rose on,' he used to say. He got me into the same habit. I got as I looked forward to that rose."

"We used to get one now an' again," I said, "—me an' Fred Wells. Remember him—his dad used to play the cornet. Then we'd go to Parkinson's tobacco shop an' buy a quarter ounce of Russian cigarettes between us."

"Scented," said Harry. "You got ten for sixpence. They were oval-shaped."

"You've got it, Harry," I said.

"A rose an' a Russian cigarette," he said, "an' yet I could never get a wench. But Billy could. He was in amongst 'um. They were always grabbin' his rose, an' he used to chase 'um. I was goin' over them days last night. I began to feel depressed."

"Do you take any sleeping pills?" I said.

"Nah, I like a glass of port before going to bed. That usually sends me right off. But lately I've been lyin' awake," said Harry. "Last night, I got up and went for a game of snooker."

"What time?" I said.

"Oh, it 'ud be well after two in the mornin'. Solomons' place over by the Windmill is open all night. It's times like that I wish I'd never left Worktown."

"I'm going back tomorrow for a couple of days," I said, "—why don't you come with me, Harry?"

He didn't answer for a minute. He just went walking along looking down at the pavement. Some years earlier he had spoken very often of a trip back to Worktown.

"I'll go," he had said, "—as soon as I've a new suit, topcoat, new shoes, an' not less than a hundred nicker in my pocket."

He kept talking of taking his father out for a drink and treating his mother to something special. Then he got word that his father was dead. He didn't go to the funeral, but talked more than ever of going back to visit his mother. One occasion he got together enough money, but before he had time to buy the clothes, he had already lost his money at the dogs. He was very determined to go and visit his mother, of whom he spoke a great deal. Then one day after we had been strolling around for a short time, he suddenly blurted out:

"I've had a letter from our Fred. *My Mam's dead.*"

"Get off!" I said. "I'm sorry to hear that."

"Her's been dead *three months*," he said. "They never bothered to write." He couldn't get over it. "Fancy me walking round London an' me Mam dead. An' nob'dy thought it worth their while to write to me."

He told me he felt hungry and we went into a Lyons' teashop: "I found a belting caff at Covent Garden," he said. "You get a smashin' dinner for three-an'-a-tanner. On Tuesday the woman who wipes the tables came to me an' said: 'It does me good to watch you eatin'. The way you clean up your plate. You do enjoy your food.' She was very nice, but somehow I've not been able to get myself to go in again. It's as though I'm being watched."

It was opening time when we came out of Lyons and we went in Henekey's wine bar in Whitehall.

Harry drank port and I had one and then went on beer. He tried hard to get me into an argument about God, for he is a dedicated atheist, but I didn't feel inclined; although I was sorry to disappoint him.

"When you can't sleep again at night, Harry," I said, "quote to yourself the Song of St. Teresa:

> Let nothing disturb thee,
> Nothing affright thee,
> Everything passes,
> God is unchanging;
> He who has patience,
> Everything comes to him,
> He who has God,
> He lacks for nothing,
> God, only, suffices."

Harry asked me to repeat it. When we were saying goodbye outside and I was catching the 24 Pimlico bus, he said, "Next Thursday have that Teresa poem written out. That's the only way I can memorise."

"I will," I said.

Then he called after me, "Have a look at our house in Partridge Street. If you see our Fred tell him I'll be coming home soon."

FRIDAY: *Nellie Lee, Weaver.*

I got on the 9.35 a.m. through train to Worktown from Euston. I always avoid the direct Manchester compartments because I like to travel with people who are going to Worktown, Blackburn and Lancashire towns of that kind. The longer I'm away the dearer the mill folk become to me. When I was ten in 1920, I was sent one Friday dinner-time to Briggs's mill in Worktown with the wrapped-up dinner of a sidepiecer called Allan. "He'll ha' drawn his wages," said Allan's mother, "an' as you slip him his dinner he'll slip you his wages. You fetch 'um back to me." It was the time when there were still half-timers working in the mill. These were boys of twelve who went to work for half a day in the spinning room and went to school for the other half. I went in just before the dinner-time break. I remember pushing the door open. I saw the small boys at their work. And that was all I did see. The humid heat was so stifling that, before I had time to turn and get out of the door, I felt myself collapsing in a faint on the oily floor. When I woke up the faces, kindly and concerned, of the spinners were looking down at me. From such bits of memories and the experience of years of living amongst them, there has grown in me a respect and affection for these people who could stand up to a life that seemed to beat me.

I got a carriage seat next to a woman with a hearing aid. "It's not workin' right,' she said, "—I keep comin' an' goin'." She had a Worktown face and I wasn't surprised to learn that she was a weaver.

I used to work in the weaving myself and I know a large number go deaf after hearing the din of the looms for many years.

She had made three attempts to get into the lavatory. "They must be makin' their will in there," she said. It was an old saying in Worktown and an appropriate one, for in those small cottages the only room that had any privacy was the closet. It was there that husbands went to sort out their wages ("So much for me—so much for thee!") before handing them over to their wives. It would have been the ideal spot to make a will. She had been ill on and off, and had been to Croydon to stay with her married daughter.

"I've been doin' a bit of *convalessitin*," she said. "Ee, it's *stuffocatin'* in here," she added—"could we have the window open?"

She told me of her daughter's husband: "He's a good chap in his way," she said, "but I wouldn't fancy him for myself. He wouldn't think of talkin' to me like you are now. Down South they seem to think folk are goin' a bit sideways once they've turned fifty, but in Worktown they've more respect for you the older you get. But I will say this—folk talk nicer in the South."

"I like to hear a bit of Bowton talk," I said.

"Aye, you like to *hear* it," she said "—then you go away an' laugh at us." She smiled: "Ee, I expect they'll be laughin' at me for talkin' posh when I get back."

Between talks I thought I detected a suspicious look in her eye as she watched me, as though she was wondering what my interest in her could be. I am inclined to be open and frank with any newly-met acquaintance, and I spoke to her of my brothers and sister in Worktown, and of my own life there. I could see she thought I was coming it when I told her I had once been a weaver at Kershaw's factory.

"You don't look as though you believe me," I said. She had a small lunch packet tied with twine, and I took two ends between thumb and forefinger and tied a weaver's knot for her. "And I used to know how to make a loom go faster," I said "—put some soap on the pulley strap." After that we were good friends. She spoke most of the time. "I keep goin' on an' off," she said, fiddling with her hearing aid. But she could follow my lips when I faced her. I asked her about things in Worktown.

"Things are all right," she said, "folk are not as hard up as they used to be—" she gave me a nudge, "you'd have a job to find a pawnshop! On the other hand I think folk have become *self-centred*. They don't listen to each other's troubles the same. Course they don't get much chance with all this television. You're not welcome these days, you know, droppin' in for a chat—not if they've got something on they like. They tell you to shut up. Mind you, it's a good thing for a lot of people. I know two brothers at a farm who used to be in bed every night at nine o'clock. Both bachelors, you know. Now they're up watching the television. They get through their work quicker, so's they can sit down and watch. They've got *two sets*—one in either room, so's they miss nowt. Ee but it has made a difference to them. Even with the work on the farm. One time of day they'd have had naught to do with silage or anything like that—but once they'd seen it on the telly, they decided to try it. An' they can talk to you about things all over the world, things they'd never heard of before. So I expect it has its uses.

"Another big change is in the evening shift at the mills," she went on. "You get ever so many housewives going off to work from half-past five to half-past nine of night. It seems a funny idea to me, but most of 'em seem to like it. It gets 'em out of the house, you see, an' that's what most housewives are in need of."

She lit a cigarette. "I don't like smokin'," she said. "I don't really. It was a neighbour got me into the habit. She kept putting a cigarette on the table every time she came into the house. I'd lost two stone in weight an' I was bad with my nerves. She said smoking would be good for my nerves. My husband said: 'I've to see the first woman yet who looks nice with a fag in her mouth.' I agree with him, and I've tried to give them up, but I was so grumpy after the first few days that he said: 'If that's how you're going to be, you'd best start smokin' again.'"

Although we chatted freely for most of the journey, she really blossomed after Manchester Victoria, where some women from Worktown and beyond entered the compartment. She began to tell them of the death of a brother.

"He never married, you see, and he lived alone. One night he came up to our house and he said: 'I feel as if I'm going all to pieces, Nellie.' So I made him lie down on the couch. 'Stay there the night,' I said, 'and happen you'll feel better in the morning.' So he laid himself down but after half an hour he got up and insisted on going. You see, he wouldn't live with any relatives because he said that would be spoiling their happiness. Of course I didn't realise he were that bad. Then they took him to hospital."

As she told her story they all listened attentively, breaking in with remarks, "Ee, poor chap," "What a shame!" "You'd done all you could do."

"Anyway, I got a telegram. When I opened it it said my brother was extremely ill and I had to go and visit him at once. I began to get myself ready. I was all nerves. The woman next door came in. She said, 'I saw the telegraph boy. You've had bad news, Nellie.'

" 'Our Charlie's extremely ill,' I said, 'I've had word from the hospital to go an' visit him.'

" 'Would you like me to come with you?' she said.

" 'Eee I would, Annie,' I said, 'if you could see your way to.' "

One woman said, "It's times like that when you need a good neighbour." The others nodded. They waited and Nellie went on with her story, fiddling occasionally with her hearing-aid.

"I didn't know where I was—or I'd have got a taxi. Anyway, Annie and me set off walking up street. And as we did we saw a bobby coming down. Annie said, 'I wonder is he going to your house.'

"I looked at him and I saw he was walking very slowly, with his beat walk like, swinging along like that. 'Ee I don't think so,' I said, '—he's walking with his beat walk. He wouldn't be having any message.'

"Anyway, we got to the end of the street," went on Nellie, "and Annie said, 'I'll just look back and see what he does.' And we looked back and watched him, and when he were near our house we saw him looking up at the door numbers. 'He's at your door,' said Annie. So we went back. And he had word my brother had died. But you'd never have thought it by the way he was walking. A fortnight later my sister was knocked down an' killed."

"Ee, you'd had a hard life," said one of the women.

"I have," said Nellie, "but when I'm t'other way about I'm as lively as can be. In fact, my husband is always saying to me: 'What're yu' takin' on other folks' troubles for?' You know, I can cry when I tell him something that's happened somebody else. Mind you, in time it goes away—that feeling you get. A good job it does, isn't it, or you'd never live if you had to bear it all your life. Time heals, they say."

The women all agreed about this, and one remarked: "Time heals all wounds." And after that they went quiet for a time.

At Trinity Street Station, Worktown, I helped Nellie out and two other women got out also. There was a woman waiting on the platform and when she saw me she hesitated and then shook my hand:

"Is it Billy Naughton?" she exclaimed. Her eyes were very blue and I knew them well, but for a moment I couldn't place her, although I didn't let on, as they say. "I used to keep the little toffee shop at the 'Cocker'," she said.

I knew her at once then. She went on as we shook hands.

"Do you remember the night you called in the shop for a packet of fags with your typewriter under your arm? I said 'What have you got there?' and you said, 'It's a typewriter. I'm going to be a writer.' Ee, when you'd gone out of the shop, I said to myself, 'Coalmen don't become writers.' Ee, but you have! And we love your stories, and your television plays. Ee, I'm so happy to see you. An' I'm so glad you've managed to do what you set out to do."

At the top of the station brew I saw one of my old coalbagging mates driving by in his lorry. It struck me that if I had my time over again, I'd hardly have the guts to keep at it. It used to take me all night to get down a couple of sentences.

SATURDAY: *Worktown; Old Mates*

By Saturday morning I had had time to get over a depressed feeling that usually takes hold of me when I first arrive back in Worktown. There are a number of reasons for this feeling. One of them is that over the years I've got used to London. Almost daily I walk through St. James's Park, along the Mall, round Trafalgar Square, and have five minutes in the National Gallery. To walk up Crook Street, in Worktown, past the ironfounders' and engineers' and the coal-sidings where I used to work is something very different. People are working—not strolling about. That's the sort of thing that amazes my Worktown friends when they visit me in London and we have a walk. They keep saying, "But what is everybody doing *walking about*? Does *nobody* do any work?" I show them Charles the First on his horse and they don't even look. They look at the throng. "Who are they?" they ask. "Where do they come from?" And I can see they don't feel any too pleased about it.

I walked down some quiet cobbled streets in Swan Lane. I was surprised to see the moss and grass growing between the cobblestones as it had years before. The main bits of character about Worktown never seem to change. I saw a newspaper placard with the caption: PANCAKE EATING CONTEST. I walked in to town.

I saw a horse-carter I used to work with before I became a driver. I was his carrier-off or "monkey" as we were called. His name was Freddy Throppershaw. He was standing on the sideset outside a pub in the town centre. He was as I'd known him twenty-odd years before, little changed except he looked more flushed on his cheeks and paler on his forehead. He must have been in his sixties, but he didn't look it. He looked like a squat robust farmer. He had his hands in his front trouser pockets, was smoking a pipe, and with his back to the pub door he appeared to be watching the traffic.

"How're you goin', Freddy?" I said. I made my tone a broad Worktown one to make up for any change in my appearance.

"Not too bad," he said, eyeing me closely.

"I'm Bill Naughton," I said, wasting no time.

He took his pipe out of his mouth and gave a big grin of welcome and shook my hand.

"I'm right glad to see thee, Bill," he said. He couldn't take his eye off my bald head and my grey-white hair. I know what he's thinking, I thought, he's thinking I've gone damned old since the time I worked on the coal job.

"Are you havin' a pint, Freddy?" I said.

"I'm just waitin' for um to open," he said.

"Now how are you keepin'?" I said.

"Oh, hearty but poor," said Freddy with a grin.

He's not changed much, I thought. There was a sound from behind the closed door. Freddy turned quickly.

"That's her now—drawin' the bolts," he said.

A barmaid opened the door and we went in together. Freddy, although a matey and popular chap on the job, always had a reputation for never parting, never standing his corner, never paying his round, if he could possibly get out of it. One night a gang of us, about a dozen, carters and carriers-off, had stayed on drinking in our working dirt on pay night (this was said to be the worst thing a man could do—to start spending his wages before he went home to his wife: and those who said it weren't far wrong).

We had all paid our rounds in pints, except Freddy, and we were in our second round, when one fellow called Boarding said: "Same again, Freddy?" Freddy, who had drunk about fifteen free pints, shook his head: "I don't think I'll bother this time—oh, but I'll tell thee what, get me a bottle o' stout. I'll tak' it home for the missus." Boarding ordered the round and the stout and said to the barman: "He'll pay!"

Freddy made no pretence of offering to pay for the drinks whilst he was with me, which gave me much satisfaction. I remember his once telling me: "It's not that I'm skinny, Bill, it's just as I'm so bloody fond of me ale that buying it for anybody else seems a waste of money."

"Are you still at the old firm, Freddy?" I said.

"Aye—int' stables," he said.

"We don't work Sat'days. Only twenty horses. Tha wouldn't know t' place."

He spat out. "*Everybody does what he bloody wants,*" he said. "We've one sod called Jober, a milk driver, supposed to be in cleanin' his horse by quarter past seven every mornin'—but he never shows up till eight o'clock. So th'orsekeeper says to him one mornin', 'Tha big idle glassbacked bastard—can't not get outa thy bloody bed of a mornin'?' An' this Jober turns to him an' says: 'Yu' twit—if I could I'da been 'ere before this, wouldn't I?'"

Freddy took a gulp at his pint and almost emptied it: "To the gaffer! That's how they talk to the gaffers these days. Everybody does what he bloody well wants. Place is upside-bloody-down." He began to get excited: "Tha knows what'ud 'ave 'appened to us if we'd ha' dared to talk to owd Tummy like when he wert gaffer."

"Aye," I said. "I were once sweepin' stables when he called me back. A coupla bloody hayseeds had blow in an' he made me sweep 'em up."

"He would," said Freddy, "he were a proper bastard. He came to a miserable end. Hadn't a friend in the bloody world."

I got Freddy another pint and I had a bottle of Crown ale. "How's the coal job?" I said.

"Everybody does as he bloody wants," said Freddy, "—the job's upside-bloody-down. Tha knows how we used 'ave to climb o'er back gates, unfasten shed, tak' buckets out, an' put coal up int' corner?"

"I do that an' all," I said.

"These sods today won't even open coalshed door! If it's not oppen they slat coal ont' bloody floor outside bloody shed. Even if it's a poor bloody old age pensioner she's got to shovel coal in herself. Coalbaggers—you've got to welcome um like bloody kings. They're payin' in at half-past three every day, an' we used to be out while six o'clock tryin' to get shut of it." He began to mutter: "Upside-bloody-down. Everybody does as he bloody wants."

Two more from my old firm came in, Bailey and Alf. I didn't know them as well as I knew Freddy, but they both remembered me.

"I hear tha's become a farm bailiff int' South," said Alf.

"Tha's heard wrong," I said. "Must be somebody else."

"I heard tha works on puttin' plays an' things together fert' wireless an' telly," said Bailey.

"Something like that," I said.

"Ist' money good?" said Freddy.

"Not bad—" I said.

"That's the main thing," said Freddy.

Alf seemed very disappointed that I wasn't a farm bailiff. It did seem a let down even to me.

I asked them what they were having, but Bailey said he would order.

"Bill's paying," said Freddy. "Don't go against bloody etiquette. If a chap's at bar tha doesn't come in an' treat him."

"You used work with old Benny up Astley Bridge," I said to Alf. "How's he going on?"

"He gets thirteen an' tenpence-bloody ha'penny a week pension," put in Freddy, "after all the years he paid into it. In them days for every tanner he paid in he coulda bought a packet o' fags, a gill o' beer, a box o' matches, an' had a ha'penny change."

"How dusta make that out?" said Bailey.

"Tuppence for a five-packet o' Woodbines," said Freddy, "tuppence ha'penny for a gill of beer, a penny for a six o' matches, an' a ha'penny change."

"He's bloody right," said Alf.

"'Course I am," said Freddy. "He paid good tanners in an' he's getting bad tanners back."

"The best thing to do," said Bailey, "with this 'ere superannuation, is to draw the bloody lot out—the money tha's paid in, a few weeks afore tha leaves. Otherwise, they dock it off thy supplementary pension."

"Aye," said Alf, "tha'rt sure of one good booze-up at least."

"An' suppose tha lives on till tha'rt bloody ninety?" said Freddy.

"They 'ave thee every bloody road," said Alf.

A man called Owd Jem came in and joined us. I was very glad to see him. When I first started coal-bagging I worked with him. I ripped my trousers the first day and he gave me an old pair of his (that had once belonged to a tram driver; he also gave me an old pair of his clogs).

Jem knew me at once. We shook hands warmly.

"You're lookin' champion, Jem," I said.

"I'm just as God made me," he said.

"He's turned eighty," said Freddy. "They'll hatta take him out an' shoot him."

Bailey bought a round of drinks.

"We've just been talkin' about the old times on the coal job," said Freddy.

"Bloody hard times they were an' all!" said Jem.

"We were happier than these young 'uns," said Freddy.

"Nowt of bloody sort," said Jem in a loud authoritative voice. "Folk are happier all round these days."

"Everything's upside-bloody-down if you ask me," said Freddy.

"They're bound to be happier," went on Owd Jem, "because *they've a bit of cash to play with!*" He stared at us to let his words sink in. "Afore the war money was that tight every penny was spoken for! But today folk have a bit of choice. An' they feel better for it. You go out an' you can see it on their faces. They're no longer frickened. They feel freer. It stands to reason."

Jem went on about this, ignoring any interruptions. He reminded them that before the war the holiday week was a week and that now it was a fortnight, and that before the war hardly any firms paid their workers during the holiday.

"It weren't a holiday," said Alf, "—it were bloody sack for t'week."

Freddy said something about gaffers not being the men they were in the old days. Something about letting the "job get upside-bloody-down." This brought about a sudden burst of talk about gaffers and bosses. I'd forgotten how much it used to mean to us, to have a boss that one could respect and, in a way, look up to. You didn't want a boss to be in any way soft—that was even worse than his being a tyrant. He could be overriding, demanding, hard, and, to a degree, unapproachable, but if he was "fair and bore no malice" then he was a good gaffer. I now began to hear lots of the sentiments I had heard so often in the thirties, and had used on occasion myself. "Aye, he were a good gaffer—when he said a thing he meant it," and "If he told thee to do a thing, an' it turned out wrong—he'd always stand by thee," and "He'd give thee a damn good ruckin' if tha did owt wrong—but once he'd given it thee it were all o'er, and he'd never mention it again." And I found myself chipping in about one boss I remembered with affection: "You could talk to him. You could speak your mind to him. But you could never kid him."

The thing stuck in my mind afterwards—how much a good boss meant to the men on a job. If he was the sort of man they could look up to, workers seemed only too eager to give him a curious loyalty, that seemed to contradict their usual attitude to the job and to bosses.

Owd Jem said: "They're not all gone, the good bosses. I've just been workin' for one who was a lot better than any of the bosses in the old days. A right toff—a real gentleman, Mister Thomson, the head director." When Jem spoke I recalled the reverence and affection with which my father, a miner, would speak of one of the pit managers, who had once done him a good turn. He used to say,

"He is a college educated gentleman. Would never go back on his word."

Jem began to tell us of his job, and although the others had heard part of the story, they let him go on with only odd interruptions, mostly of approval.

"When I left the old firm at sixty-five," said Jem, "after forty years coalbagging an' a few years sweeping up, I went workin' for this other firm, first as a night watchman, an' then as a checker at the gate. I took the drivers' load papers from them and checked up on the lorry numbers and all that sort of thing, like. It was a champion little job. Good chaps to work with, an' I was a favourite amongst all the women in the canteen."

"Not at thy bloody age," said Alf.

"No—not at eighty," said Bailey.

"I said *everythin'* were upside-bloody-down," said Freddy.

Jem said: "The women knew I meant no harm, so they were able to show me a bit of affection without bein' misunderstood."

"What a bloody tale," said Freddy. "I wouldn't trust thee as far as I could throw thee—eighty or bloody eighteen."

"Good old Jem," said Alf, "he's never short of a way of gettin' round the women."

Jem had a laugh and then went on: "It was a firm that makes furniture an' stuff—in a very big way of business. Exports all over the world. I had a smashin' job. But things were gettin' bigger an' bigger, an' the next thing they brought three security men in?"

"Who are them?" said Bailey.

"Men who patrolled the place with dogs just to make sure everythin' was all right. I think they were sent there by the insurance company. Millions of pounds involved see. And they began doin' the checkin'. It meant I had nowt to do. So I went to the gaffer and said: 'Do you want to get rid of me?' and he said, 'Not likely. There's a job here for thee to tha dying day.' So I says to him, 'Aye, but what have I to do?' And he said to me, 'Do owt as tha has a bloody mind to. Go down the fire 'ole and have a smoke. Go to the canteen and have an hour with the women. Go out for an hour if tha fancies it.'"

"That were a right bloody good job," said Bailey.

"A real doddle," said Alf.

"Aye, it were what I'd been lookin' for all my life," said Jem, "—a job wi' no work attached to it."

"Turned eighty when tha found it," said Freddy, "—bin lookin' for it seventy years."

"That's what I thought," said Jem, "but then I found I couldn't do it."

"What—couldn't do nowt!"

Jem's voice became louder and more serious: "It's the hardest thing in the world to do nowt once you've been used to workin'. I didn't know what to do with myself. Every bloody day seemed stretched to an eternity. I were in an' out of the canteen, in an' out of the firehole, helpin' anybody as 'ud let me. All the bloody joy had gone out of life." He looked round at us: "It's a bloody fact," he said.

"We'll tak' thy word for it," said Freddy. He was always the first to drain his pint glass, and I was glad to see he never made any attempt to pay for a round.

"I went to work one mornin'," went on Jem, "an' the cashier called me over. 'Would you mind going home, Jem,' he says, 'and changing into your best suit. Get back about twelve o'clock. You'll be wanted upstairs.' I looked at him but I said nowt. But I thought to myself, 'They're gettin' rid of me at last.'"

"That's what it looked like," said Alf.

"Anyway, I went home, an' washed me, an' changed me, an' put my best suit on," said Jem. "I got back dead on twelve. 'Come with me,' said the cashier, 'they want to see you upstairs.' So I went upstairs with him. He knocked, opened the door, an' sent me in first. There was a long table, covered with a white tablecloth, and on it were bottles of whisky, gin, sherry, beer, owt you had in mind. An' round it were all the bosses. An' the chief boss, Mister Thomson, this one I've been telling you about, comes up an' shakes my hand, an' wishes me a happy birthday. It were my eightieth birthday, an' I'd forgotten all about it! But they hadn't! The next thing a light flashes. It's the photographer from the *Evening News*. They weren't sackin' me at all. They were givin' me a birthday party."

Jem looked at us. "I felt a bit overcome for the minute. Yes, I did. But I soon got suppin' an' I were as lively as a cricket. Chattin' away to the gaffer."

"An' did they sack thee, when it were all over, Jem?" said Freddy.

"No, they wanted to keep me on," said Jem, "—but I gave 'um my notice in."

"It's no use putting on good nature," said Alf.

"It wasn't that," said Jem, "—but once you feel you're no use on a job you might as well pack it in. But yon boss were a right toff to me. An' they all had a collection for me when I left."

"If tha fell off co-op," said Freddy, "tha'd fall int' bloody divi."

I remembered that Alf lived up Deane Road, and I asked him if he knew Harry Crow.

"Aye," he said, "—I knew all the family."

"He's a pal of mine in London," I said. "He reckons he's coming to Worktown one of these days to see the old home."

"He's left it too late," said Alf. "They've demolished Partridge Street. It's part of Wellington Yard Sewage Works now."

I was sorry to hear that.

I haven't dared tell Harry yet. . . .

★   ★   ★

"*Is the realistic novelist to be taught to find his material not in life but in Mass-Observation?*" questioned Miss Dilys Powell in the *Sunday Times* (she is still writing well for it weekly) when M-O's book on King George VI's Coronation appeared twenty-three years ago.

Mass-Observation should be life, or at least, as a specialised study of it, brings the reader close to life. Some readers perhaps *uncomfortably* close. We know that, from working with M-O or reading its reports, writers have learnt from its methods, and widened their own creative vision. Three now professional writers who worked with M-O have helped with this volume, of whom Bill Naughton was one.

When we first met him in 1938 he was still on the coal round. He used to turn up most evenings after work at our house in Davenport Street (we had a few resident women observers). He was always well bathed and spruced up but had the dark-rimmed, coal-flecked eyelashes you see on miners. He told me it took longer to get those eyelashes clean than all the rest of him. You had to do it with olive oil, a cloth and a matchstick. To clean his hands he used a mixture of olive oil and sugar, and that took ten minutes. If he didn't clean them that way, he said, the sweat would bring out the dirt during the evening, and smudge any paper he was writing on. He wrote personal reports for us, on Armistice Day at the coal sidings, all-in wrestling, and such like. He was introduced to the giving end of radio when he went with the present writer to the BBC studios at Manchester to say what he thought of Picasso's *Guernica* in a mass-criticism programme.

"In the taxi," he recalls, "I spotted your pyjama collar sticking out from between the front of your shirt. 'He's a nice chap is Tom,' the Worktown cleaner had told me, 'but on cold days he will put his shirt on *over* his pyjamas'."

Since those days Bill Naughton has published five books, over a hundred stories, and more than a dozen major television and radio plays and features. On the evening of Sunday, 10 July 1960, the present writer, together with Julian Trevelyan, Humphrey Spender, Francis Huxley and Barbara Harrisson watched Naughton's *"June Evening"* on television in a Worktown pub., a documentary drama of the street in which the author was brought up, action on the evening of 1st June, 1921. It seemed that all Worktown was watching it. From the shoal of letters the author and the BBC received, they enjoyed it. And so did the critics.

The *Times* said: *"June Evening*, by Mr. Bill Naughton, was received with acclamation when it was heard in the Third Programme almost two years ago. . . . There is no story in Mr. Naughton's classic (a term used here after full deliberation)."

The *Daily Telegraph* headed its notice "BRILLIANT PLAY OF ATMOSPHERE". The *News Chronicle*: "It was a brilliant documentary, as carefully knitted together as a Lancashire shawl, putting to shame the attempts of some writers to present so-called life in dramatic form."

Praise came from every quarter—no not quite every. "*Cathode*", the Worktown newspaper TV critic, alone got into a fearful flap—at seeing his own near-ghost? It seemed that he felt as uncomfortable now as Miss Powell had before him. This is what he wrote (our italics):

"The trouble about the twenties in Lancashire is, I am sure, that the atmosphere and spirit is *uncommunicable* to any who did not experience them . . . I am sure that Boltonian Bill Naughton's '*June Evening*' meant as little to *people in Suffolk and Ayrshire* as it did to my own family. . . .

"The poverty, courage, squalor and humour of it were couched in a language and idiom that must have been *double-dutch* to those lacking the interpretative key. . . . It is, therefore, a *museum* piece. . . . Of what interest could such a picture be to the *people of Hampshire*? . . .

"It may be an odd thing to say, but this was *too* faithful a picture. . . .

"I doubt whether many *outside Lancashire and my generation* did 'understand it'. . . ."

The visiting M-O unit of outsiders from Borneo and elsewhere felt no such unease; instead, incited by the paper's editor, we wrote a letter (15 July) which among other things, called this play:

"A superb piece of television. Worktown should be proud of a wonderfully sincere, subtle and sympathetic rendering of its 1920 past written by its only playwright of eminence."

Maurice Wiggin, one of our own first kindly critics of 1937 (see p. 16), now TV critic of the *Sunday Times*, asked:

"How much of Bill Naughton's '*June Evening*' is actual, how much imagined?

What distinguishes his loving recapitulation of the very feel and essence of life in a poor street in Worktown . . . is that it is not, like so much writing, anthropological."

That is where Mr. Wiggin is, for once, wrong! But he may readily be forgiven here. For he is only underlining the hard fact that in fact anthropology adequately applied to one's own society requires several levels of approach, involves insight and imagination (both in preparing studies first and in interpreting them afterwards), individual records as well as numerical checks, personal cases and passionate statistics.

So relevant is this relation of the "realistic" creative writer to the social scientist, and of both to their own society—in practice they have to operate subject to close public criticism (unlike the anthropologist abroad or the psychiatrist at hospital)—that it seemed a good idea to ask Bill Naughton to add a further piece on his experiences in growing out of Worktown (in the space-sense) from coal-man into TV playwright. Bill readily obliged with the following gem, which adequately concludes this mainly Worktown part of our study.

A Man of the Old School
by
Bill Naughton

Friends in London have said to me: "What do your old workmates and others in Worktown think of you becoming a writer?" Very few of them comment on it, for which I'm glad. One called Arthur, with whom I once worked, said: "Look at the money tha'rt savin' on clothes. No need to buy new clogs, let alone graftin' irons. Sittin' on thy ass all day. What a life!" Most of my real old mates, if they venture a remark about it, say something like this: "Oh, so tha had a hand in *puttin' that television play together.*" Or, "I hear tha put a story together." One woman I spoke to, who was the mother of a boy I went to school with, said: "Ee, you might be able to write stories, but I wish you'd seen the letter our James *put together* to send to the landlord. You've never read anything like it. I showed it to your dad and he said: 'He's better than a philadelphia bloody lawyer.'"

One woman asked me did I get the title first and then write a story round it. One chap was telling me how much he had enjoyed my first book, *A Roof Over Your Head*, and how he had read it to his grandmother. He drew me aside and said in a kindly way: "We were only sayin', tha'd be made for life if tha could get somebody *to put it together into a book for thee*. A mean a book for toffs to read.

Tha's *put it together* as it's come to thee, an' tho' we like it that way (we understand it see), they may not like it. So tha' wants to look round an' see if tha can get a *publisher* interested in it, who'd *put it together* into a book." I was genuinely touched by his concern. He said the things that I should have thought and perhaps said myself at one time.

I got a remark to the point from a man who was known as Honest Harold. When we worked together on the coal job he was in his middle fifties, a big broad-shouldered man with a heavy moustache and dark grey eyebrows that scratched against his long eyelashes as he spoke. He was frightened of nobody or nothing, from the manager to the most difficult horse in the stables. Actually, when he growled "Stand o'er!" to a horse, every horse in the entire stable stood over. He was never a cruel man, but he insisted on being obeyed. If he thought there wasn't enough oats in the porven' he never hesitated to go and tell the horsekeeper about it, and would insist on some more.

He was called Honest Harold because he had never been known to cheat a customer out of an ounce of coal, nor would he cheat the firm either. It was always a thirsty job, working with him, because you never made the extra shilling or two which got you your pint of ale during the day. He even refused tips from any customers he believed not to be as well off as himself. But he was never offensive: "We get paid a fair wage, Misses, an' you get charged a fair price for the coal, so I reckon we're happy all round."

He was an intelligent man, and a good and conscientious workman, yet he seemed to be a bigger nuisance to the boss and the staff than he was to his own workmates. He would refuse to take the coal from any wagon if he thought it wasn't up to standard. "I'm not takin' that muck to my customers," he'd tell the coal manager. "Send it back to the pit." Yet he never hesitated to speak outright to the customers if he thought they were being unfair. A dentist once complained about some Trencherbone cobbles being half a crown a bag. Harold turned on him quietly and said: "A miner has gone down into the bowels of the earth to get that coal for thee. It's the best coal that can be bought. It's been brought up on the shaft, screened, and sent in a wagon to the sidings. We've filled it, brought it out here, an' put a full hundredweight into thy coalshed for half a crown. If you think that's too much I'll bring it out again. But my daughter came round to you last Thursday to have a tooth out. It took you less than fifteen minutes. Yet you charged her six-and-sixpence. I don't see what *you* have to grumble about."

Harold would never buy "Co-op cheques" or have anything to do with weekly payments. "When we got wed, Billy," he once told me, "all we had in the chair line was one good solid kitchen chair. It were mine of course. The wife had to eat *standing up*. I said to her, 'Now tha can sit on that when I'm out, and if tha doesn't sit on it too much, I'll buy thee one for thyself next week or the week after.' "

Harold was a great lover of music, of brass bands, massed choirs and Handel. "If I had my way," he remarked one day in the cab, as he was drinking his morning tea from a blue enamel tea mug, "I'd have every man, woman an' child in this country listen to 'The Messiah' next Saturday night. You'd waken up to a new civilisation next morning." A fellow called Swinger said : "What about them as doesn't like it, Harold?" Harold remarked lightly: "We could dispense with 'em. Tha can't make a human being out of somebody who doesn't respond to Handel. If the soul's dead the body isn't much use."

Although he was a difficult man to work with, and you never got your bunce or your drinks or had any spare cash when you worked with him, yet over the years I grew fond of him, and every man paid him a grudging respect. The thing about it was: you were always aware of somebody being there when Harold was around. It gave an extra bit of meaning to the day's work.

Harold would never allow any swearing, coarse language or dirty tales to come out where he was working. Yet he was never a prude, and had the old-fashioned Lancashire way of talking about sex in a straight forward way. We were once having a cup of tea at the home of an old friend of his, a woman whose daughter had been married a few months. The daughter was there, a good looking woman of thirty, and so was her husband. The mother said to Harold: "Don't you think our Ruth's looking well since she got wed, Harold?" Harold said: "Of course she is, bless her, An' she ought. She's gettin' fed at both ends." We could hardly believe our ears; but Harold never batted an eye.

On the coal job you nearly always got one woman customer on the round that took a fancy to you. I can't think exactly why, because we weren't a handsome or romantic bunch, but that's the way it was. Harold, it was thought, was woman proof in that respect (he was a family man). "I've had many a woman sailing her bonnet after me," he once said, "trying little tricks an' lures to get free coal an' something else. And I've felt like tellin' 'um they were wasting their time. A woman can say owt, offer me owt, come to the door half naked, but she'll never catch me." Then he added: "But I have been caught." His voice went low and serious: "It's when a woman's bare skin touches mine. Her bare arm on my bare arm. Her shoulder against my shoulder. Her bare bosom touches my skin in any way. Then—" he admitted openly, "*I'm undone.* Yes, if that happens *I'm undone.* I'm only human after all, and if a woman's skin touches my skin I'm undone."

I met Harold on one of my recent visits to Worktown. It was Saturday afternoon and I had gone for a long walk on the moors. I was near a lonely spot known as the Scotman's Stump when I saw a figure approaching in the early dusk. It was a tall man wearing a long overcoat and a black cloth cap. When we drew close to each other I saw it was Harold. It gave me great pleasure to see him, and I shook his hand very warmly. Although he said nothing to the effect, I had an intuition that he disapproved of my going away from Worktown. We chatted of old times and he told me he was retired.

"I'd like to live in London just for one thing," he said, "to be *near the Albert Hall.* To be able to go to them concerts they have." Then he added: "And I understand you've given up coalbagging for good an' you've turned to writing for a living?"

"You never know, Harold," I said, "but it seems that way."

He shook my hand and gave me his parting words: "Well they say the pen is mightier than the sword. *But I doubt if it's mightier than the spade.*"

Part B

EIGHT

FACES, PLACES: 1937-60

This is an illustrative section, and will be found inset following page 160.

Ship made of cows' horns seen in window of small house, Worktown, 1960.

Part C

LEISURE PLEASURES ANYWHERE

Egg-timer, 5" high, in plastic and glitter chromium; Blackpool souvenir, 1960, 3/11.

Such feelings move those images
And dreams that living creatures are,
As are inherent in our frames
Of mutable earth, air, and fire.
                    Kathleen Raine
                    "Seen in a Glass"

NINE

AROUND THE TOWER

THE FIRST Vicar of Blackpool was the Rev. William Thornber, a Lancashire-born six footer, appointed 1829, who became a famous local figure and played a great part in popularising the beginning of Blackpool as a resort. His *Historical and Descriptive Account of Blackpool*, published by J. Banks of 133 Fishergate, Preston, in 1840, includes the first ever mass-observation there. Just before the book was published he made a snap count on that August day over a century ago now:

Visitors	1,856
Inhabitants	521

In August 1960 the best figures we could obtain from official statistics and the careful observations of M-O staff on the spot gave:

Visitors	500,000 plus
Inhabitants	144,500

The Publicity Officer for Blackpool Corporation advised that over 7,000,000 people had come to the town in the past twelve months, a rough figure. However, we have pre-war figures from similar official sources giving up to 8,000,000 in one year.

The trajectory of Thornber's life was in a tempo of drama that Blackpool has constantly maintained. His own child was drowned off the beach; and he ended up himself (dying age 82) in a lunatic asylum because, as another historian mildly describes it, ". . . he erred and strayed as the Prayer Book says, and because of intemperance and breaking his marriage vows."

During the insane dotage of the errant Anglican Minister, one of the local landed gentry, Sir Reginald, of the old Lancashire family of Heywood, lived in a mansion on the seafront of the west coast of the Fylde, at what was then a small hamlet. The first definite "visitors" came to Blackpool in the second decade of the eighteenth century. 1714 is the preferred date. The first hotel probably appeared in 1735, converted from a cottage. Bishop Pococke wrote in 1750: "At

Blackpool, near the sea, are accommodations for people who come to bathe."

No one disputes that the Heywood home was turned into an Aquarium in 1874, but about the only thing known of Sir Reginald is that he gave £100 to the first Blackpool lifeboat. The first Mayor of Blackpool, Dr. Cocker, set a precedent which has been followed by many of his successors. He looked ahead and bought the Heywood mansion. Six years later he turned it, together with the by then flourishing Beach Hotel, into the Blackpool Central Property Co.

Four years after he had floated his Central Property Company, Cocker "reconstructed" the concern as the Central Promenade Estates Company, and this paid £44,000 for property which had cost him £16,000. Five years after that, the whole was purchased by the Standard Debenture Corporation Limited of London for £65,000. These people were scouting for a site to erect *a rival Eiffel Tower*. It was the time when architects were throwing up the Crystal Palace, the Forth Bridge and the Eiffel Tower, steel-girder skeletons, air and glitter between; symbols of the last iron age. Blackpool was chosen land for the English Tower experiment.

The height of the Tower to the top of the flagstaff was fixed at 518 feet 9 inches (above sea-level). A circus between the four legs formed the core of the Tower buildings, with new Aquarium on one side, and a dance pavilion on the other. The local M.P. laid the foundation stone and was promptly raised to the peerage. The Tower was raised rather more slowly and took some years. When Cocker had been bought out of the Tower Company, its new head became Alderman John Bickerstaffe, another big Blackpool name. John was the son of Bob Bickerstaffe, a local sailor, described by historian Alan Clarke as "blue-eyed and breezy like the sea he loved". Bob loved the sea so well that he also became manager of the newly-formed Central Pier. It was only after this that his seafaring powers were recognised; and when the lifeboat was launched, he was appointed coxswain. Not unnaturally his son John was one of the crew. From these thwarts he became first chairman of the Tower Company, further reorganised in 1891; with an Issued Capital of £452,500, and never paying a dividend of less than $17\frac{1}{2}$% even in the slump years of the early 1930s, it remains today the biggest single feature both of the landscape and of the economy in a town now permanently populated by 140,000 people. A Bickerstaffe is still president (capital now over £1,000,000: post-war dividends up to 35%). Admission fee up from 6d. to 3/-.

The Tower dominated (and dominates) the landscape for miles, whichever way visitors approach Blackpool. When it was finished, the shareholders presented their life-boating chairman with a silver model of it, still on hand in the Tower today. Hundreds of thousands of models of it, in plastic and cheap metals, were being bought each month in 1960, as they were when some forty mass-observers lived in Blackpool and studied the place in 1937-8. There are models of the Tower made as brooches set with imitation brilliants ("Latest Fashion"); as bottle openers, paper knives, handles of tea-caddy spoons (which include an incised clock face fixed at 4 p.m.), on a teapot stand; as cufflinks, comb cases, ball-point pencils, pen-knives; on dynamic egg-timers (5 inches high, price 3/11); as the centre-piece in shining silvery white of cruet sets (3/11); and decorating cigarette cases, mirror backs, fork handles, handkerchiefs and scarves, tape-measures, porcelain cups. On the sea theme, souvenirs include a glittering 8-inch anchor with a built-in thermometer (4/11), and a chromium ship's wheel with dolphins playing around a date-changing calendar (3/11— "registered patent applied for"); and there are "snow storms", Made in Italy. Prices are more than double those of the thirties, and the number and range of such Blackpool relics is at least trebled (see also p. 195).

Odd souvenirs have no local attribute—like the thinly silvered trophy cup with two monster handles (almost a perfect replica of the 1937 version, but on a plastic stand) inscribed:

The Worlds
BIGGEST BOOZER

as it was in 1937. Unchanged over the years, too, are "the practical jokes", popular as ever, their main sale in a shop below the Tower and on the piers;

    2/11 "*The Famous Whoopee Cushion*"
          "Causes roars of laughter"
          Joke of the Year
          (Picture of man sitting on it with scarlet face)
    1/-   "*Mucky Pup*"
          "Roars of laughter"
    6d. CIGARETTE STINKEROOS
          "Oh what a pong!"

The only other main souvenir is edible: Blackpool rock all over the town, pre-war and post; the latest gimmick is to package it in Tower-shaped cartons.

The Look of the Place and People

Someone like the present writer—who has lived abroad for nearly two decades—was perhaps entitled to expect that, on returning to Blackpool after twenty-one years, this teeming place, whose whole *raison d'être* is attracting people to spend for fun, might show major alterations, at least on the surface.

What was the result of this first revisit? Well, it seemed difficult to believe that one was not in the old, familiar, beloved Blackpool of the thirties. The people, the thronging holiday visitors, looked *slightly* different and are indeed statistically different too. More of the people from Worktown and the rest of the great industrial zone of the north who used to come to Blackpool now go to the Costa Brava, Majorca and the Lake of Geneva; many Worktowners in Blackpool now are those who could *not afford to go away at all* when Worktown had many thousands of unemployed. The casualness of dress has distinctly altered for both sexes, with one exception: the little white hats which used to be labelled "Kiss Me", "Stop Me", "Try your luck", etc., have disappeared in favour of felt cowboy hats, always in dark colours with contrasting fringes, bearing wild western names: "Kentucky Kid", "Cisco Kid", "Sheriff", "Texas Ranger" and "Wyatt Earp", with a smattering (of the same hats, priced 2/6) labelled "Elvis Presley" or "Adam Faith"—the rock'n'roll teenage idol heading the bill at the Blackpool Hippodrome this summer.

Clothes counts made on the promenade show, for instance:

82% of men in 1937 compared with only 53% in 1960, with a collar and tie. 18% and 47% respectively wearing open neck shirts.

Similarly with men's headgear:

52% without hats in 1937 compared with 69% in 1960.

The bowler, in Lancashire largely associated with Sundays and special occasions in the thirties, secured over one-third of all male headgear then, but not a single specimen now. Similarly, July/August 1960 Worktown church congregation counts on Sundays showed less than 1% bowlers, nearly all of them at Anglican churches: identical counts in 1937 gave 43% of all Sunday men's heads bowler-adorned, the figure going as high as 58% for Anglican congregations and as low as 16% for Roman Catholic (compare p. 47).

At the other extremity of the body, footwear has loosened up as well. Only half as many men wearing black shoes many more wearing brown; while the black boots worn by 4% in 1937 are no longer found in 1960. This trend is best expressed for both sexes in the statistics of sandals:

	% of Blackpool visitors' feet in sandals, August:	
	1937	*1960*
Men	0	29
Women	13	32

Again, before the war, brown was easily the predominant colour in women's coats, both in everyday Worktown and holiday Blackpool; in 1960 Blackpool brown had fallen by 21%, the lead taken by beige (19% now—less than 1% before). Bright colours, red, yellow, orange, seldom seen before, have become commonplace, with an effect which tends to catch the eye of any visitor from bright old Borneo.

Otherwise, the long-absent looker-on sees again foot after foot of the same vivid conglomerate all along the "Golden Mile"—a typically Blackpool description for a quarter-of-a-mile (nearer 400 yards) of pavement covered with almost *every* conceivable kind of stall, pressing the shadow of the Tower from every side except the sea, arteried inland through the Pleasure Beach, Winter Gardens and the back streets (in which almost every house is a boarding house).

Glittering names over the crowded arcades, occasionally new (but all the same idea and similar in content within), include:

FAIRYLAND	THE BEE AMUSEMENT ARCADE
WONDERLAND	FAIRGROUND
CONEY ISLAND—Climbing Monkeys	FUNLAND
MONTE CARLO PASTIMES	FUNLANDIA
GHOST SWING . . . GHOST TRAIN	FUNHOUSE
VICTORIA AMUSEMENTS	FUN!

Every inch of usable land is packed, in no predictable order, with amusement attractions or related food and drink (but not, in the open, ever alcoholic) supplies. Only the wide, shallow-shelving straight sandbeach and sea seem to offer a way of avoiding constant physical contact, aural and visual and nasal bombardment: but it is just these that most folk come to Blackpool to be swallowed up and wallow in. This is a land as unlike the industrial home-town as commercial Lancashire man can make it. To nearly all, until very recently, it represented and filled the picture of non-home, of awayness, of *abroad*. For in pre-war days, only a tiny élite of holidaying Worktowners ever went *across* the sea, itself a barrier to thought; Blackpool was the limit of leisure dream. Indeed only one permanent building ever managed to get immediately adjacent to sea and beach. Back in 1785, when there were already two Inns, the Metropole began to grow up in its huge red brick straggling mass. Two years later, John Bonny advertised that he had built a new dining-room, and lodging-room for twenty beds (Ladies and Gentlemen 2/2 per day each, Children and Servants 1/6, Table Beer included. Horse Hay and Grass per night 8*d*.).

The Metropole has remained in its proud isolation, though today taken over as part of the Billy Butlin Empire and is now thoroughly modernised. During September 1937 an observer living there (Ralph Parker, who now lives in Moscow) reported:

Upstairs to the bedroom you find it less strikingly different from that of any other boarding-house, than the rooms downstairs and the people. There is a jerry. On this floor of fifty rooms there is one bathroom, giving a proportion of bathrooms to bedrooms actually *lower* than elsewhere in the town. By way of compensation the bedrooms have hot and cold taps.

Blackpool's theatres have an honourable antiquity also: though Adam Faith is a new boy, George Formby is still here for the season, nearly his thirtieth year, singing the good old songs like "Lily of Laguna", "She's My Lady Love"; his show at the Queen's, just below the Tower, was packed out all through this August.

Back in the Tower itself, there are some new animals and new arrangements in the Tower Zoo. But the main attractions, by observation, are still the tigers, the difference now being that the two superb animals on show in the same small prison cages are Blackpool-Tower born from their now departed predecessors. Immediately below the Zoo, the vast Tower Ballroom offers the same main dishes on its daily menu—the children's ballet in the afternoon, and Reginald Dixon at the mighty Wurlitzer organ later on. Next door the Palace Ballroom's largest billing is for "Old Time Dancing".

In the thirties more than a million people paid to see "Colonel Barker and his *or* her bride". The huge hoarding which read:

> I AM TAKING THIS STEP
> FOR THE WOMAN I LOVE
>
> ON A STRANGE HONEYMOON
>
> LOVE CALLING
> ADMISSION 2*d*.

—is now down (see Plate 19). Colonel Barker, the army officer who was discovered to be a woman, was displayed in a pit; round the top people moved in an endless stream throughout the day. Down there, two single beds were separated by a pedestrian crossing, dotted lines between that then novel subject of bawdy jokes, orange Belisha Beacons. In one bed lay the portly frame of the Colonel in a sort of nightshirt; in the other a young girl in a flimsy. Beside the young girl generally lay a huge spotted Dalmatian dog. Under the Colonel's bed there usually lay a bottle of whisky. As the 1937 season proceeded, twelve hours a day in bed being abused and spat at from above, put over 20 lb. on the Colonel's weight. An observer's report described the scene:

> Holidayers pass in an almost continuous line, queueing during peak periods, staring down, kept on the move by attendants. Stream of remarks:
>
> A lad says: "The silly bugger."
> Attendant: "Pass no remarks, please."
> Man: "I call it a frost."
> Attendant: "They won't believe before they come in, so they *won't* have it."
> The man: "He never were a colonel."
> Attendant: "I don't care whether he was a corporal myself."
>
> Woman: "He looks very much like a he, doesn't he."
> Woman: "Yes, and she looks like a she."
> Man: "What's to stop them crossing to each other's beds?"
> Attendant: "Nothing. Only he'll lose the wager if he does."
> Man: "What if they have nightmare, and sleep-walk?"
> Attendant: "They're watched all the time. When one goes to the bathroom the other has to stop in bed."
> Man: "I don't know. I'd like to watch them myself."
> Attendant: "Well, you can if you want to, we'd be glad to let you."
>
> Man: "Oh yes, we know that."
> Woman: "Belisha's wide enough. They're expecting."
> Woman: "That's Belisha stopping 'em."
> The barker prattles on:
> > "Colonel Barker is on the left. Keep moving please. The first person in the world to have the now famous operation changing her sex from that of a man to a woman. He's six weeks and three days to go down there. The only condition of the wager is they don't cross to one another for the twenty-one weeks. They are watched day and night.[1] He's come here for a wager, I believe it's £250."

---

[1] This was not so. An observer shared lodgings and enjoyed many a whisky with the Colonel that year.

He informs that the Colonel has put on 20 lb. since she has been in the pit, but of course he only *guesses* that, he adds. "He's not *starving*. We don't say he *is*."

The Colonel, alas, died in 1959. Continual references to *not* starving were made; this was due to the desire to separate this act from another great attraction of Blackpool's thirties, the Rector of Stiffkey. This Anglican priest was defrocked after a sensational series of ecclesiastical litigations. He then put on a public fast, to prove that the Lord was on his side and that he could live without food. A cocky little man with a filthy vocabulary, he appeared in a barrel. Several million people paid to walk past him, exchanging largely unprintable (on the record) remarks. The Rector too departed, but more untimely—the next year he moved from Blackpool to Skegness, as "Daniel in the Lion's Den"; one day the lions finished off their latter-day Daniel.

The new substitutes for the intersexual officer and the unfrocked clergyman involve more people and more of a strip-tease element. One of the larger new exhibits on the Mile is:

PALACE OF STRANGE GIRLS

THE SHOW THEY TRIED TO STOP

"IT WAS HER FATHER'S FAULT!"

NO CAMERAS PLEASE

PRIOR TO WORLD TOUR

A small-bearded, glitter-eyed barker attracts with card tricks and a mild illusion of sawing a girl in a box. Further along the quarter mile *mêlée*, Montmartre Theatre (Plate 21):

DARING   SPECTACULAR
The most controversial type of entertainment ever seen...
STRICTLY ADULTS ONLY

—with a barker outside proclaiming "Girls from France, Brussels and international countries". There is expert patter, too, giving a moral tone to the affair, such as this of one girl, a small blonde who stands on the outer platform in a red cloak beside the mike:

"She isn't English born of course. She settled in London in 1957. Like other young women before her, unfortunately she got into the wrong hands. . . ."

The middle-aged, dark, dark-suited proprietor of this show told us that he is making less money than usual this season; but that the increased prices (admission 2/-; cf. old Col. Barker 2d.) kept things going fine. Certainly the crowds for this type of attraction are *visibly less* in August 1960 than 1937 or 8. But as he now put it, after many years in this business at Blackpool:

"*If Blackpool fails, Britain is finished*—BANKRUPT."

This is a widely held attitude, which does not wholly cloak a nervousness about present trends in Blackpool *within* this Britain.

The strip-tease stuff has visibly increased. In one side street is a "Folies" theatre specialising in it. The Winter Gardens this summer gave three different semi-comical versions of strip-tease acts, including one elaborate performance by a white poodle puppet dressed *en grande dame*, life-size (she only agrees to strip when a *real* gentleman in a top hat, after trying her with several offerings, wins her consent with a diamond bracelet).

Like nearly everything in Blackpool, though, the new taste for strip-tease is one of emphasis and degree, continuing a much older tradition. The Winter Gardens first opened in 1876. Soon it acquired Mr. Bill Holland, one in a long line of entertainment impresarios in the vigorous local tradition. Local historian Alan Clarke describes the result of the acquisition:

"In his first season he inaugurated those ballets which have developed to such splendour and for which the Winter Gardens has become renowned. . . . The idea of ballets with the usually scanty attire associated with terpsichorean character rather shocked some of the 'unco guid' in Blackpool, including some of the Garden directors themselves and protest was made at their introduction to the town, but time and tolerance have silenced the objectors and now the majority of folks accept such stage displays of the female form as beautiful and artistic entertainment."

Holland was a "proper Blackpool" showman. He once bought a hundred guinea carpet and advertised it all over Lancashire: "Come to the Winter Gardens and SPIT on Bill Holland's hundred guinea carpet."

There are some other fairly conspicuous "new" or part new gimmicked features in this holiday panorama, including these five:

i) Reference to *TV* (to which we will return).

ii) *Photograph Yourself* stalls, and various fairly elaborate incitements to be photographed. Automatic machines are in all amusement arcades; 3 for 2/- —sit on seat, put in money, a flash each time your photo is taken. Wait 2½ minutes until it falls down a slot (head only).

iii) Many other *modern-type* machines, serving squashes or hot drinks; juke boxes.

iv) More *American* influences, chiefly through Hamburgers and Hot Dogs replacing—though not entirely—pasties and hot pies.

v) *Gypsy fortune tellers*—stronger than ever but mildly modernised.

A Gypsy Aristocracy

The Gypsy link goes right back into Blackpool's past—the most famous clan of gypsy fortune tellers—with the late Petulengro, of sound radio fame, as their "King"—are Fylde people. Today there are nine gypsies, for instance, practising along the front between the Central Station and Tussaud's, and many others towards the South shore and around the town. They usually charge 2/6 a reading and are manifestly thriving. Benches are often put outside the stalls, and groups of women clustered round waiting are a common sight. Here is a recent observer description:

A typical booth has a roof and three solid walls, the fourth, being only large enough to enter, is hung with a curtain or has a waist-high door. The booth looks like a tiny room, always having two chairs (for the fortune teller and her client) and if space allows a table between them. Outside the booth the walls and gypsy's name are decorated with mosaic squares of mirror which glitter attracting the crowd's attention, but once inside, the client is alone in a small darkened room, cut off from the light, friends and noise outside, with only a mysterious gypsy confronting her. Certainly the women waiting outside one booth had serious and not altogether unworried expressions on their faces.

For a stall like this a gypsy (usually a woman, dressed in flowing robes) pays around £1,000 a season to the Blackpool Corporation; it still leaves enough margin to make these few square feet golden for the stall-holder. But no wonder a competitive spirit is manifest. Thus among the crowded booths of the Golden Mile, *four relate*:

1. "The Original Queen of the Golden Mile, Gypsy Rosalee"
2. "The only Real Original Gypsy Lee on this Front"
3. "Gypsy Lee. Be sure you consult the right one"
4. "Blackpool's famous Gypsy Lee".

While several bring in the modern claim to fame:
5. "Broadcasting and TV Gypsy"
6. "This gypsy has appeared on Television"
7. "Blackpool's own televised gypsy".

The gypsy majority, who cannot claim a personal appearance on TV, often have photographs of well-known people who have been more fortunate in this respect. They continue, as pre-war, to plug royal and celebrity connections as evidence of efficacy. Gypsy Rosalee, in a key position on the front (see Plate 23), excels all others in this respect. She has scores of photos of celebrities seen with her, the emphasis on radio and TV personalities—Charlie Drake, Jill Day, Alma Cogan, and locally-starring Adam Faith. But centre piece, set in a special window, is a letter from the *locus classicus* of Monarchy itself (on royal stationery):

> Buckingham Palace,
> 17th February 1960.
>
> Dear Gypsy Rosalie,
>   I write at The Queen's command to thank you for your letter and for your kind message of good wishes. . . .
>   I am to send you The Queen's most sincere thanks. . . .
>   Yours sincerely,
>   Rose Baring (signed)
>   Lady-in-Waiting.

The dual conception of being traditionally near-royal as a Gypsy, and technologically modern as a personality, is best expressed in one of the side arcades:

> GYPSY ROSE ANNA
> *Grand*-niece of the Famous
> TV and Radio *Old* Gypsy Sarah
> "A real time Gyspy of the
> ROYAL ROMANY BLOOD"

The mystique and technique of palm-reading and crystal gazing is unchanged. And even the side effects used for presentation are almost interchangeable with the thirties, as indicated for instance in this extract from a 1937 observer report:

Palmist Madame Curl exhibits outside her booth a number of telegrams and letters from royal secretaries such as:

"The Private Secretary is Desired by the Prince of Wales to express his Royal Highness's thanks for your kind message of congratulations on the occasion of his birthday".

On the other hand, there has been some reduction in pseudo-scientific side propaganda such as the 1937 "Violet Ray Ozoner". This is in line with the general if vague increase in knowledge about the marvels of science, as well as improved and free medical services, putting less of a premium on magical or herbal answers to ill-health.

It is seldom safe to take the disappearance of anything with traditional or primitive roots as likely to be definite or lasting in Blackpool. Again and again we find links back into a long past which, in a town led by showmen and extroverts, is exceptionally well documented. Thus, old-style herbalism is in Blackpool's grass roots (Plate 18); August 1960 an observer came across one practitioner carrying on business where the pavement narrows at the entrance to the South Pier:

The man kneels on the prom near the South Pier: behind him stands a card table on which are some small packages looking as though they contain pills; on either side of him lie bunches of dried flowers and a couple of Spanish onions; in front of him are silver coins, placed one on each of three lumps of ice which steam spectacularly. A small group of women and children stand around watching. He removes one of the silver coins and, chopping off a small piece of ice from the large block, pops it into a glass of colourless liquid. The mixture fizzes and a white cloud emerges above the glass.

"I've been in Blackpool for 35 years, the only herbalist left. . . . The maximum for good health is to leave the table just when you still want a bit more. Chop up an onion, boil it, add a spot of gin, drink it before you go to bed and you'll be off to sleep like a top. . . ."

The tremendous mixture of stalls, side shows, slot machines, mechanical and living attractions, prize-winning grab cranes, lotteries with electric numbers and ball games of chance, souvenir counters and specific entertainments, all mixed up together, is one of the excitements for any anthropologist in modern Blackpool (Plates 16 and 23).

Noah's Ark

The Blackpool attraction of this kind with the longest continuous antiquity is "Noah's Ark", dating back to the Winter Garden site in the eighties, and later moved to the Pleasure Beach at the south end of the Promenade. This Pleasure Beach originated from a travelling fair visiting Blackpool, periodically at first, then gradually extending, with a strong gypsy element crystallising this into a regular camp. A switchback first erected in the town centre in 1891, moved there and became—as a new version of it still is—the dominant feature.

But for pure spectacle, the eye is still caught by the Noah's Ark. A 1937 observer's view of this highly unusual attraction:

> A model of the Ark, rocking on a rugged granite rock. The deck of the ark and the clefts of the rock are thronged with animals and other figures, which were catalogued as follows:
>
>> Over the door admitting to the tunnel, fangs.
>> On the triangular cave of the top window a king and queen picture, a leaning chimney above it.
>> Frog with anteater riding it.
>> At the side a rhino, regularly opens mouth.
>> Policeman in front of steps up against Belisha beacon, has long beard, hand up to stop (or bless), and at regular intervals knees bend as in gym.
>> Procession of animals is: elephant with rabbit on back; stork and chick; frog and anteater; polar bear and foxhound; kangaroo and lamb; swan; cat and pelican; cow and wasp; emu and koala; camel and hare; top-hatted ostrich; white puffin and snake.
>> Looking from windows; Mrs. Noah and rolling pin; giraffe.
>
> Paying 6d., you go inside:
>
> 1. Along dark passage from pay-desk.
> 2. Across sort of gang-plank of round wooden stepping stones. These tip up as you tread on them and you slip into about six inches of water.
> 3. More dark passages—steps that bump up and down.
> 4. A gang-plank that bumps you to and fro like a cake-walk.
> 5. On to upper deck where there is a donkey in a stall whose tail shoots at you as you step on floor by stalls.
> 6. A rocking pig with the caption: "Thus it is written in Noah's log: Oft the crew were on the hog."
> 7. A corner of this Zoo room is walled off with a small low entrance— over it is a caption: "Within this Zoo you will find interesting animals of every description."
>
> Stoop and enter. Within is a small partition walled with mirrors.
>
> 8. Passages down into bowels of ship—sharp slopes and sudden corners— all pitch dark—more bumpy stairs, etc. Finally as you step on a board a whistling draught blows in your right ear. As you step on to the next bit of floor it gives way with a loud clank. The whole ship pitches and tosses constantly in a very realistic fashion.
>
> People come out:
>
>> Little boy (with laughter): "Oh, what a treat, what a treat!" Two boys

and one girl: "Wasn't that bridge awful? I don't mind a joke but that was one too many."

One man to another: "I thought my girl had got me when that blew in my ear."

Two girls screaming: "Oh, it's terrible. Oh, it's terrible, you go up and down and they throw you about."

In 1960, Mrs. Noah was still at her window, and there was no conspicuous change after all those years. Same old giraffe, rhino, elephant, bearded policeman and beacon, etc. A large lion replaced the kangaroo, though.

A Blackpool summary report (1939) concluded:

On the whole observers agreed that Noah's Ark was the most terrifying mental experience. . . . Many of the overheards reported confirm their reaction.

A 1960 observer confirmed too:

I *hated* Noah's Ark.

The most horrid thing was having to walk down a pitch black gangway not knowing what would jump out at me.

Blackpool Palaeolithic to Sputnik

A hundred yards from old Noah's Ark rises a post-1937 erection in towering concrete, with a waterfall cascading down between two great mask-like carvings on the top of the flanking concrete columns. These appear to be Amerindian in inspiration, Maya or more nearly Aztec? Below these near-colossi, a very fat half-life-size elephant trumpets across the foot of the waterfall. The base is moulded into massive rocks overhanging the purpose of the whole—a waterway into darkness navigated by small boats on a chain. For these are the River Caves, 6d. for children, 1/- for adults. On the outer cement face, in shining coloured mica, are big figures of prancing bison (4), huge antlered elk (2) and a bulging uddered cow, dancing. Two standing nude human figures are executed in concrete from off the floor; almost (but certainly not quite) in the Henry Moore manner. The effect is clearly intended to be "Palaeolithic Cave Art—*with* a difference"; the difference is Blackpool.

This *primitivism* underlies the whole tone of the holiday attractions. It is expressed equally in the Tower's own upright symbolism and the types inside it, Gypsy magic linked with television magic; the Flood, Aztec and early Stone Age, ancient past and questioned future. The road up from Lytham St. Anne's is flanked by two remarkable stone statues in sphinx position, but with enlarged bare breasts and

Indian type hair-does. The lamp-posts all up the Promenade are ornate with intermixed bunches of huge southern grapes, Chinese dragons, Japanese pagodas, and occasional sputniky shapes. The illuminations of Blackpool's autumn (valued at a capital cost of some £800,000 in 1960) feature a lunar rocket—but manned by Mickey Mice and engineered by Pluto the Pup. This is one of the few modern things in the universal labyrinth of set tableaux and side-shows of light at night—Pickwickian scenes, Father Christmas, Hula Hula, jugglers, jokes, fairy tales of all kinds (The Sleeping Beauty, St. George and the Dragon, Jack the Giant Killer, Jack and Jill, the Cow over the Moon, Little Bo-Peep, Old Mother Hubbard, etc., etc.). Among smaller illuminated set pieces placed along the pavement of the actual sea-front are a line of old Windmills, as well as several big orange-like, sectioned objects painted with moons and stars, evidently signifying simplified space-globes, containing brilliantly dressed Mickey Mouse, Chimp and Jumbo figures gesticulating.

There are other modern-type features at places like the Pleasure Beach—aeroplanes on a swirling roundabout; but these were already there in 1937. Brand new, though, is the huge "Flying Saucer", but constructed on an established amusement pattern: a number of cars attached at the end of separate long clamps turning to meet a central one—umbrella ribs. These cars have up-to-the-minute design: rounded sides and base, brightly painted, decorated with balls strung through the handrails symbolising chains of atoms—the flying saucers of space fiction.

Also at the Pleasure Beach the REEL has been redesigned with saucer-shaped cars, in a setting including jungle scenes and pseudo-prehistoric animals. On the GRAND NATIONAL racer, half-saucers, inverted, roof the seats with almost comical effect. The BIG WHEEL has its twenty-foot traditional clown moving as if to rotate. The stalls all around these have only changed in minor presentation—Darts through Cards, Dice, ·22 Rifle shooting, Rolling Pennies, and the rest.

Above the entrance to the Fairyland Grotto, where you take a train through scenes of all sorts, there used in 1937 to be an orchestra of animated stuffed animals in Noah's Arkish mood. Now there is a great expanse of gun metal, concrete, *papier mâché*, moulded into barren-looking rocks and pits: the surface of the moon. Gnome-like men in bright pink space kits look tiny against this background. Every few seconds a bright saucer-shaped object whizzes along a large horizontal slit in front of the space men (a space ship landing and taking off). Beneath, the usual barker shouts the pleasures of a journey through fairyland.

Slot machines have similarly altered, similarly slightly. The thousands of machines which take plenty of thousands of pounds a year, in many cases appear to be the same ones in the same places after twenty-five years. Certainly, common themes are quite unchanged, and many of them have a look which was often described as old-fashioned back in the thirties: rifle-shooting inside a glass cover; football games with two Soccer teams; "Try your Strength" by grip; punch ball; the intricate cranes with which people spend as many hours, but now more sixpences, trying to pick up a vanity compact, shaving cream, ornaments off a groundwork of brilliantly coloured sweets. One or two space designs have appeared as incidentals in machines still working on the old plan, and a few have been remodelled into very modern terms—for instance the old Steer-a-Car along a line is now "The M1 Test". Automatic palmistry continues for those who do not trust a "Lee" or "Petulengro"; but now there is Telefuture as well. JET PILOT is an old travel idea modernised by a model U-2 placed on the floor; the light indicators flicker to mark its (unmoving) journeys over a view of the world which puts Tokyo north-west of Rome and excludes the whole of Communist Eurasia. A number of slot-machines have paintings of rockets (usually a row ready to be fired) as end-pieces or back-sets, with otherwise unchanged and traditional material on the working parts and purpose. This sort of mix-up of old and new runs all through the town, and is most simply expressed in the trams: stream-lined ones as a special attraction, or the one heavily advertised antique "Built for Blackpool Corporation 1898"—along with scores of horse-drawn cabs. Thus the theme of space is growing, but slowly, in Blackpool; though still only a fraction of the whole attraction.

Immortality in Wax: Who Now?

One rather straight way of documenting Blackpool change is by comparison of the figures selected for the highly successful Waxworks exhibits of the local Tussaud's—(Louis, descendant of Madame). Entrance fee 1/- (previously 6*d*.); some of the same old faces are there, Ghandi, Hitler, Churchill, the late Queen Mary and the late Lloyd George, Anthony Eden, Disraeli, Napoleon, Stalin, President Wilson, Joseph and Neville Chamberlain; among newcomers, Colonel Nasser, Khrushchev and Bulganin, Duncan Sandys, Hugh Gaitskell and Dr. Adenauer. This kind of political or international figure forms just

Period:	20th century Living 1937	20th century Living 1960	20th century Dead 1937	20th century Dead 1960	19th century 1937	19th century 1960	18th century and earlier 1937	18th century and earlier 1960	No special period 1937	No special period 1960	Total exhibits in each category 1937	Total exhibits in each category 1960
Art, writers	1	1	1	3	4	3	2	2	—	—	8	9
Business	2	1	—	—	—	—	—	—	—	—	2	1
Crime	2	2	21	24	1	1	—	—	—	—	24	27
Fictional, romance, adventure	1	—	3	—	—	—	1	—	13	17	18	17
Heredity aristocrats	17	21	6	5	1	1	—	18	—	—	24	45
Military, Naval, Air Force	3	6	7	11	4	2	3	1	—	—	17	20
Politics	23	22	8	19	4	3	1	—	—	—	36	44
Religion	5	5	1	—	1	4	1	1	—	—	8	10
Sports	40	24	3	6	—	—	—	—	—	—	43	30
Stage, screen, radio and TV personalities	15	27	1	1	2	—	—	—	—	—	18	28
Types in tableaux (prisoners, victims, etc.)	—	—	—	—	—	—	—	—	—	30	—	30
Total exhibits in each period	109	109	51	69	17	14	8	22	13	47	198	261

the same proportion now as in 1937—a little under one-fifth of the lot. There is an increase in the number of hereditary aristocrats, due to a big exhibit of eighteenth century figures surrounding Henry VIII and his wives, attracting comment in the Lancashire manner:

"That one looks a miserable bugger."

Among the contemporary popular artistes are Sabrina, Diana Dors, Marilyn Monroe and Tommy Steele, who is appearing in person in Blackpool (1960). Autographed postcards of Tom sell briskly in the shops; but 99% of all cards sold are traditional groups—pictures of Blackpool (mainly the Tower), or pictures with *risqué* jokes.

Postcard Pornography: TV Self-See

Far and away the best-sellers of Blackpool post-carding (and that means millions) are in a style that goes back into seaside antiquity.

Beach Attendant peering over rock at massive blonde in scarlet briefs and complaining at him not telling her there's a law against bathing:

"There's no law against getting undressed lady."

In a homelier mood, a middle-aged, pink-faced couple are shown drinking beer (gills) and eating chocs under a beach umbrella, with a printed programme of pleasure, the urban holiday dream:

    9.00 DOWN TO BREAKFAST (double portion)
  10.00 DOWN TO THE BEACH (in a taxi)
  11.00 ELEVENSES, beer, coffee or tea
  12.00 NIP IN FOR A QUICK ONE
    1.00 LUNCH (six courses)
    3.00 DECK CHAIRS ON BEACH (to sleep it off)
    5.00 MORE GRUB
    7.00 START OUT NIGHTLIFE
  10.30 LAST DRINKS BEFORE TIME
  11.00 SUPPER (fish and chips)
  12.00 EXHAUSTED BUT HAPPY!

There are cards about bosses, lavatories, drunks; two storks chatting ("No real business, but I put the wind up a couple of typists this afternoon"); weddings of fat women and tiny men, and occasional introductions of the new theme, TV. TV is here used only as a medium for focusing on the old joke, though.

(a) Man gazing at strip girl in screen; wife calls him to come and do dishes in kitchen: "I'm just watching the *Brains Trust*."
(b) "Best thing I've seen on the TV for a long time"—comment of a gent in

Part B

EIGHT

FACES, PLACES: 1937–60

THESE 31 illustrations give another view of Worktown, Westhoughton and Blackpool in 1937 and again in 1960. In both years Humphrey Spender, Julian Trevelyan and Michael Wickham each actively participated in Mass-Observation, each painting and photographing at these places. M-O from the start attached importance to all methods of observing. Several other photographers and painters, including Sir William Coldstream and the late Graham Bell, also took part in these activities.

1. Worktown, 1960; a drawing by Humphrey Spender (*see p. 204*)

2. The Christian Year preserves the pre-industrial life (*see p. 61*)

3. The funeral, 1936 (*see p. 45*)

4. Bethel Evangelical Sunbeam service: strict fundamentalist sect (*see p. 68*)

5. The act of voting, November 1937 (*see p. 32*)

6. The late George Tomlinson, M.P., successful candidate in the Farnworth Parliamentary Election (and later Minister of Education) (*see p. 89*)

7. Listening to Clem Attlee, Worktown Labour Party (*see p. 85*)

8. Marking up the canvass, Worktown, 1937 (*see p. 104*)

9. Party propaganda (Municipal election) (*see p. 105*)

10. Dominoes in the Vault (*see p. 171*)

11. With the wife, Saloon Bar (*see p. 178*)

12. Corner of the bar—"a regular" (*see p. 194*)

13. Closing time (*see p. 186*)

14. Steps of the Town Hall—a temperance speaker in full 1937 blast
(*see p. 172*)

15. Children's playground, 1937 (*see p. 39*)

16. Operating the Lucky Grab on Blackpool promenade (*see p. 158*)

17. "Fruit Machines" 1937—illegal in 1960; a "decoy" bringing in the hicks (*see p. 158*)

18. Blackpool 1937: the Professor (*see p. 154*)

19. The Colonel (*see p. 149*)

20. "Win a Dolly" (see p. 157)

21. The Golden Mile: strip-tease of 1960 (see p. 150)

22. Gipsy Rosalee's 1960 booth (*see p. 153*)

23. Looking up the Golden Mile, the Tower in the background (*see p. 152*)

24. 83-87 Davenport Street, Worktown, August 1960 (see p. 29)

25. The latest in exterior decoration, next door to Davenport Street (see p. 29) (author taking notes)

26. Kids play in 1960 Davenport Street (see p. 39)

27. "Keaw Yed"—a slight spot of totemism in Westhoughton, 27 August 1960 (see p. 218)

28. Relaxed in the "Red Lion" Lounge (*see p. 222*)

29. Westhoughton Wakes' Funfair: The Baby Sputnik, the most modern attraction (*see p. 222*)

30. Worktown: a collage by Julian Trevelyan; 1937

31. Worktown: ink drawing by Julian Trevelyan, 1960

white tie and tails seeing low-neck girl sitting cross-legged on early type of cabinet set.

The main public use of TV is back in Tussaud's, where it is advertised outside and emphasised inside:

SEE YOURSELF ON TELEVISION

—and you look into a set which cleverly reflects you against the background of a wax-work setting of the Pope; with suitable effect, too:

"Can't you see that's *us* in the picture"
"Oh, it's *us*, fancy" (waves)
"Who's that, Peter." (mother holds boy's hand and points to screen).
"Oh, they've filmed the waxworks."

Plain Boarding House

Only a small proportion of Blackpool boarding-houses have TV in a public room. They want their lodgers out and about as much as possible—as do most other vested interests of holiday-making.

Accommodation at Blackpool has not changed in major respects over the recent years. There is a bit more of it; and some new "flats" for holiday lease are a novelty. The price of a bed has gone up, like everything else,[1] but still compares favourably with most seaside resorts:

	1937	1960
Boarding House (average):		
Bed and Breakfast	3/- —7/6	12/6—14/6
Full Board	6/- —9/6	16/6—19/6
Licensed Hotels		
Per day (minimum)	15/-	£1.10.0—£1.15.0

Compare a lower price boarding house (12/6) with better-class hotel (bed and breakfast, 25/6), breakfast in the holiday mood (15 August 1960):

[1] A few other examples illustrate these for:

	1937	1960
Food and Drink		
Steak and Chips	1/6—2/6	4/6—6/6
Ham and Chips (average)	1/4	3/-
Coffee „	4d.	8d.
Horlicks „	5d.	9d.
Amusements and Entertainments		
Theatre tickets	1/9—3/6	2/6—9/-
The Funhouse	1/-	2/6
Big Dipper	6d.	2/6
Swimming pool (adults)	6d.	1/6

BLACKPOOL HOTEL	BOARDING HOUSE
Pineapple, Grapefruit	
Orange, Tomato Juice	
Stewed Apples and Prunes	
Grape Nuts, All Bran	
Porridge, Corn Flakes	Corn Flakes
Grilled Bacon	Bacon (1 rasher)
Manx Kippers	
Grilled Pork Sausages	
Poached Finnan Haddock	
Fried Fillet of Whiting	
Boiled, Scrambled	Fried Egg (1)
Poached, Fried Eggs	
Toast, Rolls	Toast (1 piece only)
Marmalade, Jam, Honey	Marmalade
Tea, Coffee, Cocoa	Tea (small pot)
	(*No alternatives*)

But there is more choice of actual boarding houses you can *stay* at, for the casual visitor today. There are many more "VACANCIES" notices in windows than there ever were in an August of the late thirties—before Blackpool had to compete with the Balearic Islands under higher affluence. A series of street counts at the height of the 1960 season, gave 50% vacancy notices in *every* street and over 70% in some (even close to the front). At the same period in 1937 mass-observers sometimes had to sleep on a bench on the beach—everything else was full, unless you had booked in advance.

Considerable efforts have been made to up-grade accommodation, particularly the plumbing and washing arrangements—often the subject of detailed comment from those who had to stay long periods in 1937. In 1960 an observer's boarding house is described by her thus:

It was a two storey house, having 14 rooms for guests, 7 bedrooms and one lavatory on each floor. I was given a small back room on the top storey. Not more than 7 × 8 feet, over three-quarters of its area was taken up by a large double bed. The only other furniture consisted of a wash basin—hot and cold water—and a battered chest of drawers. There were no pictures but two mirrors hung on the pink plaster walls, and a few clothes hooks on the doors. Above the bed was a patent fire-escape—a rope coiled around a wooden pulley and attached to an adjustable cloth belt for one's body. "Do not hesitate to use this in an emergency" were its instructions. The window overlooked other back bedrooms opposite, only about 10 feet away. However, a fine view of Blackpool Tower from the adjoining lavatory window afforded some consolation.

One of the several problems that face Blackpool as a holiday resort is how to keep it "up-to-date" (in so far as that is necessary at all) without putting the prices up to a level where competitors can offer the same or "better", at a similar price. Faster and easier travel, plus more money in the workers' pockets via wage rises, has pressured that problem.

The Hire of the Labourer

Wages pre-war in Blackpool tended to be low. Much of the holiday labour was seasonal, casual and cheap. Such labour is a rarity nowadays, and manpower hard to come by:

WAGE COMPARISONS. BLACKPOOL, 1937–60

	1937	1960
Blackpool Rock making (factory)		
Girls 14–15 years	£0.14.0	£3.10.0
21 years	£1. 5.0	£7. 0.0
Men (basic)	£3.10.0	£10. 0.0
up to	£6. 0.0	£12.10.0 and over
Open Air Swimming Baths		
Boys 14–16 years	£0.15.0	£4.10.0
Women	£1.10.0	£7.10.8
Men	£2.10.0	£8.16.0 (plus bonus)
Cinemas		
Plaza—attendants	£0.15.0	£5.10.0
Catering		
Waitress	£1. 3.0	£4. 4.5
Cook	£2. 0.0	£6.15.0
Amusement Places		
Lads (average)	£1.10.0	£ 6. 0.0
Stall manager or Supervisor	£3.10.0	£15. 0.0 to £25
Speilers—barkers	£3. 0.0	£14. 0.0 to £40.0.0. (peak times)

What Next? Tensions . . .

Blackpool cannot sit back and bask under the Tower shadow. There are signs, too, that its own expansiveness of mind along the line of enlarging and expanding tried formulae and old patterns is suffering some strain from far-seeing local leaders (the town has always been rich in these). Currently there is a £7,000,000 Redevelopment Plan for the town centre, including relief of the motor traffic by a fly-over road-way. The elimination of the present railway station close to the Tower and immediately behind the Promenade is part of the plan still awaiting a Parliamentary Bill to sanction. But this project was already very much on the books in the thirties and we have a whole file of cuttings and comments on it then.

In an interview with Stephen Watts for the *Observer* (24 July 1960) the present Mayor ("ebullient, florid perhaps, and a salesman") expressed some dissatisfaction at the lack of "freedom" holidayers now enjoyed:

". . . he would like to see more freedom and is frustrated when he cannot do more about it . . . it is partly the licensing laws . . . and partly the still prevalent rigidity of the timetable."

In these restrictions of time Blackpool does not differ, however, from Brighton—or Worktown. And there is very little sign that holidayers feel thus inhibited. Yet Alderman Firclough is voicing a broader unease: an underlying suspicion, perhaps, that the basic draw of Blackpool may not be adjusted enough to these times. There is some room for this suspicion on observational grounds also. On the other hand, there is much to suggest that the Blackpool kind of "holiday magic", supreme contrast from cotton-mill or co-op shop of everyday, has an abiding attraction for very many—though this is perhaps being gradually reduced not only by counter-attractions on the Continent but by slow changes in popular taste, still largely at the level of "*Misc.*" (under 1% of *public* opinion; see also Chapter 6, and Chapter 16 below).

Licensing rules, referred to by the Mayor, do provide one particular emphasis on time and restriction—though again, nation-wide as well. The Police have a problem which has grown in recent years. "Crime" was not a visible concern in this community in 1937. Today it is all over town.

Before the war, Blackpool allowed *exceptional* latitude to the drunk and mildly disorderly—the sort of latitude normally only allowed inland on celebrations like Coronation nights (Chapter 14). On Saturday, 29 July 1939, an observer report reads:

A crowd of about 300 people pressed on rails staring at sea which is coming in with only a narrow strip of sand left. On the sand and sea-edge four boys, so obviously have been drinking that liquor smell perceptible when walking on sand ten yards from them. Fully-clothed they are running deep into the roughly incoming tide, wrestling with one another, tempting one another to go further. Some of the crowd are laughing, some are anxious and suggest they may endanger themselves and other people; most are silent. No one endeavours by word or gesture to stop them. When observers have watched for five minutes, the crowd having doubled, noticing that the boys are going deeper and deeper, beyond the likely safety mark for ones so drunk, they decide to phone the police. There is no public call-box nearer than Central Pier, five minutes away. They reach this, and press the emergency button, ask for police. Given the Central Police Station, they report what is happening; Central puts them through to South Shore Station. South Shore says they will attend to the matter at once. Observers return to the scene. Three of the boys have left the water, but one, angrily refusing to be induced by them to quit, is running well out chest high. In the gathering darkness he often cannot be seen at all. Expressions of anxiety among the watchers are much more audible, but still there is no attempt to interfere. After quarter of an hour no police have arrived. At this point one of the other boys, evidently sobered, comes running back, plunges into the sea, reaches his friend, grabs him, and half by force, half by persuasion, gets him out. Shouting and singing, dripping wet, they march off. In five minutes the crowd dispersed. Still no sign of police. (HH, JB)

These were isolates from the mass, though. There would hardly be more than a few such incidents each evening. *Very* numerous were the rough and tough, the accordion players, gangs of lads with mouth-organs. Stumping his way through the 700,000 said to be in town this week goes a lad of 22 with one wooden leg, accompanied by a good-legged comrade. They move north along the densely-crowded inland side of the prom, both staggeringly drunk:

They fall down twice in a hundred yards, the second time crash into a weighing-machine. The wooden-legged man reels about and clearly has great effort getting about on one leg. They move slowly and unsteadily northwards. One-leg's brown suit is covered with mud from falling. When he falls his pal grins and helps him up. No one else helps him. Many stop and look. Three chaps walking behind wait when he falls down, playing on a mouth-organ "When the poppies bloom again", which pal croons softly. Each time he falls some of the people around think that his crutch has slipped. Outside the Tower they fall twice more. They go on towards Talbot Square, turning off the Promenade there and heading inland. They have six falls in the 20 minutes that this journey takes them. Near the end one man, aged 30, and working class, helps by supporting one-leg on the other side. No one else helps. There is plenty of comment—the following recorded as observer passes along:
Man: His crutch slipped.
Woman: Not with one leg like that—uh.
Man: He's down again.
Woman: Uh—it makes you feel cold, doesn't it.
Man: They've 'ad two nasty falls now.
Woman: Isn't it a shame?
Man (paper-seller): Sunday Chronical Paper.
Woman: With one leg.

Man in bowler hat stops observer to shout: "It's a shame you know to let a one-legged man to get drunk like that. It's a shame. They ought to have more sense."

But today the police are faced with a fiercer if small new minority: Through the fun and slot games some young pseudo-tough holidayers stare too hard at an older one who really is rough; his knife flashes at the heart. The *Daily Express* headlines (27 August 1960):

GOLDEN MILE DRAMA

A man accused of stabbing a holidaymaker through the heart on Blackpool's Golden Mile tried to fix an alibi with a girl shop assistant, a court was told yesterday....

Maxwell accused Cook and two friends of staring at him. Cook said he wasn't staring at anyone and without warning Maxwell lunged forward, stabbed him in the chest and ran away.

In 1960 there are toughs and Teddy Boys as in any concentrated population. Now there is a great deal of local talk about them; publicity on crime; and a new stricter control of drunkenness. There is a police booklet on theft (two masked gaol-birds carrying away the GOLDEN MILE on the cover); book markers on CRIME PREVENTION through the Libraries; window and car stick-ons "DON'T MAKE LIFE EASY FOR THE THIEF" (clawing hand in centre); and a glowing poster in yellow and scarlet, giving six verses written by Constable Coxall, culminating:

> We want you all to realise,
> In spite of holidays,
> That you must use your ears and eyes
> And not be in a maze.
>
> Some thieves from near and far away
> Who come on Blackpool tours,
> Just love to have their hols with pay,
> MAKE SURE THE PAY'S NOT YOURS.

But Worktowners and others still go to Blackpool partly because they want to relax, maybe to beat it up a bit. Alcoholic drink in the company of others is one way of doing just that.

We are in a pub on the Blackpool front on 4 August 1937:

9.25 p.m.

Approx 25 men, 15 women. At one side of room 2 girls, in black coats and skirts, white silk blouses, are singing loudly, a dirty song, being encouraged by group of men at table in middle. Song is about Old King Cole, and the

people he called for, chorus of each verse contains repetition of all previous. Following are extracts that obs. was able to record:
From chorus—

> "Have it on the block, said the butcher
> Put it in and out said the tailor,
> Slap it up and down said the painter,
> Bounce your balls up and down said the juggler.
>
> Now every postman, he had a very fine letter
> Now every collier he has a very fine pick
> Now every parson has a very fine book...."

This takes a long time, and seems to be going on indefinitely. A rival female group at the other end of the room starts singing jazz songs, which are eventually taken up by their side of the room, and drowns the dirty girls.

A 1960 observer on the same spot; talks to two barmen:

"It is quite lively here, but not as good as it was. All the teenagers are delinquents these days! Last week we had trouble. One of them had a knuckleduster. The police had to come. The girls were drinking shorts, the boys draught, but there were five large taxis waiting outside."

"August has been a bloody washout. When we get some of the gangs in, you just can't take the risk, they're desperate. The kids even carry birth certificates with them now, that belong to somebody else, so that when we ask them their ages they get saucy and show one of these. Cheek you up no end they do, we've had them in at 13, 14 and 15."

To try and even things down, "No Singing" notices are up in many 1960 Blackpool pubs. In 1936 they were up in nearly every *Worktown* pub, none in Blackpool—whither Worktowners came for liberty (among other things) to sing through into closing time. Today, singing is no longer barred in Worktown, but has become something of a police and licensing obsession in Blackpool. Let us look at what, if anything, such ideas mean in another context now....

TEN

THE PUB AND ITS PEOPLE

Pub Basic

THE BRITISH PUB has numerous variants, locally and within any locality, both socio-economically and proto-historically—back a millennium. Yet little social research of a serious-deep sort has been carried out in the pub: one of the key institutions in British life. Even the basic questions of attraction towards alcohol (as well as alcoholism) have not been adequately analysed in that total human context, world-wide in some respects, within which so many of the principal features and behaviour patterns are just about the same on the front at Blackpool and in the far interior uplands of Central Borneo.

Mass-Observation made the pub one subject of exhaustive analysis within the context of the pre-war north of England. Our study covered mainly Blackpool and Southport, Liverpool and Manchester, as checks against Worktown, the chief study centre. On the whole *The Pub and the People: a Worktown Study* (Gollancz, 1943: out of print) is still almost the only full picture at this level, and remains a basic source on social behaviour in the pub and drinking patterns in general. Largely as a result of this, Sir Hugh Beaver, Managing Director of Guinness, commissioned M-O to make a number of large-scale postwar surveys on drinking; and we have remained actively interested in this field ever since.

Before looking at the national and local changes in pubs and drinking since 1937, it will be best to recapitulate here what we have adopted as a prototype observer report on a "typical" Worktown pub evening (details and comparisons in *The Pub and the People*). In the main, we shall see, this account still stands valid on into the nineteen-sixties:

"This pub is at the corner of a block of brick fronted houses, whose front doors open directly on to the pavement. The road is cobbled; the bare, flat façades of the houses are all tinted to the same tone by continual rain of soot from the chimneys of the [cotton] mill opposite and the chimneys of all the other mills that stand in all the other streets like this.

"The pub isn't much different from the other houses in the block, except for the sign with its name and that of the brewing firm that owns it; but its lower windows are larger than those of the others, and enclosed with stucco fake columns that go down to the ground; and the door on the corner is set at an angle: it is old-looking, worn, brown; in the top half is a frosted glass window with VAULT engraved on it in handwriting flourishes; at the edges of the main pane are smaller ones of red and blue glass. (Some pubs look very like nonconformist chapels from outside, but not this one.)

"The door opens with a brass latch, disclosing a worn and scrubbed wooden floor, straight bar counter brown-painted with thick yellow imitation graining on the front panelling; at its base is a scattered fringe of sawdust, spit-littered, and strewn with match-ends and crumbled cigarette packets. Facing the bar a brown-painted wooden bench runs the length of the room. Four yellowish-white china handles, shiny brass on top, stand up from the bar counter: the beer engine, nerve centre of the pub. Behind the bar, on shelves, reflecting themselves against mirrors at the back of their shelves, are rows of glasses and bottles, also stacked matches and Woodbine packets. Beer advertising cards and a notice against betting are fixed to the smoke-darkened yellowish wallpaper; and on the wall beside the door is a square of black glass, framed in walnut, that has painted on it, in gilt, a clock face with roman numerals, and the letters NO TICK. (The clock can't tick, it has no works; but if you are a regular the landlord will give you credit.)

"Five men, in caps, stand or sit, three at the bar, two on the bench. They all have pint mugs of mild.

"From the back parlour can be heard the sound of a man singing a sentimental song. In here they are discussing crime, manslaughter, and murder. A small thin man (whose name subsequently turns out to be X) appears to be a little drunk, and is talking very loudly, almost shouting. Another chap, called Y, also has a lot to say.

"X (to Y): 'If a man says you're a jailbird he's no right to say it—if he *is* a man.'

"Another man: 'He can have you copped for defamation.'

"Y: 'I've seen cases in the paper where a man's been found guilty and it's a bloody shame.'

"X (very slowly): 'I'll tell you a bloody case, I'm telling you. . . .'

"Y: 'Awright.'

"X: 'There were two navvies——'

"Another man, who has been quiet up to now suddenly says, in indignant sounding tones: 'No, they weren't navvies', to which X simply replies: 'Ah'm sober enough' and goes, on, apparently irrelevantly—'There isn't a law made but what there's a loop 'ole in it. Marshall Hall said that afore 'e was made a Sir—some big trial it were, for murder, an' it lasted a week, he'd strangled 'er wi' a necklace—it were that Yarmouth murder. He 'a won t' case, too, but for that courtin' couple, they were passing and they 'eard 'er screamin' and they thought they were only, you know, 'avin' a bit. Instead o' there 'e were stranglin' 'er. D'you know why there's a loophole in these 'ere laws. Well, them there M.P.s—'ave you ever noticed there's always some lawyer puts up. Now the reason for that—' He looks up and sees, through the serving hatch at the back of the bar, a man going into the parlour, and shouts out: 'Eh, Dick, lend us two an' six. We're skint.' Dick shouts back something inaudible, goes on into the parlour.

"The singer in the parlour, who has been steadily working through three verses, now finishes with a prolonged and loud note, and there is the sound of some clapping.

"The talkers have now divided into two groups, one around X; the other around an old man who is arguing about the age of the swimming baths. He keeps on saying: 'I remember it being built', to which another chap replies, disagreeing: 'My father works there.'

"X: 'That lad could fly through t' water like a bloody fish.'

"Y: 'Bill Howard, that's 'is name.'

"X: 'Gooes into water like a bloody fish.'

"Old man (loud): 'I remember it being built.'

"X: 'I'll tell you what 'e could do—you know when you're walking along the towing path, you an' me walking along the towing path, 'e'd keep up wi' you, you an' me, walking decent tha knows, 'e'll keep up wi' you.'

X stops, drinks and the old man can be heard stubbornly reiterating: 'I remember it being built.'

"X: 'I'll tell you the hardest feat that was ever known—for a man to fall off the top of the bath and not go to the bottom and not go to the top, as long as 'e can 'old 'is breath—I've seen (name inaudible) do that. 'e could do a 'undred yards in eleven seconds—wi'out any training. What could 'e do wi' training? I'm telling you, he could stay in t' water, not go to the top and not go to the bottom—an' I'll tell you 'ow 'e did it.'

"Y: ' 'ave another.'

"X: 'Aye.'

"While he is getting his drink a chap stands up, and says: 'I swim that road', demonstrating convulsive sidestroke movements with his arms.

"The old man looks up from his argument and remarks: 'I go left 'nd first'. And returns to the swimming bath discussion. X, now with another beer carries on: 'He'd drop into the water and neether go to the bottom or go to the top. . . ,'

"In the parlour they are singing the chorus of a jazz song, which the barmaid hums loudly.

"It is now half-past eight, and more people are coming in. Two old men arrive; both have gaps in their front teeth; wearing clogs, dark scarves knotted round pink-wrinkled necks, white hair raggedly protrudes from behind their greasy caps; their coats, trousers, and waistcoats are all different yet appearing alike to be made of a shapeless greasy grey-blue cloth. They sit together, talking in undertones. Their beer mugs are placed on the edge of the bar counter, and they have to reach forward, half standing up, to get at them. They both smoke pipes, from which drifts the ropey smell of cheap twist. At regular intervals they shoot tidy gobs of spittle across into the sawdust. They reach for their mugs together, and drink the same amount at each swig. The mugs stand untouched for several minutes, with a last inch of beer in them, then one of the men stands up, drains his mug, and bangs it on the counter:

"The barmaid has gone out, and the landlord takes her place. (He is large, redfaced, clear blue eyes, about 45, wears a clean dark grey suit, no coat, clean white shirt, sleeves rolled up, no collar or tie.) He draws off two half-pint glasses from one of the middle taps: the old man pays him, and the two empty the glasses into their mugs. During this transaction no one has said anything. Both men, standing, take a long simultaneous swig, and sit down. One remarks, suddenly loud: 'Well, of all the bloody good things at Ascot t' other week anyone following Aga Khan t' other week would 'ave 'ad a bloody picnic.' X bawls across at him: 'What dost tha know about bloody horses. I'll bet thee a bloody shilling and gie thee two thousand pound start an' I'll 'ave bloody Lawson agen 'im. Why, 'e's seven bloody winners at meeting, you bloody crawpit.' The old man says nothing.

"A group of four men has gathered round the table and is playing dominoes. Each has a pint mug at his elbow. At the end of the round they turn the dominoes face downwards and stir them noisily. They play with a lot of loud talking and joking. One says: ' 'oo went down then?' (and see Plate 10).

" 'Jimmy.'

" 'Oh, Jimmy went down.'

" 'I did.'

"My down—one an' one.'

" 'If we're down we're down, that's all. What's the use of worrying.'

" 'Come on, man, don't go to bloody sleep, th'art like a bloody hen suppin' tea; when th' art winning it's awreet, but when th'art losin' it's all bloody wrong.'

"They talk about the holidays, which begin next week. 'I'm not savin' oop twelve bloody months for t' sake a gooing away for a week. Wife's always asking what I do wi' me overtime, and I towd 'er—why, I bloody well spend it, what dost think,—and she says—Tha owt t' ave more bloody sense. . . .'

"So on, until at about 10.20 they leave; standing for from one to three minutes outside, and calling 'Goodnight' as they walk, at about two miles an hour to their private houses, which are seldom more than three minutes walk away" (see Plate 13).

Drink, Drunk and Drunks

H.M. Customs and Excise (*Monthly Digest of Statistics*) reports that in 1958 about 25,000,000 barrels of beer were drunk in the United Kingdom and in 1959 (fine summer) about a million more. For spirits, 13 million proof gallons in 1958, a million more in 1959. And the Board of Trade gives 1959 U.K. wine imports as 18 million gallons—though this has still barely touched Worktown, statistically, it will certainly do so more deeply soon (see below).

Here we are concerned mainly with what is still the mass-drink, at Worktown, Blackpool and almost everywhere else in Britain: beer.

National consumption of beer { —1936: 17·58 gallons per head
—1958: 19·70 ,, ,, ,,

This gives a beer increase of approximately 12%. Today bottled beer amounts to nearly a third of the total, and this increase (from under 3%) is a continuing homey trend.

Canned beer rates are growing rapidly, too, though still less than 1% of the market (see also *Which?*, August 1960, beer survey).

The drunkenness conviction figures, per 10,000 run:

Year	National	Worktown[1]
1938	16·84	7·52
1959	18·71	10·53

Over this period, pubs per 10,000 inhabitants decreased from 17·58 to 16·56.

In Worktown 52% of all pre-war drunks were arrested on Friday or Saturday, a point of importance to this *Pub and the People* thesis. In 1959 this thesis found encouraging support, since 51% of all drunks were similarly arrested on Friday or Saturday.

The number of women convicted for drunkenness in Worktown has remained static since 1937, the increase being predominantly masculine. This is true, too, for the national trend:

	Men	Women
1938	46,832	7,686
1959	60,216	4,842

Yet there is unarguable evidence in M-O's comparative observations and in "general experience", that *more women are drinking more alcohol than ever before.*

As we argued afresh (with evidence) in *The Pub and the People*, the long-standing teetotal argument (e.g. in favour of restricting opportunity—both in time and place—for drinking or for other *fun* with drink) has little substance (in Britain) in the control of that drunkenness, which is their main preoccupation and the alleged basis of most temperance propaganda. We have good reason to believe our arguments indeed considerably influenced these interests in the forties and since. They lose nothing by new evidence.

---

[1] Normally people so arrested in Worktown virtually and often literally force themselves on the attention of the Police (twenty of these were in a vehicle, 1958). There is evidence that police have become stricter in making arrests in many areas in recent years however.

War Shortage and Repercussion Since

During and after the war shortages of beer and other drinks made considerable alterations in the normal pattern of pub behaviour. Our job then was to find out (mainly for client interests) how much these alterations were likely to prove lasting, or how far people were likely to revert back to form if and when that became possible. The biggest study of this sort included, among the sixty-four paragraphs of the "Other Conclusions" section in the report, these which are relevant to the present time:

"1. There appears no basic change in the drink pattern between 1937 and 1947. Some trends obvious before the war have increased, others have been retarded by shortages, etc., but no fundamental alteration is visible.

"The violent changes in drinking habits caused by the war are still visible in 1947 but in a less marked form.

"2. The areas in which the most serious drinking takes place are the areas of the *weakest beers* or of the greatest shortages; they are also the areas in which there have been the most marked *advances in economic security* since 1939. It is apparent too that in the areas where living conditions are the worst, pub expenditure is highest and pub and club comfort lowest.

"6. Pub drinkers cover about *two-thirds of the population*, and about six-sevenths of all non-abstainers. Regional differences in pub-going are large but are mainly accounted for by the big variation in the number of women going to pubs.

"7. There is, if anything, a *reverse correlation* between the number of pubs and the number of drinkers in any area. The places with the fewest pubs have the most drinkers.

"15. Just as there is no correlation between the number of pubs in an area and the amount of drunkenness, there is *no correlation between quantity of beer available and drunkenness*. Shortages can cause over-drinking as much as full supply.

"16. *Drunkenness with disorderliness* (or other legal offence) is *very rare*. What is far more common is a drunkenness that is simply a *loosening of normal standards*, particularly on special occasions, and without any serious consequences.

"22. The basic reason for choosing a pub is the *company provided there*. This is again conditioned by the landlord and the type of people he attracts.

"23. Both casual and serious drinkers will not necessarily choose the pub nearest to their home, but it must be within *easy walking distance*. Few people will travel more than ten minutes to their pub but about three in four pass at least one other pub on the way to their own.

"25. The regular drinker is for the most part the *serious* drinker: the amount he spends on drink remains constant throughout the year, and is not materially conditioned by the amount of wages that he earns.

"26. The fact that most pub-goers have had more than usual amounts of beer available for drink, together with war-time restrictions (e.g. fires in only one bar) and allocation of supplies to higher priced bars have all caused a general upward movement towards the more comfortable and therefore more *expensive* bars.

"27. This does not mean, however, that *class differences* are showing signs of collapse. People state that the reason they use their favourite bar is for company and the company tends to be based on their own social groupings.

"28. Pub groups are, to a large extent, dependent on pub *lay-out*. A square room generally causes large groups; a room with many nooks and crannies causes very small groups.

"47. About one pubgoer in five is a regular *spirit drinker*; most often spirit drinkers are in the higher income groups, and they are far more frequently women than men. The most frequent spirit drinkers are often the least frequent pubgoers.

"48. Whisky and rum are *men's drinks* as exclusively as gin, port and sherry are women's. Men spirit drinkers are far more concerned with gravity than women spirit drinkers.

"49. About half of all pubgoers usually drink *mild or bitter* or mild-and-bitter. Of the remainder about a third drink Guinness or stout. One drinker in thirteen —even after prompting—can give no details about his usual drink beyond that it is 'beer'."

The main co-ordinator of the above study was also the "observer" in the pre-war Worktown and Blackpool reports above cited, John Sommerfield. He did much of the field work for the book *The Pub and the People* as well.

Pub Crawl with a Gill-Master, 1960

In the early days of M-O on the Worktown end the Civil War in Spain was one of the hottest political issues. John Sommerfield was the first person actually to impact out of the Spanish War into Worktown. He joined the Worktown Unit fresh from writing one of the best accounts of those times, *Volunteer in Spain*, still considered by specialists a mild and bitter classic of honest documentation. In the following year John became one of the inner nucleus of our Davenport Street lot.

As for now, in 1960, when he is a well-known novelist and radio playwright, John Sommerfield has once more joined in to help M-O. He has supervised the recent work and made several visits to the north to refresh his own impressions and make some very detailed observations of his earlier reports in the same places now. Among other things, in July 1960 he revisited twenty-nine of our 1937 "type pubs".

Let us go with the old master of the gill (still the standard Worktown term for half-a-pint of beer) on one night pub-crawl, 16 July 1960.

SATURDAY NIGHT.

6.45 Pub A (corner of Newport Street). Saloon bar.
14 men 2 women.
5 men under 25. 8 men with pints.
Group of men with two women got up and left 6.50. Women were carrying large, filled shopping baskets.
Group of 5 men (including 3 under 25s) had been drinking a lot. One young man refused to have a drink when offered, said he'd had enough. Another wanted a brown sherry. Two of this group were carrying carpenters' tools in bag.
This is a heavily tiled pub, with some varnished woodwork. No observable change in this, or bar layout. A tiled fireplace looked as if it might be a post-war addition. One area of newish rather drab wallpaper. No spittoons now.

8.30 Pub B (small beerhouse Chorley Old Road).
5 oldish men in Public bar drinking pints. 2 men (about 40) in lobby, drinking Guinness.

One of the men in Lobby (smartly dressed in good dark blue suit) says to his friend he's going on somewhere else, where there's some music. Landlord takes slight umbrage at this, says he's got a tape recorder. Man says "But there's not the stuff to go with it". Discussion about this, and how old you should be before you stop bothering about girls. Then a fairly drunk Irishman in Public bar says he'll give them some music, *and* buy the landlord a pint. He produces a piano accordion, and plays pop tunes loudly [and well, thinks J.S.].

On wall of this pub is a licence granted in 1882. Talk about this, and man reads aloud a long list of things not allowed, including bull baiting and cock-fighting. "But it says nowt about closing time," he adds. Landlord tells this man, who says he hasn't visited this pub for three years until now, that they don't have the Buff lodge meetings upstairs any more. The last landlord couldn't be bothered. He seems slightly defiant and apologetic about the present emptiness of the pub and talks about more people getting in later. This pub is untouched late nineteenth century. But no spittoons now.

9 Pub C (large main road but not town-centre pub).
Commercial room is crowded, piano playing. Crowded lobby bar. This pub, tiled and mahogany-panelled throughout, appears to be quite unchanged.
But, in lobby, a respectably dressed woman of about 30 is standing at the bar, drinking with 4 blue-suited men. Ten minutes later, the whole group goes and sits at a table in the Commercial room.

9.20 Pub D (a small beerhouse).

Densely crowded small bar parlour. 15 men, 8 women.
Some singing.
Majority under 25, including 5 under 20.
12 men in Public bar, 10 drinking pints.
The whole pub is clean and fairly recently repainted (including the exterior). Most of interior is the conventional brown and cream. But bar parlour has modern wall paper, and several peculiar bas-relief vases full of plastic flowers, fixed to wall. Tables are formica topped, but old type benches. This is very much a young peoples' pub.

9.35 Pub E (big pub).

This used to be a rather rowdy pub. Next to it now is the Worktown Youth Centre.
Obs. expected some overflow from this. But not many people in the pub, and *all* middle-aged or old. Sultry Spanish music coming from loudspeaker. In *all* rooms—18 men, 10 women.

As obs. was leaving a group of young men came in, including 3 youths just seen in the Bark Street Tavern. This pub has some new "old fashioned" wall-paper, and bright curtains. No other noticeable changes. No spittoons now.

9.50 Pub F.

All rooms densely crowded, including a high percentage of young men.

9.55 Pub G (town-centre "high class" accommodation).

The old Lounge here (which was somewhat apart from the rear of the pub, and considered high class) has been completely changed in layout and appearance, including the bar itself, which has a big fake canopy over it. It was too densely crowded for obs. to get to the bar and buy a drink. The other rooms in the pub were also very full. No noticeable change here, and the number and type of customer are similar to those seen very often before at this time on a 1937 Saturday night.

10.10 Pub H (old town-centre, big).

22 men in saloon—which is a big room. Formica table tops. An area of clotted-porridge type wallpaper, apparently repainted. Otherwise as before and a bit shabbier.

10.20 Pub I (small old pub).

The etched glass on the windows outside is unchanged. But interior re-done, 3 sides wood wallpaper, inside a strong brownish Bracqueish still-life type paper. Bar itself is also changed. New chairs and tables (but not "modern" at all, like the wallpaper). Room not very full, nearly all men, all age groups.

The previous evening this observer had looked into some other old haunts with fresh eye, again noting structural and superficial changes rather than anything surprising on the human side (beyond the odd women drinking standing—a thing never seen in the pre-war years):

8 p.m. Pub J public bar (small local pub).
No apparent change in bar layout and décor since last visit. Bar fairly crowded, with men, mostly in non-best suits, drinking pints.
2 groups under 25, best suits, drinking bottled light ale.
Group of 5 under 25s visible in Saloon.

8.30 Pub K (big local pub).
Obs. stood in small lobby bar, from which other rooms could be partly seen. Layout of this pub has been completely re-arranged. Where possible areas have been covered with modern wallpaper. But there is still a lot of painted tongue and groove. There is a new piano.

9.15 Pub L (near town-centre).
Here from lobby bar it is possible to observe most of the rooms. This used to be a heavily tiled pub, in the Manchester style. It still is. The only physical difference in the pub that obs. can notice is the presence of some modern wall paper. Pub is fairly crowded, piano playing. (This pub was usually sparsely populated.) Quite a lot of young men. 2 Salvation Army girls came in and made a rapid walk through. 8 copies of *War Cry* were seen to be bought (poss. more in part of best room out of sight).

10.15 Pub M (old town-centre pub).
This pub was interesting because there was a long, narrow room, divided into saloon and vault sections without any physical division, except for a break in the bar counter. This break no longer exists, but otherwise pub appearance is much the same, though perhaps more "done-up" than before, in the same Victorian style. But, though the physical division between the better and less good ends of the room is even less than it was, there were 10 men and 6 women at the "best" end of the bar, only one of these men drinking a pint; while at the other end there were *no* women and 18 men, 5 of which were drinking pints.

10.25 Pub N (Wine Lodge).
Approx. 40% women. Approx 175 people.
Arrangement of bars has been slightly changed. Also the benches, still grouped in middle of room, are new, rexine covered.
A lot of Guinness drinking, by men as well as women. Some people drinking Younger's Scotch Ale. 22 types of port, sherry and Empire wines are listed on wall.

The place too big and crowded to make detailed observations just before closing time. But obs. impression is that, despite slight physical changes in the pub, it is still used by the same sort of drinkers drinking the same sort of drinks. Few people notably drunk, but few apparently cold sober either.

Pub Changes into the Sixties

From the new field work and observations supported by conversations with landlords, background statistics, etc., some distinct conclusions are practicable, comparing pre-war and now. (Other observations by Nell Umney, Roland Currier, Rayner Atkin, Julian Trevelyan, Michael Wickham, Humphrey Spender, Bill Naughton, Francis Huxley, Barbara Harrisson and T.H.)

Firstly, there are *more* people in the pubs. But much of the volume increase is in more *drinking* rather than more people (other detailed statistics on this in *The Pub and the People*).

Secondly, these increases are far from uniform. Local and personal preferences remain important, and the landlord is still a very significant factor (with or without "renovated" pub).

Thirdly, there is an increase in midday drinking, including a smattering of reeling drunks around town in the early afternoon—something not seen at all in the thirties. This affected locally by the new system of shift work in the cotton mills, by which no one there works all day, as they did before (see Chapter 3).

Fourthly, more expensive beers are being drunk. More bitter (the rather costlier beer) and more bottled in the pubs.

Fifthly, there is a change in the balance of female drinking. Some Guinness types now over to Mackeson, younger women on Babycham (unknown 1937) and Cherry Wine especially. Thus a pub that was notably "young people" in the thirties and has remained so near the town-centre, at 9 p.m., on Saturday 23 July 1960:

This is still the "young people's" pub. About 40 men, 15 girls, nearly all under 25. Fairly crowded, but a few seats vacant.
At the far end is a piano, with a *big* notice on top PERSONS UNDER EIGHTEEN NOT SERVED IN THIS HOTEL. (This is new.)
As obs. comes in, piano is being played by a middle-aged man—the only person, except obs., over 40 in the room. He is playing "Some of these days", and there is a very loud singing accompaniment to this, plus hand-clapping in time with the music. This is followed by several other tunes from the thirties. In between these tunes, people sing (unaccompanied) tunes: "Down at the old Bull and Bush", "One of the early birds", "Glasgow belongs to me". No post-war tunes were sung or played.
People coming and going all the time, some girls carrying dance shoes in paper

bags. The same old Palais crowd. Some of the men have narrow trousers and slim ties, but on the whole they are pretty "square".
The benches round the side of the room have been reupholstered with a light buff imitation leather. The varnished wood tables and chairs appear unchanged. Also the same worn old rubberoid floor covering. The Lincrusta on the walls has been repainted. There are *five* loud-speakers on the walls, not in use.
A brand new 21" TV set at one end of the room, not switched on. This is the first TV set observed in any Worktown pub (no ordinary pub has one).
There were several groups (two's and three's) of young women drinking together without men. Most women were drinking Mackeson, Babycham and Cherry Wine. (These all post-war female drink-taste developments.) Majority of men were drinking pints. Nobody appeared to be really drunk.

Just twenty-two years before, J.S. and T. H. sat in the same bar making a marathon record of an evening's "overheards" there. Passages from this report:

At 8.38 p.m. one of the waiters-on put on a white jacket and apron. The other kept in ordinary clothes for the whole evening. When man in group ordered two pints waiter-on went to serving hatch and called out "Two buckets!" 2 young men came in at 8.58, sat opposite the girl who had come in by herself and eyed her. She came over and joined them at 9.14. All young people here, under 30, on draught beer and Guinness (girls). At 9.40 people begin to join in the choruses of old songs that are being sung by chaps at piano (played by a youth). This happened at the same time last night.
Owing to the noise of singing and many conversations it was difficult to record talk fully. Subjects overheard were horse-racing, the Coronation, women, the new clock in the bar. Next to observers were two young women wearing green coats, fur collars, thick make-up, veils. Also (a) a respectable looking young millworker; (b) thin, cheeky young man; (c) man of about 30, pockmarked with glasses. The girls try to get off with observers (who are wearing overcoats) by saying, at different times: "Are you enjoying yourself?" "Been on whisky all the evening then?" and "Is your name Sattiwell?" "Been here before?"
After ten minutes the young man (b) got into conversation with them.
The girls paid for their own drinks; it was about this that (b) got into conversation. He said: "You know the bargain don't you—the price of two Guinnesses and I'll take you home, front door or back". But they left unattended at 10.5 having arrived at 8.41, had only one drink and no cigarettes; they said twice: "Beggars can't be choosers, you know".
Directly they had gone, animated conversation developed, (a) saying: "I knew you wouldn't get anywhere with 'em", at which (b) said vigorously that he'd never expected to. (c) "The only way you can get anything from them is for money." (Another man, sitting by, solitary, says: "I weighed them up in three seconds", he never spoke again.) (a) declared it was impossible to get anything

out of them anyway. (b) agreed. (c) said: "There's about as much chance (thinking hard) . . . as an Eskimo getting sunstroke". (a): "They're just gold grubbers."
(b) (very cheerfully): "All they want is Guinness 'ere every night for it."
(c) in the face of strong opposition, seems to think that there is a chance of something further, though he admits "You pay for them inside, you pay for them outside, and by that time you're inside out." (At the end he summed up, in his peculiarly difficult style: "It's like a motorbike—putting your skill against hers.")
Not one of them considered the possibility of paying them; it was something outside their range of ideas.

Years later, another investigator has a long talk with the licensee of this pub, age 40, Worktown born and in the business for twelve years (in this pub for three). He explains about his unusual TV; now he turns it off at 8 p.m. on Fridays to Sundays "because the pianist arrives"; and how loud-speakers are arranged so the sound does not carry into the other rooms, but in this way one can reach those who may not be able to see the picture. The young, he says, "are tickled pink now that we've got the telly." The danger is that it slows up the drinking? As he puts it:

"These days . . . the kids like wine and spirits. They're good business. . . . Women, they come in much more than they used to, they drink Babycham. The young chaps drink pint splits, ½ gill in a pint glass with a Brown Peter or Maccy Stout. The girls have their Cherry Babycham and usually a gin and lemon. The girls pay their own.

"The regulars and the older people leave the place to the kids Friday and Saturday nights.

"They're a grand crowd, never cause any trouble."

Another publican, a mile away talks to an August 1960 investigator:

"People are much more particular now than they used to be; women come in much more than they did; as a matter of fast, we were just remarking about it before you came in. I think they prefer a glass of beer to a cup of tea after the shopping.

"The ladies go more for bottled beer at lunch time, but they go on to draught when they're with the old man.

"They don't come in alone so much in the evening. Draught beer is just as popular as it was but they went on to bottled beer a couple of years ago, but it didn't last. Young people, much more, too young sometimes. We have to ask them how old they are; they make themselves look older, both the lads and the girls, they mostly come weekends, about 7.30 and then go off dancing. The girls drink fancy drinks, gin and orange, rum and orange, and Cherry B and Babycham dressed up. That's an 'all in', we put in a bit of lemon and a

cherry, and a piece of sugar, and charge another 3d. The lads like to have their pints.
"Younger age spending more money, and the regulars as well. We have a crowd of lads 14 strong, none of them more than 21. I think they work in the pits, they earn good money, and all stand their rounds of pints. There isn't much trouble, I think some of the young ones are looking for a bit of mischief, but that's all, not trouble."

A sixth change is in dress. There are less men in working clothes, caps and scarves; more with collars and ties. Women in light coats (and never black shawls now) in summer and so on. As a third publican put it this August:

"The ones who used to come in their shawls, in their place we have the women who drop in for one on their way home, not so much at dinner time. We try to check up on age, but a lot come in under 18; yes, I think perhaps we do have a few more these days, but on the other hand lads have always liked a drop of the best. The lasses like Cherry B and Babycham, and a drop of gin dressed up, the lads stick to their pints. They are in a way spending more, of course they earn more, but the girls stand their whack."

Along with the up-affluencing of some pubs, all in Worktown have now abolished the once standard "spittoon". In one bar, however, an observer was surprised—by then we had covered a large proportion of the pubs in town—to notice a single one, brassbound, clean, in the Vault. The old lady, who has been the licensee for thirty-eight years and was well known to our pre-war observers, explained its survival, invoking a law even:

"Ah, yes, well dear, we're not *supposed* to have 'em. But there's one regular spits on the floor, and it's not nice for the cleaner—so I've got it there for him."

Inside and Out
Despite some changes in layout and furnishing the main pub structures have seldom changed significantly. In many cases, any change is simply a renewal of what wore out in the decades between. To quote J.S.'s summary report (14/9/60):

In others, particularly in the case of wallpaper, the changes were attempts at modernisation, which often resulted in considerable incongruity, such as a patch of ever-so-contemporary type wallpaper in an old-fashioned vault with wooden benches, brown grained woodwork, and worn lino on the floor. One pub, however, had been completely transformed and modernised. This is worth considering.

The particular pub above is in the mid-circle of Worktown. An observer had a couple in here 15 July 1960.

4 men are playing darts when obs. comes in. Lots of conversation about the game. These men exchange remarks with most of the other non-playing people in the bar—13 men altogether, 5 of them under 25, 11 of these, including the darts players, were standing up, though there was plenty of room for them to sit down if they wanted to. The 4 men sitting down were all under 25. Also there were three women (two about 30 one 40 plus). They all had wedding rings and were respectably, but not smartly dressed. (This definitely not a pre-war vault occurrence.)
A man, about 35, blue suit, no tie, comes in with a piece of paper; circulates this to people, who write numbers on it and give him sixpence. He approaches obs. who asks: "What is it?" Is told "It's for ten bob". No further explanation was made, presumably because obs. ought to know.
Despite the physical changes in this pub, obs. considers that, except for the presence of the three women, the types and behaviour of the people in it are what he would have characterised pre-war as a typical town-centre small pub vault crowd.

Compare the same observer there, 22 April 1938:

Old lino on floor, old lino topped table. Worn leather seats, large open fire. Craggy overmantel with mirrors. Vases of artificial synthetic flowers. Lots of coloured pictures. Big R.A.O.B. Certificate framed in black, quite new. Glass Wills advt. ashtrays. Gilt ornament on mantel, man with crown sitting on rearing horse. Plaster trout in glass case on wall. Everything worn, comfortable looking. Man comes in, commercial traveller, wearing cap, blue suit, stiff collar. Has a quick one, bitter. Tells me about his brother in the C.I.D. in Battersea, how he lived there too for three years. Says about the people up here being unfriendly. Goes off to meet his pal.
Small old woman, face powered dead white, shambles in and has a mild, sits crouched over it, sucking a relit cigarette butt. Says quiet here isn't it. I say it is. Conversation expires.

Even this pub, the one that has changed most of any in Worktown, keeps its "soul", as some "regulars" might say. Here is another version of it, as seen by an observer (24/7/60); the changes in glass work and wooden partitions are in line with those we have already seen so widespread in Worktown's countless renovated homes of current affluence, too:

Both exterior and interior of this pub is now *quite unlike* any kind of typical small Worktown pub. In the vault, the front of the bar, the doors, and the partitions are panelled with plain, flat light mahogany veneer. The windows are reeded glass. A formica bar top (with oblong sponge rubber mats for glasses). Contemporary wallpaper in shades of grey. An advertising calendar on the wall with a semi-nude lady, displaying abundant breasts.

Two oval formica topped tables (the formica grained like pale wood). Benches upholstered with dull reddish imitation leather. Modern lighting fittings. So far, this description could be matched in many small London West End bars. But the room is dominated by the dartboard, which is set inside a large, cream-painted ½ section motor tyre, which again is set inside a large green-painted wooden box, so that the whole thing occupies quite a big area of the wall. Beside it is an old, worn Player's ad. scoreboard.

As if to be in the progressive mood socially, too, this pub has a Ladies Darts Team, something quite new in these parts and growing rapidly in the country. As the licensee put it, after talking about the modernisation (done five years ago):

"All the darts lads drink beer, most of the women too, mostly Barley wines, comes dear in the week, by Thursday they're counting it up."

Whatever the surface changes, the Worktown pub remains as we drew it in the thirties.

Observations in London working-class districts, where pub structural changes of this kind are commoner, show an equal preponderance of not-change over change in *behaviour*. Their character in any working-class area, as in Worktown, was nicely put, in another way, by an African negro anthropologist chatting to an observer in a Hampstead pub (August 1960): "These pubs are terribly *tribal*, aren't they?"

In quite a number of small London pubs the introduction of TV *has* made a difference; it tends to interfere with conversation and restrict "sociability". However, most of the London pubs observed that have TV don't keep the set switched on all the time—usually only for certain programmes and sporting events. Only one Worktown pub observed had TV (and none in Blackpool).

700 Years and Many Earls Away. . . .

Pub changes, very closely studied, add up to notably little, in human terms. More of some things (Babycham, women drinkers, midday drunks, formica, stronger ales, etc.), less of others (spittoons, —but not pot plants). But never *much* more or much less; and many things *not changed at all*.

These changes must be related to more spending money and a lot less unemployment than pre-war (also change in mill workers' hours). Not enough is yet known to say they are the *direct* result of economic changes. In the meantime, if any of those working on the pre-war pub survey had asked, "What would happen to the pubs if everybody had a bit more money to spend?" we could have predicted just what has *actually* taken place (and in several available cases we *did*).

Evidence of no-change is more interesting and important than that of change. What hasn't changed is *behaviour*. You may wear a tie instead of a scarf, your second best suit instead of the working clothes that had once been your only best suit, drink "best mild" instead of ordinary, twenty-two pints a week instead of twenty, and maybe put in an hour in the boozer dinner-time, which your dad in 1937 couldn't afford. But the way *you behave* in the pub—the rounds you stand, the conversations you have, the games you play, the outings you go on, the raffles you join—is very little different from the way your dad and his friends carried on pre-war. Again and again we found this.

Worth quoting as an example of the persistence of pub behaviour patterns is the "Man and Scythe", Worktown's antique.

Back in 1937 J.S. had filed a report on the Man and Scythe (5 May) thus:

Man and Scythe, 1937
This is a particularly interesting pub for the observation of class differentiations. The vault door leads into a very long, narrow room, in the middle of which is a notice (indian ink on cardboard) Parlour prices beyond here. There is a gap between the bars A and B (see plan). Bar A is wooden, bar B covered in zinc. The passage is stone floored throughout, but in the B section there are rope mats. Both bars have a sawdust ditch but the sawdust at A was much more scattered and spat on than in B.
In A there were 3 men sitting, 8 standing.
In B there were 11 men standing.
All the men in A wore caps.
With one exception, the men in B wore bowlers or good trilbys. The exception was a small chap of about 45 standing at the end of B, who wore a cap. He looked in the direction of A and there was a considerable gap between him and all the other men in B who were pretty close together.
There were 3 men standing at the serving hatch.

Again, three weeks later (26 May 1937):

Man and Scythe
Vault 9.30.
14 men, 9 sitting.
The man with cap, who stood at the end of the gentleman's bar last time I was here, is still standing there, looking as if he hasn't moved since. The parlour

price bar is about 6 inches lower than the other. The barman told us its history. The present landlord came in about 12 years ago and introduced the division "to make it more select". But since the introduction of the extra penny on beer the prices are now the same. However the notice is still up "to keep out undesirables."

Revisiting the pub twenty-three years later, we thus found that the gap between the bars had been filled in (by a flap on which a cash register stood). It was now one long, continuous bar counter, and there was no notice about parlour prices being charged at one end. Three sets of observations, at different times and on different days, failed to discover *anyone* sitting down at the old vault end, whilst in every instance *some* people were sitting at the parlour end.

Also, there was always a higher proportion of pints being drunk at the vault end, and no women present.

The physical vault-parlour barrier had been done away with at least twenty-five years ago, and today there is no barrier whatever (or price difference?) between one end of the bar and the other. Yet the people in the pub are still maintaining the same traditional pattern of behaviour as they (or their fathers; or their grandfathers) would have done if these changes had not taken place.

In 1960 another observer, post-war vintage, talked to the present licensee, Mr. P—, age 47, Worktown born, in the "Man and Scythe" two years (after twelve years in engineering and another twelve in London pubs). He noted the absence of young people in his pub and, in general, the way old-time regulars now have to bring their wives, and don't themselves spend so long in the pub. "All bottled stuff nowadays . . . it's the old people who hang on."

Of all its pubs, this Worktown one has changed perhaps the least, not only in a fifth of a century but in five. It has even rated a twelve page, sixpenny booklet, published in 1952.

"YE OLDE MAN & SCYTHE INN
specially written and compiled"

On the outside wall in Churchgate a stone tells another part of its long story.

"In this ancient hostelry, James Stanley, 7th Earl of Derby, passed the last few hours of his life, previous to his execution. Wednesday, 15th October, A.D. 1651."

In a happier day the foundation stone of the largest single building erected in Worktown in the past quarter century, which among other things houses the fine new Museum, was laid (in our presence!) on the 20 June 1939—as a stone at the entrance to this Civic Centre proclaims—by "The Right Honourable the Earl of Derby, K.C., P.C., G.C.B., G.V.O., D.C.L." (since succeeded by his grandson).

The Everlasting Weekend Trajectory

Pub patterns do not only persist over decades. Despite being acted upon by forces of change, they also persist, in a sort of underground way, after they have been apparently forced out of existence. The effect of war-time and post-war beer shortage shows this very clearly.

M-O's 1947 survey showed that in Worktown, as in the rest of the country, shortage of beer had altered what seemed one of the truly basic aspects of drinking behaviour—the emphasis on the last hour in the pub. Just as the weekend was the climax of the week's drinking, with more people in the pub, drinking more and faster, so the last hour was always the peak of the evening's drinking. Limited supplies of beer changed all that. People went to the pub at times when beer was most likely to be available; drinking tended to spread itself more evenly throughout the whole week, and the *middle* of the evening rather than the last hour was the time at which pubs were most crowded.

But, as the beer shortage was overcome, the old pattern returned and today the last hour and the weekend climax are as basic to pub life as ever before.

In some parts of the country a shift in payday to Thursdays has moved the "weekend" trajectory forward a step, but the fundamental *rhythm* remains unchanged.

The following table is the result of five Worktown counts, taken during the week beginning 26 May 1938.

	Monday	Tues.	Wed.	Thurs.	Friday	Sat.	Sunday
A	15	25	14	20	50	67	41
B	28	31	30	28	52	54	38
C	28	20	23	19	47	61	40
D	17	18	15	19	39	46	38
E	45	46	36	52	84	100	87

A, B and C were taken in big central pubs, at 8.30, 9 and 10 p.m. respectively. A was taken in the lounge, B and C in the vault, D and E were made in an average corner pub D represents the total in the whole of the pub at 9.30, and E is the result of a count made right through the day.

The diagram is based on percentages of the respective Saturday night figures. The important, and truly representative count, is E. The relative abnormality of A, B and C in relation to the ordinary pub is important, because despite this, and despite the small figures concerned, the correspondence of the curves is close. And these figures do not vary very much from one week to another. For instance, C's Saturday night figure is sixty-one. On a Saturday during the previous month sixty-one also were counted, at the same time, and in

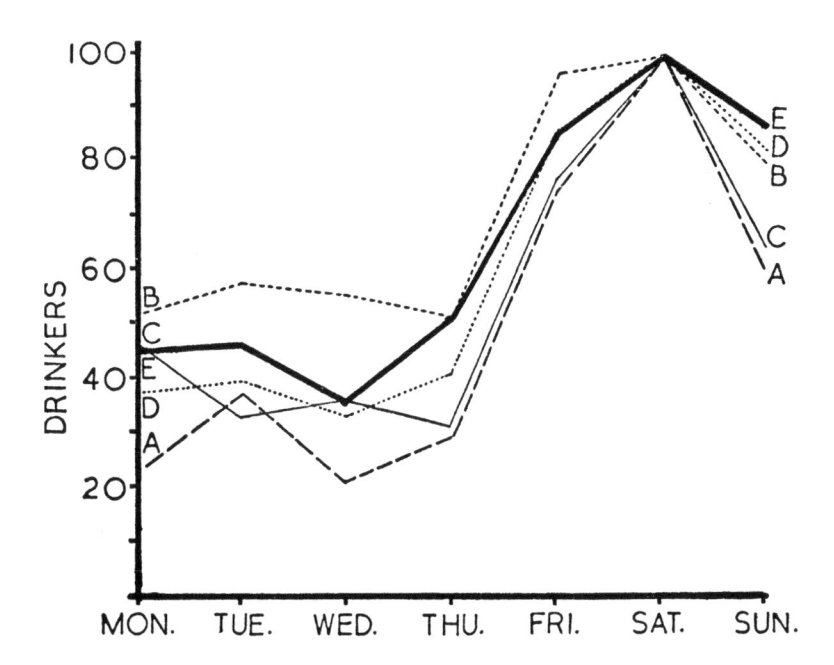

the following month sixty. Bearing this in mind these curves can be considered as generally applicable. The Saturday night pub population will be about twice that of Monday, though this will not necessarily apply to very small numbers, or to single counts made before the peak hours; the widest variation from the norm, for instance, being found in A, which was made at 8.30 p.m. Compare Rowntree's until-now-unique pub counts at York, 1899, for six pubs on a Monday and a Saturday, 233 and 342 drinkers respectively. Then pubs were open *all day*.

As distinct a variation in the number of drinkers from day to day, is that from hour to hour. And, just as the weekend peak is the dominating feature of the weekly cycle, so is the last hour peak that of the daily cycle. Landlords, when questioned by observers, have used identical words for describing this. They all said their best custom was "in the last hour".

The table below and the diagram show this quite clearly. The counts were made at the same beerhouses and during the same week as before.

	1 p.m. to 3	5.30 to 7	7 to 8	8 to 9	9 to 10
Monday	8	5	3	12	17
Tuesday	6	6	7	9	18
Wednesday	7	2	4	8	15
Thursday	4	8	10	11	19
Friday	8	12	11	15	29
Saturday	18	12	11	14	46
Sunday	34	—	17	29	38

The Friday and Saturday last hour rise is nearly three times as great as that of week nights, while the Sunday rise, though high, is spread out over a longer period.

The analogy between the last hour and the weekend is striking as is the particularly marked weekend last hour increase, thus suggests a possible explanation that will be common to both phenomena.

In 1899 York, Seebohm Rowntree found that with pubs open from 6 a.m. to 11 p.m. "while there is a considerable rush of customers during the hours 12.30 to 2.30 p.m., the attendance during the evening is considerably smaller than on Saturday night", and on every occasion peak time was 9-10 not 10-11.

Change in quality there is today, of course. Affluence has enabled drinking to be more extended and produced the occasional *midday* drunk as a new phenomenon in the North.

Back in the thirties lack of cash restricted this.

"Landlord A wrote: 'the most customers only come in on the last hour, unless they are carrying extra cash.' Landlord B says to observers: 'the drinking is all weekend'. He 'thinks' that if the pubs were shut at the beginning of the week everyone would be satisfied; doesn't think lunchtime opening is worth the trouble. Barmaid C: 'They just wait for the last hour; never mind what time you open or what time you close. It's all they've got the money for'."

Today, such restriction is economically eased; but socially, psychologically, the substance continues in the still run-of-the-mill Christian and commercial weeks. In some ways the weekend pub climax has heightened now. The larger number of people with cars has enabled a minor mass migration out into the fields and moors on week-end nights especially in summer. Some town pubs with "classy" tone suffer a little in consequence. The idea was there long ago. In the thirties young people hiked out and older ones bussed for a gill or two in the outlying villages. Should affluence cease, so would the increased excursions of today. At present, the build-up on Saturday nights in quite "remote" high villages, such as Entwistle, is impressive. Small pubs, extended and modernised (within the old framework), specialise in non-beers, such as the Bradshaw Road pub that plugs (with a poster of a nude):

TRY A BLUE ANGEL
THE HEAVENLY DRINK

—which consists, as there served (8 July 1960), of Bols, Blue Curaçao, lemonade and a dash of lime with a cherry: several middle-aged ladies with dyed hair indulging. . . .

The Speed of a Gill

There is, clearly, much fundamental research to be done yet on alcohol and pub aspects, even as regards simple matters which affect immediate licensing policy. We have already indicated here that the views on drunkenness as put forward in detail in our earlier *The Pub and the People* only add point to what has happened since. Drunkenness is (in this sense) only a trivial index of drinking and drinkees. It need not be connected *at all* with licensing laws, numbers of pubs, music (a pre-war obsession with the Worktown magistrates; and Liverpool would not even allow *darts*!), prices, juveniles or crime. The controlling factors—both much simpler and more subtle: some of them—have yet to be fully and consistently analysed. In view of the vast vested interest in (and against) alcohol as a whole, it does seem extraordinary that, for example, things like the effects of fast and slow round drinking, and the things which determine drinking rates, have, so far as we can learn, never been further studied since M-O's pioneer observations in this field before the war. We make no excuse, therefore, for drawing attention to our rather specialised, small, but quite suggestive results. These serve as a good example of the sort of pure observation lately completely out of fashion in the whirlpool of opinion polls and interview questionnaires.

We timed over a thousand drinkers sipping their gills (half pints) under natural conditions, not knowing they were observed (a difficult job requiring the highest standard of observation, incidentally). The following table shows average drink speeds throughout a week of random observations, and in the second column a control group of 443 drinks taken at the same (four) type pubs during the last week of May only.

Day	Random average	Control average
Friday	7·5 minutes	8·2 minutes
Saturday	7·9	8·8
Sunday	9·7	9·7
Monday	10·7	12·8
Tuesday	13·5	11·3
Wednesday	12·1	11·1
Thursday	10·7	10·6

The graphical representation of the above shows substantially the same curve as that representing the variation in the number of drinkers throughout the week (compare figure opposite with p. 187).

The observed variation between week-day and weekend is evidently not so sharp in the case of the speed of drinking as that of the number of drinkers. None the less, a corresponding weekend peak does exist, if not so strongly marked; and indicates that an explanation common to both phenomena should be sought.

The diagram overleaf shows a graph of the frequencies of all Sunday timings between four and sixteen minutes, for two minute intervals —i.e. all the times between four and six minutes are added to make the first point of the curve, all those between six and eight minutes the second point, and so on (p. 192).

63·8% of all times were between six and ten minutes, the day's average being 9·7 minutes. Only 9·6% of the times were under six minutes, and 26·6% were above ten minutes. Also there were eight timings, not included in the above figures, that were seventeen minutes or more, including a group of two people who both took thirty-six minutes over a pint. (Isolated cases of this kind, both unusually fast and unusually slow, are recorded for every day. The fast ones are usually due to people coming in swigging down a gill and going out again right away; the slow ones are often accompanied by deep conversation—though there are more slowing down factors than there are those of speeding up.)

Out of the 173 timings for this day, ninety-eight were times for groups of two or more, and seventy-four were of single drinkers (see Table). Tabulating this difference in the speed of single and group drinking for the other days of the week for which we have enough single figures for a basis of comparison, we find that there is a definite tendency for group drinking to be faster than solitary drinking.

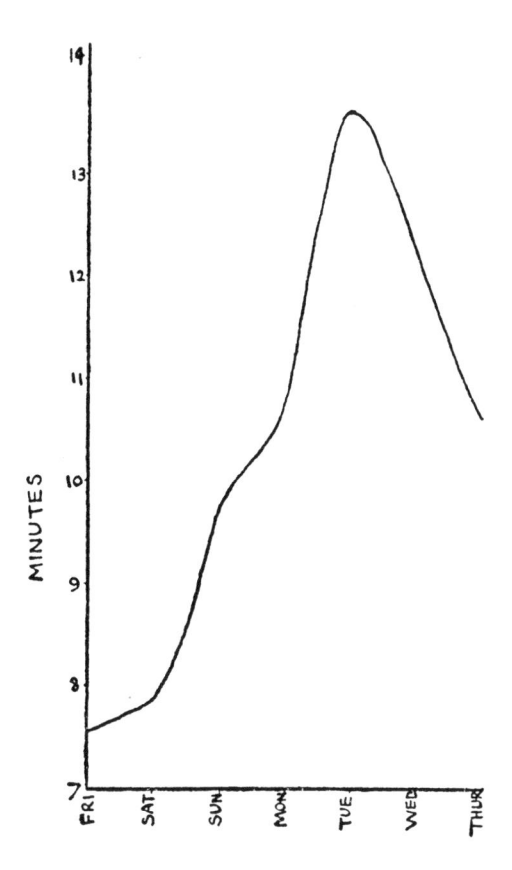

| | Averages (minutes) | |
Day	Groups	Individuals
Tuesday	13·1	15·1
Wednesday	11·0	13·6
Thursday	10·7	10·7
Friday	6·7	9·5
Sunday	9·2	10·4

What are the implications of this rhythm? That the social and the alcoholic motives of pub going, instead of being mutually exclusive, actually reinforce one another? The man who goes to the pub by himself and drinks alone would seem to be more actuated by "alcoholic" motives, and the man who drinks with others to a large extent be participating in a social environment. *Yet* the solitary drinkers drink more slowly. Again and again our studies are mutually dependent.

People don't go to pubs to drink, or for company—they go for both these reasons, an idea many planners and reformers appear unable to grasp.

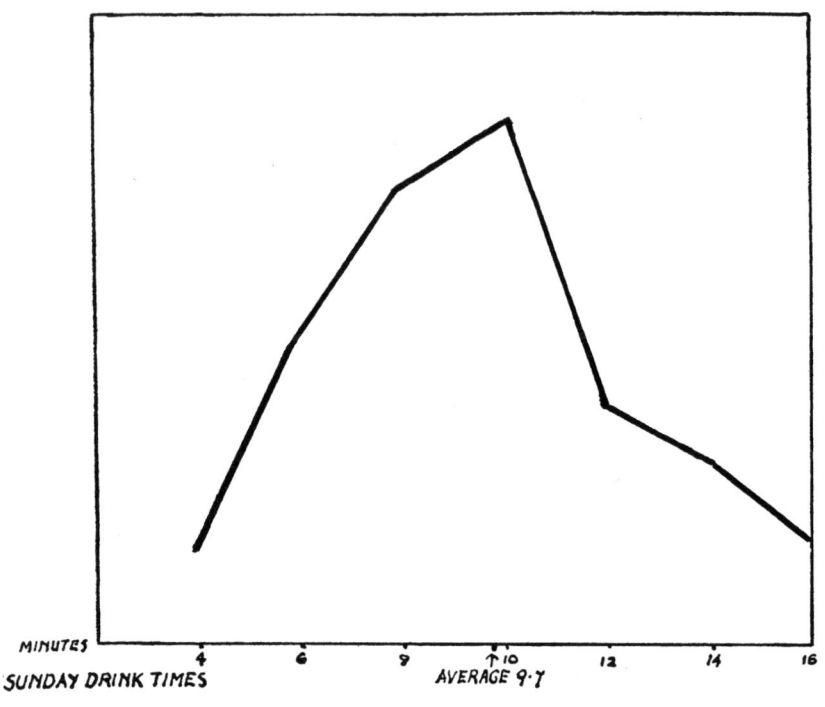

SUNDAY DRINK TIMES — MINUTES — AVERAGE 9·7

A local drinker (ex-policeman) who was asked to spend an evening in his usual pubs and write down what he saw, noted in the first report that he ever wrote for us:

Beers are being consumed steadily at the rate of 15 minutes per gill; at each fresh order an interval of five minutes invariably elapses before it is drunk, and then only a small sip. The three men all follow suit as any *one* reaches for his glass and show wonderful anticipation in drinking equal amounts, so that all three glasses register the same level after each drink.

But all our observations show that the majority of pubgoers tend, when drinking in a group, to drink level; and very often there is not a quarter of an inch difference between the depth of beer in the glasses of a group of drinkers. (Gill glasses are about 2½ inches wide.)

The greatest lack of uniformity in the rate of drinking in a group is when they are halfway through their glasses; they will, as the report says, start all together, and there is a very strong tendency for

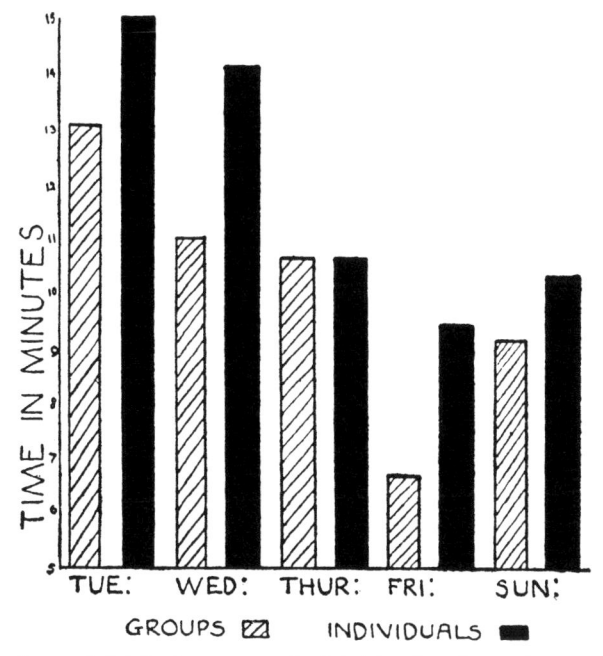

Comparison of drink times: people drinking by themselves and with groups

them to finish at once, or nearly simultaneously at any rate. The simultaneous emptying of glasses is the most frequent form of level drinking; and it is, for reasons connected with the ritual of standing rounds, the most likely form of level drinking to be due to "anticipation". But in the case of glasses in twos and threes, each group with almost identical amounts of beer in them, it is not necessarily the result of a *conscious* desire to drink level. The following incident is difficult to account for on that basis:

Regulars drink quietly. Two women, ancient by 1937, are sitting on opposite side of the room; haven't got much face left (one is syphilitic, previously observed here). They are joined by an oldish man with similar facial decomposition; he is accompanied by an old woman with a shawl over her head; she supports on her arm a blind man. The three sit together *and drink level*.

After this a sharp lookout was kept for more *blind* men. The next time one was sighted the observer followed him into the pub.

... the blind man and three others sit round a table and order pints. As soon as the mugs are brought they lift them to their mouths with a slow "follow through" motion, and keep them there for about four seconds, then put them down simultaneously. All, including the blind man, have drunk about a quarter of the mug, almost dead level. After this they take smaller gulps, sometimes the blind man starting, sometimes the others, in no special order of beginning or finishing; but gulp for gulp they drink level to within a quarter of an inch throughout.

Level drinking is part of a basic pub behaviour pattern—of round standing, each paying his turn and usually a gill of beer (or more). The other half of this basic pattern is the remarkably stable variation *throughout* the pub evening and *through the week*, of the speed of drinking, amount drunk, and relative numbers of people drinking.

The Unruffled Surface of a Gill

The outstanding impression left by revisiting the pubs of the thirties in the sixties is one of unchange rather than change. The apparently random, unorganised, uninfluenced and spontaneous behaviour of people in pubs does, in fact, follow quite rigid "rules"—the same rules today as pre-war; and probably centuries before?

The final paragraph of John Sommerfield's own notes on his 1960 return to the same old northern gill reads:

"Despite the telly, despite increased working class car ownership, despite the whole complex of commodity fetishism which *looks* as if it is changing the way ordinary people in England live, and particularly those ways of life represented in the old-fashioned pub community, the pub still persists as a social institution. Qualitatively and quantitatively. Never having had it so good doesn't only mean washing machines and holidays abroad; it is also more beer. In an old-fashioned way. Go into almost any pub and you would never deduce that this is the era of nuclear fission, computer thinking, sputniks, the cold war and all the rest of it. The winds of change *have hardly ruffled the surface of a single gill of best mild.*   J. S. 8/60."

The same observer has also reported pub sociology in another way. In *The Inheritance*, John Sommerfield has written quite extensively about working-class pubs; though not stated as such, these and other passages in his novels—which sell particularly well behind the Iron Curtain—are often based on actual Mass-Observation material. As he wrote to me (14 August 1960) regarding one of these passages:

"It is based on Worktown conversations, plus bits I made up. Can you spot them?"

I think I can. But anyway I preferred the Blackpool closing-time scene from that book (published by Heinemann, 1956):

"A white-faced young man, in a spiv collar and tie, yawning drunk begins to sing a sad Irish song all by himself his face being held very carefully (to avoid interference with his jaw movements) between the hands of a friend sitting opposite him. But he doesn't get very far with his mournful solo. The two tough girls in the far corner start 'Lily of Laguna' and in a moment almost everyone takes it up, carried away by the rich, sloshy rhythm of their anonymous voices.

"The noise is tremendous, drowning all conversation. Lucy, beating time with one hand, warbles in a loud, cracked soprano: Annie's mouth moves as if she too were singing though in fact nothing but a thin, tuneless sound like wind sighing through a keyhole emerges from her. But she's happy, Lucy is happy, everyone is happy. And, later, when the pub has closed, when the absolutely final frenzied bawling of the Landlord and barmen has driven them all out into the street, to merge and mingle with thousands of other closing-time refugees in a similar state of euphoria, they are still exalted and carried away by the sound of their voices, and the feeling of the drink inside them, and their *togetherness* which isn't dispersed in the open air and under the windy sky because they're still jammed into a crowd that is just the same as it was in the pub, only very much larger.

"It's windy outside, the sea hurls itself upon the beach with a regular roaring sigh but no one hears it. . . . The sea smells too, the saltiness in the air, the whiffs of rotting seaweed and wet sand, are obliterated by a pervading odour of beer breathed out by the swirling, moving mass of people along the promenade."

Thus we end this chapter, as we did the last, in Blackpool by the often unregarded (there) sea. What next?

Blackpool Calendar

ELEVEN

UP IN SMOKE

DRINKING ALCOHOL AND smoking tobacco are often coupled together—by economists, novelists and TV comedians alike. Alcohol reached into the far corners of the world before written history. Smoking is of more recent diffusion, but, as Dr. Kenneth Oakley of the British Museum suggested in conversation the other day (27 August 1960), the smoking idea may go back into the roots of human animal need, primitive ideas of fire, warmth, comfort.

One measure of the strength of the appeal of smoking lies in the size and number of the obstacles which in its history it has managed to overcome. It has survived seventeenth-century suppressive measures, including imprisonment and Papal excommunication in some European countries, and torture and the death penalty further East. It has continued to thrive and increase in spite of (perhaps partly because of) condemnations as immoral, relics of which linger in the argument still sometimes advanced that smokers are lacking in moral fibre. It has largely outlived social ostracism on the grounds that it was vulgar and fast.

Nowadays, from the equator across Borneo to the tower at Blackpool, there are still a few who *violently* oppose both smoking and alcohol as morally wrong (for humans). Some Australians have recently been able to prevail, for instance, on the people of the far Borneo interior not only to accept that it is sinful to smoke oneself but equally so to grow tobacco leaf for barter to others—long a main source of obtaining outside goods to bring into this remote people's hinterland.

Despite centuries of argument (almost worn out for the time being in Britain, but fresh as frangipani in Borneo or the British Solomons), extraordinarily little and feeble research has been conducted into *why* people do these things; particularly why they indulge to the excess that rouses most of the hostility.

Mass-Observation has from the start been as interested in smoking as in drinking. Both are good subjects for visual observations, general, individual or statistical; they can be observed independently of verbal explanation or corollary. Indeed, these two are among the few things people do, while awake, the act of which makes it more difficult to talk at the same time.

Smoking was one of six subjects reported upon in some detail in M-O's first publication of results.[1] In this early study it was suggested that one function of smoking was to break down a sense of strangeness. This sense of strangeness extends beyond people to places, things and ways of behaving. To a British Islander, Asian places, things, and ways of behaving are still quite alien. But so also, to some extent, are all other places, things and ways of behaving than those which he himself knows and uses. In so far as they own and use the same or similar things, in so far as they have the same or similar ways of behaving, to that extent he has a social bond with them. He can feel the force of this social bond without "knowing" all the people who share these places, things and ways with him. By "changing for dinner" he feels a social bond with "the upper class". By following football on the radio (or Gordon Pirie on TV just now) he feels a social bond with millions of people who do likewise. Moreover, it has often been noticed (and Mass-Observation supplies plenty of evidence of this) that he can feel this bond even when he is *alone*, just as the English or Belgian "sahib" changed for dinner even when there was no one to see him do so on pre-Lumumba evenings.

The British pub recognises social status by distinction in drinking places and the prices therein. In the whole country there is hardly anywhere a public structure based on any conception of one "democratic" or equal society. The same sort of attitude is adopted by British Railways in the four categories used for railway coaches, two by class (instead of the earlier three), and two according to smoking habits (we have heard it suggested that on the excursion trains from Worktown to Blackpool two further categories would be appropriate: DRINKERS and NON-DRINKERS).

In 1937 a detailed study was made of opinions about reasons for smoking. Among a regular M-O panel of smokers and non-smoking correspondents (*not* interviews with strangers but personal, subjective reports at the "private view" level, to us at M-O, in confidence), each category was found to hold several broad (verbal) views about the other, for instance:

[1] *First Years' Work* by Mass-Observation, edited by Charles Madge and Tom Harrisson, with special help from Woodrow Wyatt and Peter Jackson, and an essay by Professor Bronislaw Malinowski (Lindsay, Drummund, London, 1938). Other subjects dealt with include Pool, Drink, Jokes, Press, Research Methods.

	Smokers to Non-smokers %	Non-smokers to smokers %
Pity	14	28
Admiration, envy	21	13
Hostility	17	11

Examples:

1. "There is certainly a fellow-feeling between smokers, and if a man refuses a cigarette there is a slight barrier set up in intimacy."
2. "I notice that I have never taken to people who are habitual smokers. Most of my friends are non-smokers or moderate ones. But I do not object to smoking as such."
3. "I notice I sometimes find myself inclined to 'look down' on non-smokers. This may be quite unreasonable; but, on the other hand, I have noticed in many cases (by no means a general rule, of course) that there is something 'queer' about men (this does not apply to women) who are non-smokers. That is, they quite frequently have eccentricities, and even unpleasant traits, which are not so noticeable in smokers."
4. "I always feel that there's a milky babies' breath smell about a man who doesn't smoke; he seems to me not quite a man. He repels me in somewhat the same way as does a scout-master. Quite unreasonable of me, I know, but there it is—if a man hasn't the smell of tobacco about him he doesn't seem to me quite wholesome, and I can't like him, no matter how."

The sociability of smoking as a habit is indicated by replies to a self-documented question on *when* smokers smoke more or less:

	Smokers answering this		
	Men %	Women %	Both %
Smoke more in company	52	75	60
Smoke more alone	31	16	26
Equally in both cases	17	19	14
Use offer of smoke to break ice	83	89	85

One common reason for *starting* to smoke: "because it is forbidden". In answer to a question, "Do you ever feel *ashamed* of smoking?" 86% deny, often indignantly, anything to be ashamed of; however, there is a minority of 14% who frankly admit they are ashamed. But to: "Do you feel that smoking is a bad habit?" 48% of smokers admit it as bad, often adding "when carried to excess". They frequently compare their habit to drinking, in this respect.

Tapping: Which End in the Mouth?
One of the most persistent pieces of smoking behaviour in the thirties was *"cigarette tapping"*. It was erratically distributed, individual, variable and in the strictly smoke-value sense often useless, non-functional—by this stage in manufacture, the real *effect* on machine-packed tobacco was negligible.

Observation in Worktown and elsewhere showed that between a fifth and *over a half* of all cigarette smokers frequently (often invariably) tapped one or other end of their cigarette. But which end? The *declared* purpose was to tap down the tobacco before putting the end in the mouth. Yet observation frequently showed that, while many people tapped and then put that tapped end into their mouths, many others put the *other end in instead*. At times, the same smoker kept under observation would vary this polarity.

Put to M-O's panel of self-observers for personal documentation, plenty were puzzled when they had exactly to examine an everyday habit of their own for the first time. After taking both thought and stock check of self, 54% reported themselves as more or less regular tappers. Of these tappers:

—52% decided they tapped the end put into the mouth,
—21% smoked the untapped end,
—27% couldn't decide on any regular pattern of their own.

Considerable anxiety and even antagonism was expressed by the different "schools" of tapping. Several in the large minority who put the untapped end in the mouth did so (they wrote) because this was clearly the sensible thing to do; they were obviously in the right. Some of these smokers were distinctly *annoyed* at or contemptuous of those who used the opposite end. One put it more "logically" than most:

I tap a cigarette and place the tapped end in my mouth. A staff-room colleague once remarked on this, and I explained that I put the tapped end in my mouth because the tobacco was less likely to work loose. He said that he tapped the end he was going to light, so that it would light evenly. Another friend of mine once said he tapped a cigarette to make the packing more compact: he said you could sometimes get the tobacco in a cheap "fag" to go down as much as a quarter of an inch. The action is probably a relic of days when cigarettes for some reason needed tapping; most people seem to do it without knowing why—or for very varied reasons.

From Tap to Cancer

To tap or not to tap, to mouth or not to mouth if tapped—these are no longer such burning issues for smokers in the sixties. More of those who still tap today do so, seemingly, in connection with silver cigarette cases or some other personal pet characteristic. Fewer young people tap now. In a week's trial look-out about Worktown not one under twenty was recorded doing so, for emphasis on improved packing, widely publicised in the intervening decades, has reached mouth-tap antithesis in the vast expansion of filter tips (pre-war for the more refined minority only).

Filter-tips received a big further fillip in the fifties, with the lung cancer "scare". Today the lung cancer issue is certainly the burning one. It would be no surprise to the sociologist with his eye on the top to learn that all the mass propaganda about cancer and smoking (much of it rooted, albeit unconsciously, in already mentioned latent hostility) has not appreciably decreased the smoking rate of smokers: sometimes the contrary.

After years of war shortage, in 1947, smoking was really hit by the doubling of the tobacco duty, the shilling increase on the price of twenty. A 1948 Hulton survey showed an immediate drop in consumption of 25%—a drop which deepened slowly during the following year, then showed signs of recovering itself, but in 1954 still stood around 25% and has only since picked up.

The capacity to "recover" from almost any attack or knock-down is an abiding feature of both smoking and drinking—as it is, in a deeper sense, of human civilisation. No harder knock hit the cigarette habit than that cancer scare in the fifties (and continuing). M-O's eyes follow this new aspect of smoking, especially the cancer fear aspect, which in 1937 appeared once or twice as a "Miscellaneous". It will be recalled that a connection between lung cancer and smoking was first demonstrated by R. Doll and A. B. Hill in the *British Medical Journal*, 1952 (vol. 2, p. 1271), supported by two further reports there 1954, 1, p. 1451; 1956, 2, p. 1076; also P. Stocks and S. M. Campbell in *B.M.J.* 1955, 2, p. 923).

These papers caused a tremendous furore. The repercussions of "don't smoke" implication penetrated into the highest inhabited place in Central Borneo, the long-house at Bario, thanks to radio. *But* all that these investigators actually found was a *statistical* connection between (a) smoking and (b) lung-cancer. The *statistical probability* of smokers getting lung cancer more than non-smokers was shown. But all manner of other matters relevant to any supposed *cause and effect* link were not—and were not in the early research intended to be—taken into account.

The results were not interpreted with this limiting qualification. As with opinion polls or questionnaires on voting intentions, the emphasis subsequently placed upon the meaning of the results may well be unjustified in the meaning of the research itself. The published opinion *effect* was similar to that obtained—to use two analogies easily seen through—if:

(i) Demonstration of possession of a TV set as an index of affluence, plus statistical results showing a tendency for lower ownership of TV sets among book publishers, demonstrated a tendency to de-affluence among the latter.

(ii) A demonstrated connection between not voting and not worshipping in Worktown (see p. 104) were taken to infer that you'd better vote for someone if you want to go to heaven.

In 1959 Professor R. A. Fisher, foremost biological statistician, severely manhandled the cancer-cigarette hypothesis (*Smoking—the Cancer Controversy*, Oliver and Boyd, Edinburgh, 1959); and various others pointed out that *inhaling* may in fact have an ameliorating rather than an aggravating effect in smoking, incidentally.

Professor Fisher had suggested that there could, however, be a common reason for both observed results: lung cancer and cigarette smoking; and that this would not involve any assumption that one directly *influenced* the other. He further suggested the possibility that pipe smokers differ from cigarette smokers for some inborn genotype reason—though there was then no evidence for this, and it is by no means implied in the general *chanciness* of factors passing as "choice" in smoking (or non-) habits, or in a multitude of other behaviour patterns (not forgetting voting), studied even superficially by modern social science.

Under the supervision and control of Professor H. J. Eysenck of the Institute of Psychiatry, London, Mass-Observation carried out a field study to test this and related types of hypothesis, under the auspices of, and commissioned by, the Tobacco Manufacturers' Standing Committee.[1]

The object of this operation was to examine further the validity of an approach free of any "direct link" statistical assumption. Owing to the poverty of factual data, fully adequate hypotheses from the

[1] See *Smoking and Personality* by H. J. Eysenck, Mollie Tarrant, Myra Woolf and L. E. England, published in the *B.M.J.* 1960, 1, pp. 1456–60. M.T. and L.E. are Executive Directors of Mass-Observation, and M.W. on the staff. For a significant discussion of the methods used see *Discovery*, July 1960.

statistical or medical side, the problem was tackled theoretically on the basis of Professor Eysenck's own formulations of a "general dimensional theory of personality". Professor Eysenck has written extensively on this broad hypothesis; most recently and fully in his *The Structure of Human Personality* (2nd ed. Methuen, 1960) and as editor of *Experiments in Personality* (2 vols., Routledge, 1960).

An eight-point questionary, based on Dr. Eysenck's own personality measurements, was tested, modified and adopted for field use, by a team of whole-time M-O investigators, covering 2,400 selected persons. To obtain a correct sample, it was necessary to talk to many more people than those required for final analysis, in order to ensure suitable sampling groups; over 7,000 persons were contacted for this initial purpose.

To quote the *B.M.J.* 1960 report:

"Sample Tested
"The design of the experiment makes use of 24 groups of subject divided equally on the basis of age (40–59 and 60–70), class (ABC and HE), and smoking habits (non-smokers, light, medium and heavy smokers, pipe smokers, and ex-smokers). The hypotheses only deal with the relative positions, of four groups —namely, the non-smokers and the light, medium, and heavy smokers; no prediction could be made with respect to ex-smokers or pipe smokers. There are 100 subjects in each of the groups except among the older non-smokers."

Sampling was conducted in three stages, to ensure accuracy:

"Stage 3.—At the final stage the selection of individuals to be interviewed was not made randomly, but by the method of quota sampling. Interviewers were allocated quotas on age, social class, and smoking group, so that information was obtained from the required respondents. A looser control was placed on occupation so that the distributive trades were not over represented, as tends to be the case with quota sampling."

After this, six categories of smoker (from non- to ex- and "separate" pipe) were formed. The method then followed and the statistical checks employed are described in detail in the *B.M.J.* The *results* seemed to support, broadly, the genotype hypothesis approved. To quote from the final discussion by Eysenck, Tarrant, Woolf and England:

"They [the results] do not prove that smoking does not cause lung cancer, but they make more reasonable than had previously been the case the proposition that both smoking and cancer may be causually related to certain underlying genotypic factors. Perhaps the most appealing hypothesis is that extroverts live at an accelerated rate, drinking harder, smoking harder, living more irregular lives, staying up longer, and generally 'living it up' more. They may thus (a) lower their resistance to disease, and (b) expose themselves more to conditions which may directly cause the disease in question. This would agree well with findings of Pearl (1928) and of Hammond and Horn (1954) that the general death rate among smokers is similar to that of non-smokers of a more advanced age. (It may be that, in addition, non-smokers are biologically self-protective, as Berkson [1958] hypothesizes, and that biologically this is correlated with robustness in meeting mortal stress from disease generally. Such an additional hypothesis is not strictly necessary, and does not appear very likely to us.)

"Some such theory as that outlined above would account for all those features of the evidence which had caused difficulties to the proponents of the 'direct action' hypothesis. Inhaling now becomes irrelevant; unless it can be shown to correlate with introversion; it does not provide an obstacle to our theory. The relationship between smoking and non-cancerous diseases also finds an explanation. Lastly, the fact that pipe smokers are not particularly prone to lung cancer finds an easy explanation in terms of their quite different personality structure."

The Professor and his M-O colleagues go on to emphasise that this study is only preliminary and "should be repeated" more extensively on lines planned to test these tentative findings. And, finally:

"Much the most important, *a direct study should be undertaken* of the personality of victims of lung cancer; if they could be shown to be more extroverted than a carefully chosen control group the theory here advanced would receive considerable support."

With further direct study as suggested, it *could* be that we might presently learn more about smoking than almost anything else so far in British social science; might be even able to detect a man's private sex life or future income potential by timing his pipe or cig-rate, watching his tapping and X-raying one lung (correlated). We must beware, though, lest a new set of statistical correlations are taken as themselves valid beyond the limits of such crude measurement for man.

Meanwhile, through centuries of vicissitudes and a half-decade of shock, smoking carries on seemingly as strong as ever. In Great Britain there are now 20,500,000 smokers, of whom rather under 13,000,000 are men. Out of these twenty million plus, only one and a quarter million are *not* regular cigarette smokers.

TWELVE

THE TELLY: HOW IMPORTANT?

Large advert. in Worktown shop window (July 1960)

THE THING THAT will most strike the man back from Borneo as *new* in the air of Worktown or Worksop (Plate 1): television antennae. There were plenty of plain radio aerials in 1937, though. The great growth in shops selling TV appliances catches any passing eye. Sets of only a few years antiquity are sold off, too, at

THE TELLY: HOW IMPORTANT?

> SLOT TV
> 96 HOURS FOR 1/-

> TV SET 99/6
> IDEAL FOR SPARES

> GENEROUS ALLOWANCE ON
> YOUR OLD SET
> AGAINST ADVANCE PAYMENTS

The last of these in a Worktown shop-window poster caught in Julian Trevelyan's sketch, where out-of-dating your set reaches caricature.

Looking outward up among the wheatears and pipits, above the first Lord Leverhulme's vast and crumbling Rivington "folly" of the twenties, high over Worktown on Winter Hill, highest—and hitherto barest—point in South Lancs, four great aerials, taller than Blackpool Tower, now dominate as the new boys of Commercial TV.

Yet when one gets down to it, at the impartial level of social research, it grows distinctly difficult to avoid feeling that the vast importance attached to this novelty has, in the past five years, been misplaced—in some respects, exaggerated enormously and deliberately (both by those promoting and those detesting it).

Television has clearly had important effects, as did sound radio before it; the comparable "revolution", reversing the sequence of sense, was when the talkies brought sound to the visual screen of the cinema; or technologically, when the "wireless" brought sound regardless of gramophone.

It must be at once stated, however, that research material of a high standard is—in view of all the publicity and argument—remarkably weak as regards TV's actual impact, in depth. The Nuffield Foundation's careful but necessarily limited study of youth reaches some strikingly negative conclusions, several of them in flat (but fair) contradiction to data lately put forward from TV sources. A neat instance of Government's feeling of responsibility in this field was provided in the House of Commons on 27 July 1960 when the Postmaster-General concluded a longish interchange at Question Time:

"MR. DRIBERG (Barking, Lab.): Has the right hon. gentleman read both last week's report and the Nuffield report which led to this, and, if so, in view of the evident differences of opinion, why does he not positively encourage the research which is demanded in that report?

"MR. BEVINS: Because it is not *my* function to encourage research."

Emphases and Exaggerations

Unfortunately, research of this sort, sponsored by vested interests in so controversial a field, is liable to be inadequate in conception from the start. The whole issue has been clouded by both deliberate (for or against) and imitative *published* opinion over emphasis, of which a fair specimen is the responsible prestige column of "Atticus" in the *Sunday Times* (31 July 1960). He gives half a column to quotations from an anonymous policeman (not even his rank or zone are stated) attributing 100% novelty and power to (presumably) films when shown on TV only.

"*The New Crooks*

"'There's a new crook coming into the business these days, who's getting most of his education from the telly. In the old days it used to take a house-breaker several years to acquire his professional qualifications and by that time the police had generally had a chance to get their tabs on him.'

"It was a policeman who was giving me his views of one of the causes behind last year's spectacular rise in crime.

"'But now', he went on, 'the do-it-yourself boys are moving in, especially in the provinces. A lot of them seem to be picking up the tricks of the trade from the documentary crime serials. That's where they learn the elementary things like the proper way to break open a door or how to watch a building before they do a job.

"'Of course they make their mistakes. Television doesn't tell them *exactly how much gelignite to use* when they are blowing a safe and several of the new boys lately have been using a spot too much. But the most useful thing of all a criminal can pick up from the television is a really accurate impression of the way a policeman's mind works.'"

If TV could do what is claimed for it in this last sentence, it indeed would put sociology, criminology and psychology to shame as a serious medium for presenting accurate study-results!

M-O's own researches on TV began in 1938 (when the present writer did one of the first tele-feature programmes, on "The Lambeth", an Alexandra Palace presentation of observation material on the phenomenon of this obsessive dance (as described in our Penguin Special *Britain* that year). They have continued closely interested ever since. Here is a paragraph from a recent M-O report referring to the Manchester area:

"Perhaps the greatest power of television in the homes of relatively unsophisticated (in the cultural sense) Lancashire people, is in presenting something which they have been doubtful, suspicious, about, as if it was a *fait accompli*, an ordinary accepted part of respectable thinking and opinion, controversial or otherwise. The moment a thing has got on to TV it exists in another level of reality, so to speak. Perhaps the best of all examples of this, in local terms, has been the distinct growth in prestige of the painter Lowry since he was shown at work in his Salford home on TV."

Back in 1949 an M-O study (published as M-O *Bulletin* No. 30 in August 1949) sought to examine what people expected to happen as TV inevitably grew:

"Radio was most often thought likely to be the first casualty of television, and nearly all assumed that radio listening would grow less although few thought that it would be ousted altogether:

" 'I should probably have a television set on sometimes but as my home leisure pursuits chiefly involve the use of hands and eyes together, I do not think it would displace the wireless altogether'.

"And there were many who intended to share time between television and the radio and so create a balance between the two:

" 'Television would complement rather than interfere although I cannot quite decide what would happen if both radio and television provided personally interesting programmes at the same time' (35 year-old housewife).

"About two in five thought that they would read less with television, and a not uncommon complaint in consequence is that the list of things that ought to be done in the house, the books that ought to be read, the wireless programmes that ought to be listened to, would grow longer and yet have less chance of achievement."

In the result, TV's growth temporarily affected people much as they expected. But there are numerous signs that these effects are now wearing or easing off, as the adaptable Briton makes new adjustments. Nor do these adjustments differ *essentially* from others required by the same technology which has made TV possible; the technology that has produced Washing Machines, Spin Dryers, Refrigerators, Hifi, cheap and common place now where before they were for the few and well-off, if at all. Much of the leisure which TV is taking up is thereby a new leisure, too.

Here we come to a vital question which is seldom asked by those who feel that TV has "kept people indoors when they should be out", and all that. What *did* people do on a winter's day or a Sunday afternoon of rain before TV—especially if they hadn't much money? The short answer for millions of people then: "NOTHING MUCH". They "messed about" or did odd things (e.g. read pulp mags and Westerns, argued, titivated each other), which can hardly be said to be "worse than looking into polypact television. This is a simplified abbreviation of the past: but no one who lived long in a working-class street in the thirties can really dispute the basic truth.

The simple fact is, that on a winter's evening *before* the days of television, in a less affluent society, the great majority of people spent their time half-listening to the sound radio (on Sunday largely commercial sound), and doing all sorts of odds and ends indoors. When they could, they also went out to the cinema, the greyhounds, all-in wrestling, the sea-side (though seldom into the sea), and so on—but not very frequently; and some of them never went out at all in foul weather, or on the Sabbath. There has been some movement away from going out to these things, though it is doubtful if this movement is necessarily permanent. On the other hand, many of the people who no longer are going so much to cinemas (for instance) are no longer doing so for two quite other reasons:

1. Because they are going and doing other, and often more expensive things—such as driving out in a car, which they now own; sailing a small boat on one of the reservoirs; fishing; running a motor bike into a city for something there; going on evening train excursions; taking meals out in a new growth of restaurants and cafés.
2. A lot of people were getting fed up with the standard of cinema films in any case. The same applies to other sorts of outing as well; but most sorts of choice at this level, in a modern society, require money.

Another one of the several factors operating to make television a sort of scapegoat among those who suffer from it either directly or indirectly, is that a very large proportion of intellectuals and the sort of people who make most noise aurally or in writing in Britain, do not like—and often do not have—television. Even within Worktown, there is a distinct group in 1960 who either ostentatiously do not have television, or if they do have it go out of their way to explain that it was given to them, or that they got it to see a special programme, or that they only look at it very occasionally. Such people generally refer to it by derogatory remarks, "the little box" "the ghastly", instead of the ordinary reference to "telly", "goggle box", etc. All that is fair enough, but in shutting themselves off from television or adopting some special attitude towards it, they assist their own innate intellectual tendency to exaggerate its importance or to attribute to it effects (largely evil or apathetic-making), which in fact they would find it more difficult to support if they viewed television regularly. They would then also realise, as a great many ordinary viewers are doing, that it is just as possible to be selective about television as it is about cinema going or drinking, or equally possible just to glance at it and take little notice (as with sound). But *to be eager to be selective* very much depends on having enough affluence to be able to employ the alternatives: as well as enough intelligence or *experience* to be aware of it. And the alternatives to television tend to be, now, more expensive or more difficult.

Television itself provides significant answer as regards the second of these factors, the intelligence. Television is constantly presenting to people in their homes things that they may never have seen outside. Ballet, Ibsen, art galleries, music festivals, painters at work, beautiful places, tropical countries, ancient monuments. Thus television itself operates to stimulate people to get away from it into such "creative" outlets. Though this effect is still rather small, so are many of the other much emphasised effects of television. It is an effect, also, that is cumulative and relates to parallel (and sometimes much stronger) influences—such as holidays on the Continent.

On the whole, Britons tend to be able to avoid picking on scapegoats, which can develop in the scapees' vicious behaviour patterns: e.g. anti-semitism. But there is a powerful psychological influence in many minds, and particularly those of the powerfully non-conformist north, in the direction of locating sources supposedly leading to unoriginal sin. At present television fills this bill better than anything else, on many counts. But look back through the records of the last thirty years—and longer: you'll find that there has always been something of the kind upon which has been laid juvenile delinquency or sexual abnormality, unreadiness to work or excessive alcoholism—or whatever else were the troubles headlining at the moment. In the thirties, when the football pools grew into their present mammoth influence of trivial impact, all sorts of sins were attributed to them; even unemployment, which was then not infrequently explained (by the better off) as being assisted by an unreadiness to work when there was a chance of winning a big prize in Littlewoods.

None of this is to suggest for a viewer moment that TV cannot be or is not "influential" at all. We are suggesting that—like the Beaverbrook Press with politics in the thirties—it is far less influential than it thinks. That the main impact is minor, or as an enlargement of existing but previously more limited experience (notably Sport; and Royal Occasions, Chapter 14). As with the Press over the years, a *negative* result is often the easier to achieve, especially where institutions and ideas outside the ordinary run of economics (e.g. personal buying habits) are involved.

The Negative Aspect

Here is a recent note on this negative aspect (15 August 1960, T.H.):

"Through TV people can know very much more than they did before, how politicians do talk. And in particular, how careful all of them are not to step out of party line. What could pass as freshness and personality a few years ago is now stamped unquestionably as 'party politics'. The sense of this word has not really altered; the understanding of it has. In fact, politicians were always talking like this; but very few people realised it—because very few people had time to go and sit in the House of Commons, where anyway the seating capacity is very small, and where also the differences have a *meaning* in the context of partisanship within that building itself.

"This change, a very important one in the long run for Britain, is one of the most definite and distinctly identifiable which can be related to the growth of television. For the first time, people have seen many politicians on television. Series of programmes show them, again and again, in stereotype.

"More than this, this change can be directly attributed to the growth of commercial television. So long as there was only the BBC television, the whole controversial side of politics was avoided. The introduction of ITV brought in all these people, and also forced the BBC to bring them in to keep up with things.

"For the first time, nearly everyone has seen them having to behave as individuals when they cannot in fact behave as such in public."

During the summer of 1960 M-O carried out one of its regular nation-wide sample studies on relevant topics, including TV. In one question people were invited to rate in order of importance the relative *usefulness* they attached to various sorts of public figure. Crude and conventional as these categories are, they do give some insight into—and amusement about—present public opinion in a slightly offbeat way:

Rating	Job	Percentage of nation-wide sample saying: This job "very useful", etc. %
1.	Doctor	97
2.	Policeman	90
3.	Grocer	79
4.	Atomic research scientist	68
5.	Member of Parliament	63
6.	Clergyman	62
7.	Television Entertainer	24
8.	Fashion Model	10

Opinion on most of these jobs was *emphatic*; but scientists scored 10% of uncertain, fashion models and M.P.s 2%, TV entertainers 0% of that (see further Chapter 15).

Politicians have lately lost prestige, we think, through being shown (not shown *up*) on TV. Hitherto people knew little of them in detail. TV itself has begun to be in danger of losing out on a "flying start", for much the same reason. This reason: a chronic underestimate—lately extending into the BBC and perhaps least so far in Granada TV Programmes—of the intelligence of people and their ability to see through formulae; and in particular the way people notice little things and (even if slowly) add them up to a real-life total of doubt in the long run.

The tendency to underestimate public intelligence has for years been almost built-in to some newspapers. Those papers which do not think that way tend to increase circulation, in relation to the others. This trend is likely to continue and accelerate? Into television, newspaper dogmas have also been carried over—partly by newspapermen—into stereotype ideas of 'the sort of things people like". The sponsors of such ideas, always anxious to be reassured by the holy sanction, nowadays, *of market research and opinion polls*, have no difficulty in being so assured—since much of the research is orientated in the direction of superficial questions, which only give quantity and not *quality* of viewing, and are sponsored by interested parties. So long as people do not actually switch off a Western programme, it is able to rate a higher popularity than a documentary which bites deep. An *index of effective depth*, such as the BBC in a small way endeavours (privately) to use, can give an entirely different picture. Too little research has been done along these lines. There is now a vast (and growing) sector of negative viewing, comparable to the long recognised pre-war habit of "keeping the (sound) radio on all day" by housewives. It is difficult, even in this sphere of exaggerated statement, to exaggerate the importance—or, to be exact, the insignificance—of *negative televiewing*. It offsets a very large part of all the positives which TV and other interests attach to the impact of programmes in statistical terms. Yet it still provides statistics to record huge responses at the surface of the retina.

Past the Cathode Peak. . . .

Among the thousands of persons listened to about TV in the summer of 1960, few of those critical or afraid of it (for many varied reasons) showed the same degree of fear or hate as hitherto. The fairest test in context is the evidence from Worktown, where views are expressed with least effect of "stranger factor" (interview) as freely and closely as one can get it, among friends.

We have earlier seen (Chapter 4) that church attendances are slowly falling in Worktown. Also that Bill Naughton's *June Evening* play about the place was a big hit there (Chapter 7). The minister of the only Congregationalist Church which has suffered *no* perceptible decline links the two, talking:

"TV is new of course. There has been a decline in evening Service and an increase in morning. But it does not affect the *young* people so much. I was very annoyed the other week, I had arranged a special Sunday night Communion. Then I realised it would clash with the TV play 'June Evening'. To my great surprise, I had the largest attendance I can ever remember."

No Worktown church has yet itself used TV, though some use microphones for special occasions (ex sound radio). But nearly every strong man of the church is deeply TV-conscious; many are noticing a change in trend with it. Another Congregationalist:

"When it first came it tended to dominate people's lives. Five years ago it made evening visiting difficult, you felt as if you were intruding, but they turn it off now. It doesn't mean so much to the *teenagers* now, their natural instincts to want to do something for themselves, are asserting themselves now."

The two leading Presbyterians differed on this:

1. "I'd like to be the censor, it's one of the miracle inventions and opportunities of the world and age. It could have terrific powers if it were properly used . . . (it's not important at present). Worktown is growing into something which has made the whole system of living good. I'm proud of Worktown, I wouldn't go anywhere else. The people are a grand lot. A Minister shouldn't swear, but I have to—when I think what a mess the architects have made of the town centre."
2. "Worktowners are *Conservative* in their outlook, they prefer dramatics to Rock'n' Roll. TV has no influence . . . (Schooling) . . . the standard is high, we have a lot of Grammar School types, and Further Education, but of course they put their homework first."

A Methodist minister nearly echoed one of our Congregationalists,

"It is made more difficult to recruit people since the advent of TV. The middle-aged groups are the ones most affected. 7 years ago, they would not even bother to turn the thing off when I called, now, if they don't turn it down, they turn it off. I don't know whether it is respect for my dog-collar, or that familiarity with the gogglebox has bred contempt."

While a couple of Church of England parsons:

1. "TV inhibits creative activities, but I think the younger people are beginning to get a bit bored with it, they almost look upon it as old fashioned."
2. "TV is not affecting as much as it did, 7 to 10 years ago it made a difference. People are much more critical now of TV. It is a powerful medium if properly used."

Secular views *were* more emphatic—having little to "fear" from TV of course:

Chemist:
"TV has not had any effect on youth, contrary to a lot of opinions. The apathy of the general public to youth problems is appalling. . . ."

Baker:
"(Young people) have much greater opportunities. And they make the most of them. They're tired of TV now, they get bored with it and are getting out more and finding other interests."

Radio Dealer:
"TV hasn't the same interest it had. If they want a new tube or anything doing to it in the summer, they don't bother."

While of course the effect of commercial TV in altering varying preferences is attested on many sides.

"TV has done a lot to promote the sale of some patent things." (Herbalist).

"TV has helped our trade, people come in and ask for styles like Alma Cogan or anybody else they fancy". (Hairdresser)

"TV has a lot of influence, if we display a dress which has been on TV it is noticed straight away. Magazine cuttings are a good fashion setter too." (Dress-maker)

"Young people have more money to spend . . . a much better dress sense than they had . . . fostered by the magazines and TV." (Fashion Shop)

"I think TV has helped a lot, because they see other women *like themselves* wearing hats, so that makes them want one as well." (Milliner in Market Hall)

But:

"Teenagers are slowly becoming more hat conscious. It usually needs one of the more popular artists to take the lead. The matron of these days no longer wears the type of hard hat she used to, in fact some of the prettiest creations are worn by the older women. Take the Queen for example, I wouldn't say the Worktown woman is influenced by TV. She knows what she wants, and is one of the straightest and nicest people to deal with."

A new trend, in two directions, is observed in a radio and music shop:

"Before the war, record sales had dwindled to only very small proportions, this was because of the ever growing popularity of sound radio. By 1940 however, the demand for records had increased. Ballads were the most popular —Bing, The Ink Spots, Vera Lynn. This demand grew, reaching an all time high, in 1956. The advent of TV might have been expected to have had an adverse effect, but the opposite was the case. The coming of Rock 'n' Roll and Beat in 1956 brought into the record market an entirely new type of customer—the teenager, who, by that time was beginning to have far more free money to spend. They created a Pop market which has been one of the greatest the trade has ever known, and continues to this day. The ballad and good music was almost eliminated, but it is *gradually coming back*. A little danger now to the record market is the advent of the tape recorder by which means they can milk TV."

One is often left with the feeling that TV so easily provides a source of facile "news" that much of the apparent weight attached to it in 1960 is due to repeated, elaborated Press emphasis. For instance, our colleague of this book and 1937 Worktown days gets a slight indisposition and is confined to his London home, so that he misses a TV performance. The local paper treats it as a semi-royal event, bulletining progress on its *front page* (16 July, 1960):

"WOODROW WYATT IS 'MORE PERKY'"
"Mr. Woodrow Wyatt, who is ill in bed with a virus infection, today told a reporter over the telephone 'I feel much more perky today, and I hope to be out and about again on Monday or Tuesday.

" 'The doctor does not seem to think it is anything too serious.' "

In all this, there is always the intellectual difficulty of separating the superficial from the enduring, the new material impact from its temporary or lasting effects. This is one of the main roles of an adequate social science: and one it too seldom fulfils at present.

One particular difficulty for the sixties is that in Britain it is *too late* to do any large-scale social study on a controlled-comparison basis, because there are no longer large defined groups of the population without radio. This research can (and should) be undertaken at once in countries like Austria where the deep Alpine valleys make picture relays very difficult. The writer spent some days in such an area around Bad Gastein during the summer of 1960; and noted, for instance, that several of the things so often attributed to TV and related influences over here are fully present there (e.g. Teddy Boys, tough girls, Mopedmania, among the upper valley farm kids). It is possible, though, that at a later date moves away from TV in other ways could appear in the not far distant future. Suggestive in this connection is a new noisiness on the Blackpool Prom; as one observer reported it (and all agreed):

Portable Radios—General Behaviour.
Holidaymakers are often seen about with portable radios. Music from them is generally listened to while their owners are sitting on the piers and prom. Also, people carry them around when they are playing and gusts of sound can be heard for a second as they pass. One couple walked into a small pier café, carrying a radio which was full on. They put it on the table and music from it could be easily heard by everyone around. However, few people looked round or took much notice.

Two Set Farm, Three Set Pub

Perhaps the modern man of 1965 may be he who has a set in each main room—like Bill Naughton's two farmers outside Worktown (Chapter 7)—or the pub with three sets that shows the bleeding Cow's Head in nearby Westhoughton (next Chapter). Who has that, *and* treats it as he already does the sound radio, cinema, Blackpool fun, gramophone records and the popular Press—with a quietly selective and often gently negative British commonsense (which many of these media continue to underestimate—to their loss—yet which remains basic, abiding, and at times the distinguishing hallmark of the British as a whole and in the last analysis)?

It is not intended to imply that TV *could not have a much greater* effect than it does have at present. But this requires radical re-thinking in its own production organisations at many levels—and is not at present in sight.

Meanwhile, there is little evidence indeed that all or even most of the changes in recent life widely attributed to TV are not really due to very complicated sets of inter-related, underlying attitudes—the same *kind* of complexity as links, perhaps, lung cancer, cigarette smoking and filter tips.

THIRTEEN

TOTEMISM IN OUR TIME—WITH A SPOT OF SPIRITUALISM

"On the road between Worktown and Wigan is the small mining town of Westhoughton. Arriving there on Saturday, August 27, anthropologists of British culture had a busy day. It was the beginning of the 'Wakes' week, the local holiday, and this traditionally falls on Bartlemas, church feast commemorating the flaying alive of St. Bartholomew. Calling in at the 'Dog and Pheasant', prosperous public house run by Dick Tyldesley, England and Lancashire slow-bowler, observers found announcements of the 'Keaw Yed' festival and effigy. In a room upstairs at this pub locals were admiring an elaborate construction. A large canvas was painted with the landscape of the neighbouring hills and through this landscape protruded the stuffed head of a cow. By this stood the effigy of a farmer in the act of sawing off the cow's head which was apparently stuck through the bars of a gate. Laid in front of this scene, as though sacrificial offerings, were a tankard of beer and a pasty on the black-painted stump of a tree. On either side were pots of flowers and strewn below were cabbages, turnips, carrots and pasties."

THE ABOVE MENTIONED British anthropologists (an M-O unit led by Charles Madge) went there on 27 August. Of what year though: 1938 or 1960? Those opening sentences of the report could apply equally to either. They were published, in fact, on 27 August, 1938, as the opening paragraph of "A Slight Case of Totemism", in M-O's best-selling pre-war Penguin *Britain* (1939). Apart from the names of persons and places, most of what was there described could as well have happened in 937 B.C. or A.D. 1960.

Little has been heard of Keaw Yed since then. It hasn't made the bright lights of TV for instance. . . . So, on 28 August 1960, another M-O unit went to see how years of supposed sophistication and new technology had affected this pagan, primitive "Golden Bough" ritual —"the cow was often used as a form of corn spirit . . . and killed to promote fecundity", Sir James Frazer wrote, continuing:

"For instance at Pouilly, near Dijon, an ox is led round the field when the last sheaf is left, when a man dressed as the devil cuts the last ears of corn and kills the ox. Part is eaten at the harvest supper, part kept till spring sowing. Near Bordeaux an ox used to be killed immediately after the end of threshing. The last sheaf in many places is called Cow" (Frazer, Vol. 1, p. 289).

The Story of Farmer saws Cow, and consequent Pies, Pastry

The story begins (anthropologically) long before Christ or coal-mining. The cow-beheading is a relic of widespread rites and early worship of the ox and cow, surviving in Westhoughton only—but without any written history here before the last century. Most locals —who laughingly allowed themselves to be called *Keaw Yed*—believe now (as they did in 1938) that the rite has been going on for ever. Ditchfield's 1896: *Old English Customs Extant at the Present Time*, mentions "a huge pie made in the shape of a cow's head, which is eaten on the day of the Wake, the Sunday after St. Bartholomew's Day". The pie has gone, replaced by thousands of very big oval-shaped pasties (thirty-six dozen sold in a single pub on the night of 27 August 1960). These are, however, never now made of the cow, or even beef, but *chicken and pork*, as a partly conscious substitute for any last trace of residual totemism (eating your own name animal)?

The justifying story has remained unchanged since 1938, though. It is simple enough: a cow got its head stuck in gate. A farmer came along. Faced with the cow-and-gate problem, he solved it by sawing off the cow's head. This sort of story is world-wide: in the middle of Borneo a man saws off the branch he is sitting on (see *Sarawak Museum Journal*, 1958, for example). The short answer in outcome is: *what a fool.* It is a joke, self-ridicule—but charged with earnestness.

In 1938 few questioned that this solution was absurd: though the problem would not in life be an easy one either. The only "smart answer" then recorded by way of covering the farmer's action:

"*He wanted some beef.*"

Noticeable twenty-two years later is the growth of a new apologism, a good-humoured self-consciousness about the continuation of cow-heading: telling the outsider that the story does not show the farmer was anyone's fool. On the contrary, he was smart. His gate was threatened, and he saved it:

"It weren't *his* bleeding Keaw."

White Cow in the "Red Lion"

Dick Tyldesley, the cricketer, is dead,—there have been two changes of publican at the "Dog and Pheasant" since. The stuffed head he borrowed from the Town Hall is back there, on the wall; it is off the ox barbecued for the 1914–18 War Armistice. As the present publican of the "Red Lion", Mr. F. Baker, remarks:

"The kids all danced round then, they say, and everyone ate it. But it's not right, as I see it, that that was an ox. It must be a cow. And it's pointless to have a *stuffed* head at that."

Mr. Baker is entitled to talk that way: for of the five Westhoughton pubs who showed heads (four fresh-killed) in 1938, only his did so in 1960 (Plate 27).

The "Red Lion" is the modern big pub in town, with five different drinking rooms, from an old-style Vault (see Chapter 10) through to a prettily redecorated chintzy, *art nouveau*, lounge. In this lounge, straddling it, on Friday, 26 August and the next night, a roughly made "four-barred gate" was placed, with the cut-off head of a white cow (given to the landlord by a Blackpool friend; he lived over there until this February).

Had a tribesman from the Congo or a Kelabit from Central Borneo (passing by on a British Council scholarship) dropped in for a gill, he might have been excused for expressing either delight or (more probably) horror at this savage scene. Also: amazement that all around sat local ladies and gentlemen in their week-end pub-best, drinking best mild, gin and tonic, Babycham or Guinness, while they talked of holidays, the Mediterranean, wage rates, soccer results, neighbours, a new local suicide, and most other things (except politics, world affairs or the blood-dripping object alongside).

Under the head a notice in red read:

"IT'S GETTIN' IT YED FAST IN GATE"

There should be an apostrophe after the IT, though, in Westhoughtonese—a postcard on local sale has it correctly, with the further phrase, spoken by the top-hatted farmer at work holding the beast's stuck head:

"IS'T AT GET IT' 'EAUT SOME ROAD"

And getting it out somehow he is—with a saw. No need to repeat here the full account of background facts published before the war.[1] Let us rather indicate changes and new emphases since then.

First, the rite has actively survived, where it might quite easily have been expected to perish in the new phase of Welfare State hygiene (which has exercised its striking negative effect on all the area's pubs: caused the spittoons to be taken out, and sawdust strips for spit brushed off (Chapter 10). That the head rite itself has survived in one pub only is not so slight as it might sound. In other ways there are signs that the

[1] Interested anthropologists who wish further particulars may contact M-O at 148 Cromwell Road, London, S.W.7.

rite is on firmer footing. There are three main changes of emphasis that here relate:
1. A new industrial relationship
2. A revived church interest
3. Participant function of the Fair in Mill Square.

1. *Industrial: Wakes Week and Holiday Festival*

The cow-head, in pastry or flesh, was at one stage closely linked to St. Bartholomew's Day in the Christian calendar and to the "Wakes", which from a pre-industrial summer (agricultural) festival were incorporated into the cotton mill and coal-pit pattern of the mechanical year—as holiday time. In 1938 the link was still strong; Wakes were taken as holiday week in direct conjunction with St. Bartholomew's Day and the cow. Then, as the 1939 *Penguin* account put it:

"Industry is practically at a standstill in the town, there is 50% unemployment and those who are in work find employment *outside* Westhoughton. But this has not made the people any less keen on their Keaw Yed festival. Some change in emphasis there has been, but the traders and publicans on one hand and the spontaneous pleasure in their legend of the Westhoughtonians on the other keep the ceremony very much alive."

Now, in 1960, the whole economy of Westhoughton has altered— coal mining, its root and base for decades, is done with (only a single small pit still working).

Instead, national and international companies, such as Metal Box, Asbestos and de Havilland, have set up factories locally, absorbing every willing adult or adolescent in Westhoughton. Indeed, the clothes on these pleasant people and the goods in the shop windows struck the present writer as almost dramatically different from his thirties' memory. The firms, which also draw labour from surrounding other towns, cannot find it convenient that this small one should take its holidays *en masse* in its own special Wakes week, as of old. By rearrangement, therefore, Westhoughton now adopts the same industrial shut-down as Worktown; two weeks, the end of June and beginning of July. But the traditional pattern cannot be completely ignored. To meet the need, the Keaw Yed people work four Bank Holidays in the factories, and take off four days *after* the cowed weekend following St. Bartholomew's Day—as a residual and special separate holiday now doubly divorced from its original (religious and early industrial) setting, holding on as fossil in the stratified deposit of Lancastrian time.

2. Christian: Patronal Festival, Pasty Social

As usual (see Chapter 4), the Church of England is closely linked with the established rites. The Parish Church of St. Bartholomew, built nearly 100 years ago, is inescapably connected through three corbel figures at corners of the grey stone tower. A casual observer could easily take these for gargoyles—and apparently they were overlooked by mass-observers earlier on. Yet they have cows' horns on conventionalised heads, beyond argument. But then, in 1938, the Parish Church had let this business go rather dormant. The present Vicar, who came here soon after that, has taken a positive and lively interest. He pointed out, in 1960, where the fourth gargoyle-cow had fallen off, while refraining from offering one possible explanation current in Westhoughton folklore of today:

"The first girl who goes in to be married who is a virgin, the cows will all nod their heads, but it ain't happened *yet*."

Something of an enthusiast, the Vicar elaborated:

"The basis of the Keaw Yed is religious, but over the years, the story has taken on various aspects. My own belief is, that the Wakes, 'The Watch' which goes back to mediaeval times, always included the roasting of an Ox. According to records, Westhoughton and Daisy Hill used to have a scrap for possession of the head, and when the locals won it, the Keaw Yed originated."

He put it more particularly in the Parish Magazine (August 1960):

" 'Wakes Sunday.' Again we take the occasion to remind our townsfolk of the significance and origin of this great local celebration. The word 'Wake' comes from the Anglo-Saxon and means 'to keep vigil (or watch)' before a Festival. It refers now to the local annual Festivities observed originally on or about the Feast of the Patron Saint of the Parish Church. St. Bartholomew's Day is August 24th so the 'Wakes Week-end' and 'Wakes Sunday' come *on or after* that date."

Although the actual Wakes holiday is now altered and reduced, the Church still celebrates the *previous* Sunday—the one immediately following St. Bartholomew's Day—as Wakes Sunday, which is liable to get rather confusing for the anthropologist a century from now? St. Bartholomew's Day itself (this year on a Wednesday, 24 August) is celebrated with two Holy Communion services in the morning, a Commemoration of the Church Consecration in the evening, followed at 8.30 p.m. by a Pasty Supper and Social (tickets 1/6), with a local artist's rendering of the Cow and Gate incident, 6' × 3', in the place of honour (and subsequently exhibited in the church vestry with pride). Suitably enough, too, the religious leader of the community receives his symbolic share of the totem animal on the Saturday night before his Wakes Sunday (i.e., in this case, 27 August 1960). As our friend, the Vicar, said it:

'I don't ask questions, but after midnight on Wakes Saturday, I always find a large pasty, and a draught of beer on my doorstep. And two years ago there was a cow's head tied on the Church lychgate on the Sunday morning. I understand that the local slaughter house had been broken into during the night."

This last incident, by the way, characterises primitive rites in many parts of the world, including the middle of Borneo. An occasion of this kind always tends to trigger off similar and associated behaviour, not necessarily relevant and occasionally very irreverent to the central rite, yet clearly inspired by it. In 1938 we noted (see *Britain, op. cit.*) two particular instances of this, one involving a goat stuck in some railings! Alerted to be on the look-out for similar phenomena in 1960; sure enough, the newspaper from the next door town, while ignoring the Westhoughton affair, held this choice item on 27 August:

"Cow Fell on His Leg"

"Fourteen-years-old Eric Watson, 187 Eskrick-st., had his ankle injured yesterday—by a cow.

"As he was leading it back the heifer slipped and fell on his leg. Eric was treated in hospital, but went home later."

3. *The Fair*

". . . bright with lights and loud with music; in the evening it was packed tight with people, and at 9 p.m. it was like this: Raining hard but the Fair doing a roaring trade."

This, from the 1938 report, equally fits 1960. There are differences though. Notably absent now are the Wall of Death (with monkey), Boxing Booth, and a girl handling snakes. The passive spectacles, where you pay to look on, have gone. On the other hand, participant amusements and games of chance have heavily increased. Housed on the thick black mud, under the rain, a whole row of coconut shies, several dart-throwing stalls (three darts for 6d.), ·22 rifle shoots, all for prizes (principally coconuts and cut glass). On the gambling side —chance rather than skill:

—24 roll-a-penny, on to cards
—40 sets of Bingo (numbers game)
—c. 90 Numbers machines (for Jackpot)
—10 Ball-into-Pail rolling.

The Fair was thus very distinctly old style in tone. This was emphasised again, in the six different sorts of moving vehicle available at 6d. a ride. These involve sixty small vehicles in all. Five of these on a rotating vertical wheel were labelled SPUTNIK RIDE, but were otherwise unchanged from the usual design, with much worn and battered tin sides. Only strictly modernist item was a small circular dome surmounted with antennae in space ship style, which was quite popular on the children's round-about, though rather less so than a stage-coach labelled Wyatt Earp. Far and away the most popular participant pleasure—full to capacity at 1/6 a time throughout the evening—was the bumper car arena of pre-war vintage.

Submerged by City?

The "Red Lion", with its Keaw Yed, did the biggest business in town and the best the landlord has so far known there. With a live orchestra playing in one bar and a juke box blaring in another, the talk and laughter of the drinkers and pasty eaters was by no means drowned. And the last word was with these voices, joined in singing out the evening on "Auf Wiedersehen, Goodnight", a very old friend.

As one observer went upstairs to bed, he found the family's grandfather looking quietly at the play on the pub's third TV set; he was wearing a cloth cap, which he courteously doffed with "goodnight". Another observer helped the rest of the family and friends clear up the mess. As he was Michael Wickham, staff photographer of Condé Nast Publications, *Vogue*, etc., and as he had also worked with M-O in 1937 in Worktown, he was impressed to find two high-quality German cameras being used for final photographs of the by now rather sad-looking creature's head—in 1938 he cannot remember finding anyone around these parts to talk photography with.

The "Red Lion" people say they will carry on the Keaw Yed for sure. It certainly still means a good deal, even if only in terms of pasty eating and booze-up. Without a single head, it might feel rather different. Of course, there are always different pressures at work; nowadays always tendencies to organise, rationalise, eliminate the curious or unhygienic. Moreover, Westhoughton as a whole is threatened with a new and massive impact from the City of Manchester which is tending to eat up and detribalise so many lesser communities in the northern midlands. Manchester is proposing to build a satellite dormitory town within the bounds of Westhoughton, which will nearly double the present population. Some see this as the end of more than Keaw Yed:

"The village atmosphere will go, and the true Westhoughtian will be in the minority. It will happen of course, and once it does, then it'll be goodbye to the Keaw Yed, they'll take the mickey out of it."

Others assume and accept the elimination of local self without regret:

"They'll come all right, but only from Manchester, not Zululand—they'll bring industry and business with them. They'll never travel back to Manchester to the jobs there. There's another thing, we'll have better schools—we have no real Secondary Modern as such now. It'll get people out of a rut."

Will there be a Keaw Yed in 1980? In some form: yes. What is significant is the power of most things to survive, amidst vast material change, as touching the human spirit. When they don't, man may be in peril more mortal than most know?

Beyond: the Human Spirit

On observer's left is a tiny woman, only four foot six, with a hunchback . . . on his right a working-class woman of 45 with hands lined with grime. In front is a woman in a red velvet suit with henna'ed hair, scalp showing some of the dye.

The sort of Lancashire people indicated above may seem to have little in common with the mighty Odysseus, portrayed by Homer, as he cut the throats of rams over a trench. "And the dark blood flowed forth, and lo, the Spirits of the Dead gathered out of Erebus." Nevertheless, the purpose for which these women, and fourteen others of similar working-class background had gathered together in a small dusty hall (devoid of paraphernalia or ritual objects) on a winter evening in 1937 was no different from that which brought Odysseus, 3,000 years ago, "to the limits of the world, shrouded in mist and cloud, where never the sun's rays shine." The purpose of both was the establishing of communication with the dead, who, it is assumed (in smoky Worktown's Spiritualist Centre just as in Homer's greener Greece) will be in a position to give consolation, advice, and information about the future. In Worktown this can be done in a kind of vacuum, by only a tiny minority, without much popular support.

Those women came in 1937. They still come, in similar small numbers, in 1960, to one of the two recognised spiritualist sects. The religious service which usually ushers in the mediumistic sessions is comparable, in general tone and atmosphere, with that conducted in any other Christian church (Chapter 4). Hymns and prayers addressed reverently to a God in all essentials identical with the Christian God, and then a sermon, or some sort of address, in which all Christian ethical standards are endorsed:

"Only through the Fatherhood of God and the brotherhood of man can we earn the eternal progression of every human soul...."

concludes the Spiritualist address heard one evening in July 1960.

Only *after* this comes the specifically *Spiritualist* business. Believers with the aid of a medium seek contact with dead friends and relations. Seven men and twelve women, most over 40, are present on this 1960 occasion. The medium, Mrs. W., begins her demonstration:

" 'If I come to you,' she says, 'Give me the vibration of your voice. Sound and vibrations all work in the spirit world. I work under a spirit who has been blinded and tortured, and your voice helps him to come into contact. Madam! [to one in the congregation] I have been watching various spirit lights forming round your neck. Do you see spirit lights ever?'

" 'Yes, I do,' replies the woman.

" 'They are turning into flowers,' continues Mrs. W. 'Little Dorothy Perkins roses, which are so popular now. . . . Brought by an elderly gentleman, very fond of gardening. . . . Now they are turning into a Christmas crib with a beautiful little boy in it who has been quite a time in the spirit world. . . .' "

The woman addressed recognises this description. She nods eager assent, and the medium goes on, with frequent halts and pauses:

" 'So beautiful, one can understand why he was taken . . . There are conditions round your child, called Florrie? . . . Florence?'

" 'Yes, that's right,' says the woman.

" 'Not till Christmas will the conditions be ready. Take care. . . . Watch your vitality.' "

After this advice, Mrs. W. snaps her fingers, in sudden inspiration; shouts:

" 'Arnold! Listen, Arnold!'

The husband of the previous woman claims knowledge of an Arnold; the medium continues:

" 'He says look after your back. When you come home, cross, tired, take a warm bath, a massage—excuse me being *familiar*, it is Aunt Mary calling you.' "

The medium pauses, looks along the rows, finds new inspiration in an old woman with a red beret:

" 'You with the red beret! I want to come to you with an old Methodist hymn' (hums it).

" 'Yes!' exclaims the old woman.

" 'You know who sang that, in her little cracked voice?' ('Yes.'). 'Her spirit was sitting between you and the gentleman, and when I talked of personal responsibility (in the address) she was very shocked—she believes she was washed in the blood of the Lamb. She passed into the Spirit with cancer?' ('Yes.') 'Is there someone in the flesh with that condition?' ('Yes.') There is an anniversary around October 21st or 25th—watch cancer conditions then.' "

So definite—and indeed alarming—a piece of advice was exceptional. Mrs. W. now comes to a quiet middle-aged woman, sitting by herself.

" 'Are you fond of babies?' ('Yes.') 'I see masses round you. Do you know you travel in the spirit world at night?' ('Well I do dream.') 'No, you don't dream, you *travel*. In the sleep state you go to the home of little unwanted babies who have died before they were born, who've been got rid of, and you come back refreshed. It helps you in two material conditions.' ('Yes.') 'As we give to spirits, spirits give to us. When you go into the Spirit that will be your job, looking after the little babies. You say: "Jesus wants me for a sunbeam", don't you? Well, don't be afraid of being a *great sunbeam*. We need them.' "

Part D

OPINIONS AND PROJECTS, NATION-WIDE

The new and almost universal style of tombstone in Worktown cemeteries: in addition brilliantly green-dyed "marble" chips made of glass are strewn on the surface in place of grass or flowers (see page 45)

> I burn their horns to give me light,
> I burn their dung to keep me warm,
> and if the slaughter last all night,
> by dawn they shall be fossils calm.
>
> — Kathleen Raine, "Cattle Dream"

FOURTEEN

ROYAL OCCASIONS

"The Queen and Prince Philip had a no-fuss night out at the theatre last night—just two in the crowd.

"They arrived by taxi at the Haymarket Theatre to see 'Ross' a play about Lawrence of Arabia. They were ten minutes early. They walked in unnoticed and sat down in the wrong seats. . . ." *Daily Express*: 13 July 1960.

"I had a sudden feeling, craning at my glimpse of the bare-headed Queen at her anointing, sitting motionless with lowered eyes under her gold canopy, a sensation that was like something spoken aloud: 'There is a secret here'. It came again at the crowning . . . what that secret was, I could not say. No doubt it was the primitive and magical feeling which ancient and beautiful ceremonials still evoke, no matter in how rational a breast." The Queen is crowned—Margaret Lane—*New Statesman*. 6 May 1953.

"My son made the Crown, the Orb and the Sceptre and displayed it. He fashioned it out of stiff cardboard and the jewels—he made out of Rowntrees Clear Gums!" (Male Nurse: 57.)

"What's the use of royalty? They don't do anything." (Factory Worker: 26.)

THE ROLES APPARENTLY assigned to the monarchy in mid-twentieth century Britain are two—intelligent non-interference in government, and active, benevolent interest in most other aspects of the nation's life. In most published comments on royalty, emphasis is now in the high sense of duty displayed by royal people and upon their "human" democratic behaviour. As if, in a welfare state, a concept of the welfare monarch is called for—the ruler whose claim to allegiance is his proved utility.

From time to time, this particular façade cracks. The Press strikes a different note and a picture of the traditional monarch emerges, a dedicated and splendid personage who, it is implied, is perhaps not quite so human after all. This happens on the big royal occasions, most noticeably at Coronations but also at royal weddings, births, funerals and lyings-in-state. Then many British people begin to talk or act much as if their monarch was no less important to them than any primitive king to his tribe; as if he were the victor not the vanquished in the historical battle for democratic power-control.

A crisis in kingship, the abdication of Edward VIII, helped bring

Mass-Observation into being. This event brought into the open fears and beliefs which would ordinarily be hidden. On the face of it, a constitutional question whose issue, however settled, would have a negligible influence on people's every day lives, it high-lighted kingship's symbolic values (the king as leader and guardian of public morals). The matter was complicated by the fact that Edward VIII had gained the reputation of people's champion against poverty and officialdom; *potentially*, he was the first "Welfare King". Thus, there was a double loss to face—of traditional and new-style leader at once. We wrote about this in 1937:

"THE KING WANTS TO MARRY MRS. SIMPSON: CABINET ADVISES 'NO'

"Confronted with these headlines, a nation of fifty millions gasped in astonishment. Institutions which had been accepted as part of the course of nature were now thrown open to question. The fixation to the symbolism of monarch, so abundantly displayed at the Jubilee of King George V, and again at his death, was now shocked into awareness of itself. Millions of people who passed their lives as the obedient automaton of a system now felt they had to make a personal choice—in favour of the hereditary monarch or in favour of their elected representatives."

It was the traumatic behaviour of British people, the cross-cutting of feeling through age, class, occupation, and the silence of the Press till the crisis came, that helped the founders of Mass-Observation decide that their first major study of the "anthropology of ourselves" should deal with behaviour towards royalty. The result was the publication of *May 12th, 1937* (Faber & Faber), an account of the preparations and events leading up to the Coronation of the new monarch George VI and of Coronation Day behaviour. Since then, M-O has made regular studies of royal occasions and of attitudes to royalty.

'*I was there*'

"Have I seen royalty? No. You see I work in the pits" (South Wales miner).

"By accident, George V passed by when I was doing the door knob and he waved." (Old Age Pensioner).

"I could have put my hand in old George's. He came to Cammell Laird's in 1914" (Corporation Labourer).

"Princess Elizabeth came to the flats and I stood very near her" (Working-class housewife).

"The Duke of Gloucester rode on my tank in the war" (Newsagent).

"I saw the Queen and the Duke of Edinburgh going to the Cup Final. My bus stopped just close to their car" (Bus Driver).

At some point in their lifetime, three in four Britishers have seen at least one member of the royal family; and of the rest, all but a negligible number say they would like to do so. Most often, it is the Queen whom they want to see, although when the question was last asked, Princess Margaret and the Duke of Edinburgh were both fairly high up on the list.

To have been near enough to *touch* royalty, or in a better position than others to *see* them is a source of particular pride. Especially if this is on one of the important royal occasions:

Child: "Is that it?"
Father: "Yes! Quick! Wave your flag!"
Child: "Oh, I can't see a proper coach."
Father: (excitedly) "Now you can see. You can see the top of the coach. Wave your flag Maureen. Wave it high! Yes. She's inside it, she's *in* the coach. There it is, the top of the golden coach. There, you've seen the gold coach, Maureen."
Mother: "You *saw* the gold coach, Maureen, didn't you. Now, if anyone asks you, you *saw* it. Don't forget!"

Belief in the Divine Right of Kings is still far from remote in twentieth century living. And issues which according to the text-books should now be academic only, e.g. the royal prerogative in government, are not settled in people's minds. The survey results quoted are from an M-O survey carried out three years after the last Coronation— i.e. when the fervour of royal occasion feeling had had a chance to recede.

92% agree with the statement that a country with a King or Queen is less likely to go to *extremes in politics*.
65% that the Queen is expected to *work too hard*.
57% that the Royal Family does not have enough *privacy*.
38% (women rather than men but 30 in every 100 men nevertheless) that the Queen should be able to change what Parliament decides *if she disagrees with it*.
36% that the Royal Family costs too much *money*.
34% (women more than men but nevertheless 28 men in every 100) that the Queen is someone especially *chosen by God*.
10% that it would be better to have a *republic* rather than a monarch.

Again, in 1960, a rather different question was asked with results identical with 1956: *only* 10% said that if they had to vote tomorrow whether England should be a monarchy or a republic with an elected president, they would vote for a republic.

Eight Occasions

In the last twenty-five years, Britishers in large numbers have participated in these eight major Royal Occasions:

1. The Abdication of King Edward VIII.
2. The Coronation of King George VI.
3. The Wedding of Princess Elizabeth.
4. The funeral of King George VI.
5. The funeral of Queen Mary.
6. The Coronation of Queen Elizabeth II.
7. The birth of a royal heir.
8. The Wedding of Princess Margaret.

All these events were centred in London; but participation in the wider sense is nation-wide and often survives long after.

In 1957, three people in five *throughout the country were still keeping souvenirs from the 1953 Coronation*; and three in ten claimed to have a picture of a royal person in their house. Half the pictures were of the Queen in her Coronation gown or wedding dress, a quarter of Elizabeth and Philip together. In 1960, a repeat question showed over two in ten still owning pictures of royal people.

On the 1937 Coronation we wrote (at the time):

"Each person meets in his daily life a large number of people. Some he meets every or most days; his family, people living in the same house, tradesmen, people working in the same shop, office, factory . . . all these we shall call people in *area 1*. In *area 2* are strangers and people met for the first time. In *area 3* all people like prime ministers, film stars, celebrities, historical and mythical figures, collections of people like the Church, the Conservative Party, etc. These are not normally met in the flesh but their actions, faces, words, etc., may be just as well known to you as those of your best friend, and have just as great an influence on you."

The Monarch is the archetype on *area 3* personages; and, at the time of Coronation, he must show himself in fullest majesty. Now he seems in fact what he is in theory, the all-powerful ruler with an unquestioned place at the centre of our social system. The nearer the event, the more the mounting excitement makes converts out of possible critics. Pre-Coronation surveys in 1953 show that criticism of the cost, although never very marked, was less widespread *one* and *three* months beforehand than six months previously.

Persistent Pattern

With the aid of our 1937 and 1953 Coronation records, it would not be very difficult to predict ahead likely patterns of behaviour and feeling on big royal occasions. Both Coronations (as well as lesser royal events) show a distinct tendency towards repeat patterns, equally in official and unofficial behaviour. In official organisational planning this might be expected, although plans for 1953 were on a more splendid scale than for 1937. But many of the controversial issues of 1937 were raised and battled over again in 1953: Do Coronations cost too much? Are things over-commercialised? Are official seats fairly distributed? Should working people have more official representation? Are decorations good or bad? What Coronation souvenirs should be given by local councils? Whom should they benefit? Is the religious significance of the ceremony appreciated? Or are people just out to enjoy themselves? Easily interchangeable in spirit, if not incident for incident, these:

Coronation Spending
1937: "We are going to burn £200 in a fire on the Links. In a few moments it goes up in smoke. Do we expect the disabled and unemployed to throw up their caps in jubilation?" Letter to a Scottish newspaper—5 March 1937.
1953: "The eagerness with which the Government produces money for the Coronation contrasts most strikingly with the cheese-paring policy towards education and welfare." *News Chronicle*—21 May 1953.

Ox Roasting
1937: "Since the Committee [Souvenir and Entertainments Committee] last met, he [Councillor Reeve] had spoken to many who objected to the idea of roasting. They did not object because it was a pagan custom, but because they do not favour such a celebration." Extract from *May 12 1937* by Mass-Observation.
1953: "May I . . . appeal to all vegetarians, humanitarians and progressive thinkers . . . to make a strong last minute protest and every possible effort against it (open ox-roasting)? This mentally degrading exhibition of English paganism can—and should—be easily dispensed with." Letter to a daily newspaper, 27 May 1953.

Desecration of the Flag?
1937: "As an Englishman I was disgusted to see displayed in the shop window . . . a Union Jack in the form of a rug and I would like to appeal to those who have fought for our flag in the past and to those who may fight for it in the future, to remonstrate against this desecration of our national emblem. . . ." Letter to a newspaper—28 April 1937.
1953: "A stormy argument broke out in the *Manchester Guardian* yesterday over the publication of a post-Coronation cartoon by David Low, entitled 'Morning After'. The cartoon showed grim-faced 'Reality' gazing out of a TV set at the debris of a children's party, labelled '£100,000,000 spree'.

Toy soldiers, a drum, a triumphal arch, flags and bunting lay in an untidy heap with books called 'Fairy Princess Tales' and 'Snow White'.

"One reader complained that Low had put the Union Jack 'In the most insulting possible position on the human frame—that of a romper." *Daily Worker*—6 June 1953.

Planning: official and unofficial levels

All through the Coronation activity, one finds a dual level of planning: the official, and the shadow effect unofficial. Thus, a local council plans its programme of celebrations, and, at the same time, unofficial street party committees will be planning their own *extra* programmes. Or the Council plans to decorate parts of the town or village, while at the same time individual shops, streets and people still go ahead on their own. Official plans usually show a bias to "worthwhile causes"; and there may be friction over how to spend the money. Shall there be permanent memorials of the Coronation? Or is it best to "blue" most of the cash on one big celebration? In a smaller way, the street party committees face the same problem: how much on souvenirs for children, how much on beer for adults? For example:

"1. *Conversation with Clerk to the Council*: 'We started *last* July because we wanted to put up a good show. We've met every month and we've allocated £6,000 out of the local rates. We reckon to spend about £1,000 on the actual decorations and floodlighting, £400 towards the old folks free television show, £150 towards a display of sculptures and a printing bill for 5,000 brochures. Another £100 towards the cost of a garden party—various local notabilities, by invitation only. Then there are floral decorations at points along the route for the royal drive through London. Next? Floodlighting the War Memorial, something for the fireworks display, contributions to the vegetable, flower and bird show prize money, a local art exhibition, and a swimming gala, 1,000 Coronation Souvenir beakers, £1,000 rose garden as a perpetual memorial, and an aviary for about £150.

"In deciding what to support we judged things on their social value to the community, even their moral usefulness. We didn't want just to support tea parties for spivs, if you understand me."

"2. *Conversation with a County Councillor*: 'The Coronation Committee got going in February at a public meeting. At this meeting they decided to get Coronation seats, as well as to have a bonfire and fireworks, and this decision has been held to, unfortunately. As we are trying to build an annex to the village hall I and some of the others were keen that the money should go towards this. I suggested they might pay for the library room and put up a plaque. But they decided on seats which are being made locally and painted green, quite nice and will be used but don't make as much difference to the community as a village hall.

"'At one meeting there was discussion about gifts for old people (tea caddies and a pound of tea) and invalids. . . . The County Council will give mugs to primary school and pencils to secondary school children. . . . I asked to see the mugs to know if we had a good design. Was told we are getting them wholesale. Believe they are awful.'"

In the London borough whose official plans have just been described, between £10,000 and £15,000 was the estimated figure for "unofficial" group celebrations. Round about £100 was collected in each individual street; a street organiser described how:

"There's no committee working with me. When I see some of the people in the road they come up to me and say: 'Mrs. Brown, I really feel ashamed to look at you—we've let you down so, but you know we rely on you. You're doing a grand job'. There's only my son Billy and my niece Maureen, they go down the road every week no matter what sort of weather. We started last September. Every Sunday Maureen and Billy go round with raffle tickets. I buy something to raffle, say 10s. worth of groceries, or half a tea-set, or a basket of fruit maybe and I deduct whatever the cost of the prize from the money collected. Up to date we've collected £75. 3. 9 that was up to last Sunday."

Street Parties

Street parties, organised by residents, often preceded by months of planning, were a characteristic feature of the 1937, even more of the 1953 Coronation. The streets became, for once, close neighbourhood units, appointing a chairman, secretary, treasurer, etc. A day of entertainment would be planned, always with a children's party, usually with celebrations of some kind for adults. The groups were very much "in-groups", people from other roads rarely qualifying to join.

To some extent the street parties became an issue; were they parties for parties' sake, or a spontaneous demonstration of good will? A local paper put the case:

"The Earl Marshal had problems to solve and difficulties to overcome. But he had the help and finance and manpower of the great service of the State. The street party organisers have had to start from scratch in money, material and people. . . . They cannot refer to precedents and where the Earl Marshal gave orders they can only make requests. They have achieved success and will go on doing it until the last Coronation party has been held, because in every street and every house the aim is the same—to give the children so good a time that they will remember the crowning of Elizabeth even *without* the help of the radio, television and the cinema. The cynical may say that the Coronation is merely being used as an excuse for a party. But there is much more to it than that. The Coronation has deeply touched the emotions of the people. Deep emotion must find some means of expression and as there is no kind of affection more pure and disinterested than that of parents for their children and of a great many adults for all *children*, what simple or more direct means could be found than giving a party?" Editorial—*Willesden Chronicle*—12 June 1953.

At the children's parties, there was nearly always a Queen to be crowned: the local group substitute for the monarch. Some parties went quite a long way towards copying the finer points of the Coronation ceremony, handing over a home-made orb or sword or sceptre, or using a special form of words. The street group movement represented a determined effort not to be left out, a distinctly practical essay in *sympathetic magic*.

"Dressing Up" 1953

"We shall not be sorry to see the end of decorated London—this litter of strung bits, bearable only as the days mount to *the* moment, intolerable hereafter. Tom-toms cannot din louder than the pelmets so unrhythmically hung in some of our streets. Age-old pianos cannot jangle so preposterously as pale blue and pale-pink festoons lolloping round antique lamp-posts swathed in brown spirals." John Summerson: *The New Statesman*.

"Isn't it lovely . . . look, there's the Lion and the Unicorn up there."

"It's like a fairy tale."

"It's wonderful. Makes you feel proud of London."

"It's marvellous. It's a tonic."

"Better to spend it on this than guns."

"Why don't they have flags instead of roses, daddy?"

"They caged Eros in. That golden cage looks lovely."

"They don't care so much up West. They don't do it themselves. It's done for them."
Miscellaneous overheards.

A characteristic feature of all Coronations is dressing up: of people, shops and houses, sometimes of whole streets or areas in a town. The movement is part official, part unofficial, a method of mass-identification which is also a form of mass-pressure. A minority withstand the pressure to the end, but on the day itself most people and—especially in working-class streets—most houses, have made some attempt to "join in".[1]

---

[1] For the three months preceding the 1953 Coronation observers checked consistently on the increase in decoration on selected streets in two working-class and two mainly middle-class London boroughs, checking on the rate at which house or street decorations appeared. Other observers reported on streets outside London and on village decoration. Similar checks were made on shop window contents—i.e. the proportion and types of articles showing some sort of Coronation influence.

The pre-Coronation "dressing up", while generally acceptable, is too much for *some* people's taste; for in the last few months before the day, there is hardly an article sold commercially or an advertisement which does not in some way cash in on the Coronation. This has an effect presumably other than intended when it leads people to say that "I've nothing against the Queen. I'm just absolutely *sick* of seeing her face on everything from tinned peas upwards"; or "Them moogs. I'm fair sick o' the sight of them. An' who wants moogs any road?"

The 1953 Coronation was different from the 1937 Coronation in one respect—contemporary design and unity of design was more evident in officially planned decoration. On both occasions, unofficial decoration mostly kept to the traditional, i.e. the more the red, white and blue and the brighter the colour, the better it was received. In 1953, official design had some impact, nevertheless—for The Mall was much admired and many miniature Malls appeared with home-made triumphal arches, bells or balls attached, framing the entrances to small working-class streets. . . .

A Miniature Mall

"There are 42 houses in the Walk, which, incidentally is on the 'condemned' list of the local Housing Committee but because of the shortage of accommodation in the Borough and the difficulty of finding residents alternative accommodation, continue to remain liveable. Most residents are working class and most jobs labouring jobs—e.g. coalmen, dustmen, and building trade labourers. . . .

"Down the entire length of the Walk there are rows and rows of bunting, white paper garlands, and lines of small Union Jacks are strung across from top windows on one side of the road to the windows opposite. *Every house* has pictures of the Queen, Duke of Edinburgh, Prince Charles, and Princess Anne pasted in the parlour window and the two small top bedroom windows. Over the doorways are fixed crowns, gold and silver, large and small, posters with the wording 'God Save Our Queen' or 'Long Live Our Queen', with the initials E.R.II. The outer walls of the front parlours are completely hidden with Union Jacks, more gold and silver crowns or coats-of-arms.

"At night, the Walk is floodlit—men have extended electric wiring into the street. Each house has also planned to wash down their part of the passageway so that the entire road is clean.

"At the end of the Walk, three wooden arches have been erected; decorated baskets of pink roses hang from them. On the centre arch is a picture of the Queen and a gold crown, red, white and blue paper flowers twine round the posts and a large 'ALL WELCOME' notice has been put up."

A local newsagent described the dwellers in the road as "mad for royalty".

Towards the Climax

> Woman 1. "Do you think you'll see anything."
> Woman 2. "I think I'll see a little *something*."

Just as in everything that leads up to Coronations there are repeat feelings and actions, so at the event itself there emerge broadly duplicating patterns of group and crowd behaviour. On the day and night before, for instance, "squatters" arrive and take possession of vacant pavement space on the processional route. It is *officially* recognised that they will do so, and plans will have been made. There will be food-stalls and lavatories.[1] The BBC will have arranged to relay music, news and the Service itself; the Police will have a network of communications covering the whole route, First Aid facilities will be ready,—and so on. The route will be lined with troops, who finally take their stand in front of seat-holders and squatters alike.

On the Sunday before Coronation and on Coronation Eve special services of vigil and prayer are held in many churches. A different sort of vigil takes place in the streets as people arrive on the processional route ready to spend a night in the open. These royal occasion squatters regularly behave in the same mildly unorthodox fashion, backchatting with police and newspaper sellers, going in for spasmodic community singing, brief bursts of dancing, derisive cheering of the unexpected. Ultimately a few square miles of central London resembles a cross between a public dormitory and a number of small, individual "homes"; and the determined domesticity of the scene is constantly noted by observers. Most people prepare very thoroughly, in fact, against the hazards of their brief incursion into public mass living; they bring food, flasks, rugs, rubber cushions, extra clothing and mackintoshes, first aid equipment—aspirin, glucose, brandy, eau-de-Cologne; some bring soap and towels, even nightwear, many bring "time killers" such as newspapers, books, radios, cameras, knitting, games or toys for the children. It is indeed rather as if everyone had come expecting the worst to happen.

Once established on their personal pavement, people start to make friends; a "family" atmosphere develops. Small groups of ten to a dozen people, who have perhaps come in pairs or families, become a unit—talking to each other, sharing food, laughing at each other's

---

[1] But never enough! Among the most frequent "overheards" at this time are of people asking one another where there is a lavatory. The question of how they (i.e. people in the Abbey, the Queen, etc.) "manage" is also a subject of frequent and anxious speculation.

jokes and, most important, guarding vacant places if people get up and walk about.

The Coronation crowd has come determined to *see*. This means staking a claim and then holding it; here group support is invaluable. Good-natured as the 1953 Coronation crowd was, any Coronation crowd is an edgy one—since it is often not clear till the very last whether one *will in fact be able to see anything or not*. Anger rises if others try to usurp claims, or if troops or police unexpectedly take their position in front of would-be spectators (as they often do).

Thus in 1953, just before the Queen was due:

"Suddenly the soldiers who have been lining the pavements for ten yards or so into Glasshouse Street marched out and formed up across the entrance to the street, forming a continuous line with those already in Regent Street. There is a big stir of resentment from the crowd. Three women call out immediately:

" 'Oh look. We can't see a blamed thing now.'

" 'Oh.'

" 'Oh, we spent the whole night. . . .'

" 'Oh, no!' "

"Others then start to call out, too:

" 'Oh look, the policeman's going to stand there as well.'

" 'Officer, we can't see a thing!'

" 'Oh, it's not fair!'

" 'Look. They've put the Air Force in front of that.'

" 'Oh, crikey!'

" 'Look. They've left a tiny space there.' "

"Someone calls out, raising his voice:

" 'Listen. Can't we come in the middle?' "

"Someone pleads to the soldiers:

" 'Look. Can't you join on *that* end?' "

"A little later a mounted policeman rides down towards Regent Street. The crowd thinks this is something else to block their views. There are cries and shrieks of horror:

" 'OH, NO!' "

"Then he turns and rides back again up Glasshouse Street. The horse neighs and someone calls:

" 'See. Even that horse is neighing in horror!' "

While they wait for the event, some try to tease or feed the soldiers. As we pointed out in our 1937 Coronation Survey, the troops get treated rather like pets or mascots.

"*Conversation in 1937*

" 'Did you see us throwing sweets out of the window? We were feeding the troops—just feeding the troops.'

" 'I loved it when they ate the oranges.'

" 'I wouldn't throw them at the horses though. It's hard. It comes down with a force.' "

"*Observation in 1953*

"Some people from one window two stories up in Piccadilly threw toffees down to the soldiers.

"A young girl suddenly ran along the front of the crowd towards a group of Air Force Cadets. She thrust a cake at one of them. He was embarrassed but apparently pleased. He started to eat it, looking round at the rest for approval."

Laughter gathers, too. The first seat holders run a gauntlet which may be embarrassing. In St. James's Street in 1953:

"They more or less all wore a uniform, men in grey, a lot of the women in duster coats with a contrasting dress and little half hats usually made of flowers and tulle—a lot of grey and white. Among these seat holders were a lot of preparatory school children, girls in grey fitting coats and white gloves, boys in navy blazers or grey suits. . . . *Everybody was now standing up and gazing at these seat holders.*"

It is not only seat-holders who wear "a kind of uniform"; the overnight squatters tend to look much alike in their "dress down" rather than "dress up" uniform.

Waiting for the Great Moment

Events most likely to arouse crowd feeling are those which somehow indicate or resemble what is expected. A frequent activity is to cheer anyone or anything coming along the route before the procession itself is due. Cheers echo down the line, turn into laughter or mock cheers if dustcarts, watercarts, police or BBC vans go past; cheers increase when the connection with the central event is clearer. Early on the day these semblances of reality are welcomed enthusiastically. Patience recedes as the event itself comes nearer. Up to Coronation night at least, the crowd is a well behaved one, but the growing demand is that things shall *now* start happening. Pass-the-time activities become more preparatory: learning how to work periscopes, "playing games" with the police, i.e. do what you are told to do, then, when the police turn away do what you were doing before. There is a kind of "royalty substitute" behaviour; admiring or joking with people who appear on balconies on the route; and there is continued cheering and laughter over BBC relays of weather news or news about the crowd itself.

"*An Observation at Marble Arch—1953:*
7.15 a.m.
Victor Sylvester music announced. Claps. More rain. *Daily Express* seller passes, dressed in blue and white. Stands out clearly from all other paper sellers. Man selling sandwiches passes, one selling Coca-Cola (these dress in maroon), another selling home-made periscopes, small mirror fitted on a clothes peg wired to a stick. Charge 1s.

Two sandwich men pass. Their placards say 'The Wages of Sin is Death' and 'Jesus Christ is everlasting life'. Small group of young middle-class men watch. One says 'This is all rather embarrassing. I mean what are we supposed to do?' They open a suitcase, take out cards and start on Pontoon. Everest news is given again. Two women comment:

F.60.D. 'Oo. Isn't that good!'
F.45.C. (Lancashire woman) 'What?'
F.60.D. 'The expedition's won. Wonderful, isn't it?'
F.45.C. (seems uninterested) 'What weather,' she says.
F.60.D. 'Not like we had for the Jubilee, was it. That was glorious. Daresay it will clear.'
F.45.C. takes out a bottle of milk which has a 'God Save the Queen' top on it.

8 a.m.
News again. The pips get cheered. Announcer says, 'This is the Coronation Day of Her Majesty, Queen Elizabeth'.

F.45.C. 'As if we didn't know!' But there are claps, cheers and some shushing. The announcer talks about those sleeping out. 'At times,' he says, 'the temperature dropped to 44 degrees'. A little laughter and more when he talks about people dressed in newspaper and blankets who were sleeping soundly....

The radio announces community singing—a number join in with 'Two Lovely Black Eyes', 'You know what Sailors are' and 'Nellie Dean'. Sun comes out and is greeted with uproar. One man pretends to salute the sun. From the radio comes, 'It ain't going to rain no mo' no mo'. Much laughter.

"*Observation in the Mall:*
7.30 a.m.
Something goes by. Cheers. People rush forward. Periscopes go up. Observer counts 100 periscopes easily. Two old fashioned coaches go by driven by footmen in yellow livery. More and more cheers right down the route.

Loudspeaker commentator reads patriotic poem but not much sign that anyone listens. Periscopes are all at the ready. Someone says: 'There's another coach coming'. People crane to see. Overheards: 'She didn't half look nice. All in white with fur on her neck'. 'Did you manage to see it in the periscope?'

7.50 a.m.
Cheering in the distance comes nearer, passes away as a lorry load of troops

goes down the route. More distant cheers and a band. Lots of people stand with their backs to the direction in which things are coming from, trying out periscopes."

High Point . . .

The excitement continues, develops along the same lines. The climax draws nearer:

"*The Service begins.* . . . Of some 50 people near observer, 4 are following the loudspeakers with copies of the programme. Looks as if more on the stands are following. Most heads bent down. A noticeable silence. Music ceases and the relayed voice says the Queen is now seated in her chair. A little more talking but not much. Cries of 'Paper' in the background more noticeable than formerly. People continue to listen, or at least they do nothing which suggests they are not.

Commentator says the Archbishop is presenting the Queen four times to her people. The voice of the Archbishop: 'Sirs, I present unto you Queen Elizabeth, your undoubted Queen. . . .' Cries of 'God Save the Queen' from the Abbey and our group. 'Good old Charlie' cries a boy—'Is she Queen now?' he says. No one answers.

Now there seem to be even fewer people walking about, more concentrated listening. The Queen's voice says 'I will'. There is practically no noise at all. 'All this I promise to do', she says. There is a little murmur from the crowd and silence again. Observer is conscious of annoyance at the continued cries of newspaper men. The Queen goes to the altar. Still silence, perhaps little embarrassed. A man lights a cigarette, puts it out again. The Queen takes the oath and there is anything up to a minute's complete silence. M. 14. D. calls out impatiently: 'Is she Queen yet?' No one answers him. Then the Communion Service. Music begins, some talking starts . . . the Creed is not followed with any attention. The Anointing . . . silence from the Commentator but no corresponding silence from the crowd. Some talk starts:

M.22.B.—'I expect the crowd will go crazy. I know I shall'.

M.25.B.—'The pubs shut at eleven tonight'.

M.22.B.—'Must get some hooch. (Raises his bottle of whisky "Here's to Everest"'. F. 25. C. watches fascinated as he drains the bottle. Another young man drinks . . . 'Just what the doctor ordered' says F.25.C. 'She kneels before the altar' says the Commentator. M.22.B. says 'shush' and the people round him are surprised and do so. Renewed attention does not last long. . . . 'The Queen is in Cloth of Gold' says the Commentator, 'She is bareheaded, she goes towards the altar . . .' 'She looks at Prince Charles'. This remark is received with pleasure by the women of the group. 'He's there, then!' Suddenly, extremely heavy rain and heavy guns. Everyone jumps or squeaks. 'Some one's dropped an atom bomb', says F. 60. D.

This is the moment of crowning. No one gets up and the effect of the guns is to make people laugh with sudden shock. Then everyone starts to push forward. Observer finds herself two ranks nearer the front, and separated from the people she had been with. The Service continues. There is always more noise now than formerly . . . a Park van goes down the route and is cheered. Then comes 'Our Father . . .' a few mouths move silently. 'God Save the Queen' is played very loudly. The Service is at an end. Several move . . . no sound. Then an older man and woman start singing strongly and soon more or less everyone sings. *There is another press forward*, as if there is a feeling that any minute the Queen *must come*. It is still a long time to 3.30."

"*In Piccadilly Circus, another observer reports:*
12.35 p.m.
Sound of muffled guns. People in a doorway call out quietly 'The guns! The guns! No general reaction or movement from the crowd. Eros steps covered with people partly covered with umbrellas and newspapers. A very silent crowd. Faint sound of a radio coming from a building . . . people here not the 'have been up all night' type. Better dressed . . . (Overheard): 'Shall we go home now? We can come back later if . . .' Some sort of police changing of the guard is going on . . . the sound of military type commands can be heard . . . the crowd had umbrellas up, newspapers over heads, macs wrapped entirely round stooping figures or held over heads. It is *very* silent. There might almost be an Armistice Service going on. . . ."

"*Over at Hyde Park Corner* the procession is coming into view:
2 p.m.
A group near observer gets furious with a man who gets on a stool to take a photo and blocks their view. They call out 'Be fair'. 'That's not allowed'. 'Get down—let others see', 'Be a good job if somebody stepped on that camera'. The man gets down, but during the next thirty minutes or so gets up several times. Once he is prodded by a stick, and someone else tries to kick away the stool.

Troops continue to pass and all are cheered. 'Hear, hear'. Perhaps there is a feeling that everyone should be welcomed on this occasion whatever one's private feelings about them. Bands follow . . . the Carriage procession begins . . . tremendous interest in the Queen of Tonga who sits in an open carriage with the rain pouring on her . . . the Prime Ministers pass but only Nehru and Churchill are pointed out. It is really Churchill, they are waiting for . . . cries of 'There he is, there he is' go down the line.

Next the royal carriages. There is mounting excitement. Someone says, 'She's nearly here now'. 'There are the Kents. They've all got their coronets on'. The biggest cheers yet for the Queen Mother and Princess Margaret.

M.8.C. sitting on his father's shoulders cries out, 'She'll be here soon now'. The crowd quietly manœuvres for position. People stand on tiptoe and become almost silent. Finally, comes the State Coach drawn by eight greys. M.8.C. calls out wildly, 'Mummy, Daddy, the Queen, the Queen!' and the crowd cheers with a tremendous roar, jumping up and down trying to see more, pressing forward and forward. These cheers are at least six times as loud as any before—people's mouths look as if they are stuck wide open with the cheering. But the most anyone can see is a brief glimpse of a pale figure in a shining white dress, smiling and waving her hand. . . ."

"*Overheard on the way to Hyde Park Gate:*
F.16.B. 'Princess Margaret looked perfectly sweet. And the Queen was lovely . . . lovely. . . .'
F.20.B. 'The Queen Mother looked absolutely sweet."
M.18.D. 'Did you see old Louis? I was surprised to see him riding.'
M.20.D. 'Oh, Louis' one of the boys.'
F.35.B. 'The first thing I want is a hot bath.'
F.64.B. 'Well, it was worth it. Every minute of it.'
F.45.C. 'If we hurry, we can see them on the balcony on television.' "

The walk down towards the Gate is through a sea of damp, clotted paper, drenched, untidy people, periscopes trampled in muck, paper cups all over the place, bits of broken stool strewn on the grass. . . .

Coronation Night: "Doing an Eros"
"Our civilisation has turned people into eager nomads, the crowd into immensely respectable members of a summer school or youth hostel. The old Victorian mob seems to have vanished in London—you could never have been frightened by this crowd."

Thus "Critic" of the *New Statesman,* on the Coronation crowds. The traditional tough, rough-tongued crowd is not much in evidence these days. But there were few signs of normal "summer school" respectability about the Piccadilly Circus night crowd. And until rain started at 3.30 a.m. there were several occasions on which the crowd nearly became a "mob":

"M.35.D. is sitting astride the top of the Coventry Street side traffic lights. He is dressed in grubby worsted trousers rolled up above the knees, short socks, black shoes and a dirty open shirt. He smiles and waves at the crowd, behaves as if on a stage, with wide sweeps of the arms and a nodding of the head as the crowd cheer. He stands on one leg the other outstretched, posing for about 5 or 6 seconds as Eros. The crowd yells approval. Somebody throws up a half full quart bottle of beer. He catches it in one hand and drinks and someone else throws a piece of orange peel which hits the side of his head—he takes a mouthful of beer, holds it in his mouth and squirts the contents where the orange peel thrower stood—the beer hits several people all of whom push backwards and some shout out. Others further away in the crowd laugh and clap. Someone in the crowd hands up a half pint bottle of beer. He drinks this at the same time as the other bottle thus having the necks of two bottles in his mouth at once. While drinking he stands on one leg and kneels on the other, with one hand holding the bottles.

"M.30.C. next to investigator says 'Trying to do an Eros' . . .

M.25.D. a sailor, climbs another traffic light at the Piccadilly end of Shaftesbury Avenue. A very loud shout of approval from the crowd. The F.30.D. assisted by several helpers climbs sailor's traffic light. He helps her up and they clasp and kiss. A terrific (loudest yet) roar of approval. The couple stop, laugh, wave hands and continue kissing. After ten minutes the girl slides down the post amid cheers and the sailor shouts, 'Next one, please'."

"Things continue wildly round Eros: M.36.D. the first climber, again poses as Eros, this time as with wings. A barrage of things are thrown up, some miss, others he catches and throws back, others hit the shop fronts behind him, at least one other breaking some of the neon lighting which breaks on to people below. M.30.D. climbs the light beneath M.36.D. and half sits with him. They put their arms around each other and sway cheek to cheek. The crowd laughs and roars. On the other traffic light a policeman snatches at the sailor's feet, telling him to come down. The crowd at this first intervention by the policeman roars and surges forward. The policeman stands down and talks, telling the sailor to come down. The sailor seems embarrassed and after a while does come down and the policeman goes back. Immediately an M.24.D. scrambles up the traffic light amid loud prolonged laughter from the crowd. Two sailors try to climb the light but are pushed down by M.36.D. who lunges with his feet. The sailors catch the bottom of his trousers and pull. The trousers are torn, the shirt is ripped right off his back. Now M.36.C. is being dragged down and his trousers are in tatters. His torn underpants are visible and people jump up and down to see what is happening. Now he is on the ground surrounded, pushed about from person to person. Women giggle and scream. . . ."

But now the mood begins to change and toughen:

"A group of young males, seemingly led by M.26.D. who is wearing a long loose-fitting suit and has heavily greased hair, is seen. A car comes up behind them driven by M.36.B. with F.35.B. beside him. M.36.B. blows short impatient blasts at the piled crowd in front. People shout out, 'Quiet', 'Shut up' and someone taps on the glass of the car's front door, then someone taps the bonnet. M.26.D. stands in front of the car with arms outstretched barring its way, and then hits the car bonnet quite hard. Suddenly everybody around is hammering hard with their fists and blows are raining on the car from all directions. Someone starts to rock it from side to side. Others join in. At times it seems that it is only because people on one side stop it that it is not sent right over. Some men lift the car from the mudguard and bounce it. Some policemen in a group are looking at the scene and laughing, 'He's having a rough time' says one, 'He'll be all dents when he gets out the other side' says another. They make no attempt to interfere. Slowly the car edges forward, suddenly gathers speed and is away.

"This same group of young males is now outside Boots. M.26.D. stands in front of car after car with arms outstretched and legs apart until the cars stop, and if they do not (about a third seem to) they are bumped about and blows are rained on them and everything in fact except being actually overturned."

Finally, the lamp-post climbing gets faster and frenzied:

"A large group of people has gathered around M.36.D. (of an earlier lamppost) who is now perched on the top of another one. Someone throws him an old sack which has been ignited at one corner and is burning. He waves it. The crowd cheers. He puts the burning sack on his head so that the top burns brightly, holds it in various positions on and around his head, still burning. One large piece of orange hits him full on the face and M.36.D. immediately throws the lighted sack at the crowd. Many scream. The sack lands near a clear space and someone throws it back to M.36.D. who catches it and swirls it round and round his head making it burn brighter and brighter until it is a mass of long flames. He lets go and it lands amongst a group who scatter, shout and scream. Police push their way through to the still burning sack, and trample on it."

Now it is 3.15 a.m. of this June morning; still drizzling rain:

"At this corner of Lower Regent Street a lot of policemen are concentrated. They circle around, breaking up large groups of people and try to get people to go home. 'Come along now, there's nothing to stay for', 'Don't be a lot of sheep', 'Break it up', 'Time to go home now'. Very slowly people start to drift away. . . ."

The Television Coronation

The televising in 1953 of nearly all the Coronation Service and procession gave more people than ever before a chance to see and in a sense participate themselves, and for the first time *outside* London. This brought about a strong sense of "being there" and "belonging". An "oldest inhabitant" who had seen both Queen Victoria and Queen Elizabeth crowned wrote to us about the 1953 Coronation:

"People are fortunate now in being able to see and hear the actual Service. The Queen is brought nearer to us, which is different to the old days when we only read about these things. I remember Queen Victoria's Diamond and Golden Jubilee and once Queen Victoria's train broke down near our farm and she got out and sat on the bank. I am very interested in the new Queen because she passed very close to me at a big show in Swansea and I shall never forget her friendly smile . . . most likely this is the last Coronation I shall see (I am 92) but it was the finest I ever enjoyed. I say 'Long Life and Happiness to our young Queen.'"

Like many other pensioners this man could attend a free television show arranged by the local Council. And, in all, it was estimated that of the adult population 56% were viewing (more than half of them in public places or other people's houses) and 32% listening in on sound radio.[1] The "telly" was the focal point for innumerable parties. Local Councils arranged viewing for special groups, old people, invalids, etc., publicans put sets in the bar, some shops had sets going in the windows, seats on the route were sometimes advertised with "full catering and television facilities". Like the street parties, some of the television parties were planned weeks ahead with special food and drink and carefully chosen viewers. Sales of television sets soared. Television owners, then a minority, could invite or refuse invitations as they chose. Some TV parties cut right across class and "stranger" barriers; and family and neighbour feuds might be put aside in the interests of the "treat"....

One of the regular Day Diaries kept for Mass-Observation illuminates:

7.30 a.m.   All up and dressed slightly earlier than usual as children's daily washing has to be done early.

9.45   Everything packed on car. Cakes and other food made the previous evening ready to take over to wife's parents in Croydon twelve miles from here. They have television. Good deal of traffic on the road and many people walking (presumably most going along to others with TV sets). As 10.15 approaches, traffic thins and many cars parked by the roadside.

10.30   Arrive. A buffet lunch arranged in the dining-room, which is decorated for the occasion with the national colours, souvenir spoons and beakers for the children and a large iced cake. Two other visitors, sixty-year-old relatives, have motored up from Devon for the Coronation. Baby is put up to bed.

10.45   Christopher, the three-year-old, soon has enough of watching TV and is put in the garden. The five-year-old watches intently, without comment and everybody admires the picture, which is excellent. I see little of this as I am constantly running out to Christopher who is liable to be up to mischief.

11.45   Both children have now had enough, though all the adults have still to move from the set. I decide the best thing to do is to take the children in the car over to my parents, five miles away. Streets very empty on the ride over, occasional little groups of people staring at TV in shop windows.

[1] Estimates kindly provided by R. Silvey, Head of BBC Audience Research. He remarks that television audiences for the Coronation and for Princess Margaret's wedding in 1960 were of quite exceptional size.

12.00	My parents not listening on their radio *as expected*, but had been invited upstairs by their tenants in the flat above who have a TV. (Surprising this, as they had not been very friendly lately.) *We* did not go to the flat upstairs in our house, but apparently they too laid on a special meal for the occasion and provided drinks all round. We only stayed half an hour—my parents anxious to get back to the set.
12.30	Start back to Croydon. To fill in time, stopped to look in some shop windows. A group of people, watching TV in shop window, made room for the children whom they presumed wanted to watch. This was the actual crowning ceremony, so I managed to see it after all.
1.30	Arrived back. Everyone still watching except mother-in-law who is boiling potatoes, and my wife who now had the baby on her lap. Saw the end of the Communion Service as other hands had now taken over the children. The ceremonial seemed to me, an irreligious man, to be magnificent.
2.00	Stand-up lunch. Set switched off and all agree on a first-class performance. Everyone moans about the weather. Father-in-law says that anyone who could get a look-in at a TV set and goes to see the actual procession, must be mad. I felt that the size of a TV screen prevents a lot of the splendour of the spectacle being on the grand scale which is necessary to fully appreciate it.
2.20	As television starts again everyone returns to their places. Christopher, fortunately, has gone off for his afternoon sleep and the baby plays on the floor outside. Erica, almost five, is prepared to watch the return journey and thinks the 'carts' are lovely.
5.10	I go into the dining-room for tea as the procession has returned to the Palace. My father-in-law stays watching with the relatives from Devon and Erica. I have had enough TV for today."

Royal Dukes and the Private Lives of Princes

In the last fifteen years, there have been two royal weddings, the wedding of the present Queen and of her sister, Princess Margaret.

The 1953 Coronation left a greatly renewed enthusiasm for royalty. It is not a primary function of the ceremony to have this effect; but it has happened that sovereigns who sit on the throne for very long periods tend to gain rather than lose thereby. Passage of time need not dim the crown gilt of Kingship. But there have been signs of a new disinterest and growing dissatisfaction with the whole system on an impersonal basis, triggered off by the Abdication of King Edward VIII and continuing, if mildly, in the forties. The present Duke of Windsor has maintained a special kind of minority devotion for over two decades—well expressed in a couple of 1953 overheards from the Portobello Road:

"1. 'There's only one King and we haven't got *Him* on the throne. I bet when he watched it on television he said "There but for the Grace of God" . . .' "
"2. 'I bought this (he shows flag with Edward VIII on it). I got it in 1937 and couldn't use it then, but I've brought it out at every Coronation since. *He* was the one!' "

From time to time, the Duke revives his "image" by some form of public appearance within Britain. This has the effect of reviving old reactions. In Summer, 1960, a series of articles appeared ("My Page") in the *Daily Express*; in one of these he remarks:

"In those days a loyal crowd would have been after me, footing hot on my heels. For photography, killing the private lives of Princes, had made me familiar to all. Today, few people recognise me as I stroll through the streets" (11 July 1960).

Reaction to this particular re-appearance (as followed up by M-O) shows many people comparing the Dukes of Windsor and Edinburgh —along the lines:

—both dislike red tape,
—both are out for the general good,
—both are genuinely "democratic",

while remaining ducal.

Comparisons tend to be in Prince Philip's favour:

"He cuts across all the ballyhoo, too. But as a family man *he* gets away with it."

Emerging from the pre-marital status of non-royalty, the Duke of Edinburgh is by way of acquiring much the same *kind* of position in public opinion as the Duke of Windsor enjoyed in the thirties. He is felt, though, to signify a *continuation of the Coronation* trend: that is, to be *seen* to exist and *felt* to belong. Since the Coronation of 1953 there has been a slow but unmistakable growth in comments on this account, the main point being that the Queen herself is becoming perhaps a less "human", although a more royal figure. During the summer of 1960 Mass-Observers investigated this aspect in some detail:

"1. 'I think it's wrong to expect a young Queen like Elizabeth to detach herself from her people.'
"2. 'As the Queen gets older she is becoming more stately. It's a pleasure to watch her. So many gestures and other characteristics of Queen Mary in her . . .'

"3. 'She keeps herself aloof from her people. I expect that's because of her position.'"

Or these two working women looking at a picture as they chat in a (Leeds) shop:

"F.60.D. 'Eee. I wouldn't like 'er job!'
F.65.D. 'Eee, no. Poor luv. No *privacy*. Can't do what she wants and 'as to pretend she likes it. Not like Queen Victoria!'"

Compare, too, the sorts of feeling commonly voiced about other royal figures in 1960—(we have deliberately avoided turning these results into their statistics of pro and con, as invidious to the Royal Family; and therefore have taken special care that these selections of sentence comments are representative in each instance):

Duke of Edinburgh: Gets about more and mixes with people. More intelligent, not so snobby as some of the others. Gets talking to ordinary people as well. He's a bit nosey. He's had a worker's training and been brought up to know what money is. He's too quick-tongued, and likes his own way. He's the force behind the scenes. He's natural and easy and popular with all classes. The Queen's lucky to have married such a fine chap. He's no stuffed shirt.

The Queen Mother: Kindly and considerate. Typical Scots gentlewoman, dignified and gracious. Homely type. Rather like the *Pearly Queen* with all her furs and feathers. Wasn't born a royal lady and has more feeling for the people therefore. An understanding person. She has a radiance about her.

Duchess of Kent: Looks regal and serene. Has had a tough time. Beautiful and well dressed. Dignified. Doesn't look bored.

Princess Alexandra: Natural and unaffected. Good sense of humour. Could be anybody's daughter of the upper middle classes. Mixes with the people more than the others. Not a bit starchy.

Duchess of Gloucester: Charming. Works hard. Looks dignified.

Duke of Gloucester: Not much in public eye. Does all the donkey work and gets no credit for it.

The Royal Occasion of 1960: Future of Mister?

One royal person, Princess Margaret—like her uncle before her—recently stepped determinedly out of the traditional pattern, and married a commoner. "The task of all concerned," says the *Economist*, "is to show that the British social revolution is by now old enough and wise enough and flexible enough to treat this sort of problem as a challenge to be met." The reaction of the public to the fact of the marriage was one of pleasure (the occasion itself brought out the squatters, the large television audiences, the usual arguments about cost versus enjoyment, etc.); although reaction to the bridegroom was not always as favourable, mainly because of his lack of status. But there is also the feeling that this is a marriage which brings "them" nearer to "us"; in some sense, it is a victory for the people, though again ambivalent enough:

" 'I'm delighted Princess Margaret is going *to keep up with the Joneses*. That makes her one of us now, doesn't it.' Painter's wife: 33.

'Princess Margaret is a bit of the arty kind herself and I think they're well matched. But it doesn't give us much to *look up* to, does it?' Typist: 20.

'She's done the right thing in marrying a commoner. He's one of us, and his family's *paid Income Tax*.' Tobacconist: 57.

'I'm glad she's got a husband and like all stories about Princesses *it'll have a happy ending*. I thought she might be left on the shelf. This young man strikes me as being all right. I did think she'd choose someone in her own status, but that's her affair.' Old Age Pensioner: 65."

The presence at Britain's top level for traditional symbolism of a true commoner—Prince Philip came of royal stock—could, in changing events, have an effect on the exact status of Royalty in general. It will be particularly significant for the sociologist to track his future in mass-terms. Will he become first a vaguely and then a manifestly "royal" figure?

Either way, and whatever the future of the newest royal marriage, it seems unlikely that existing attitudes to royalty will be drastically or lastingly changed. The mould has a B.C. patent. We are probably far from opening the door to "let the prisoners out"; and the *ideal* royal person still seems to be someone who, like the late Queen Mary, can be described as "out and out royalty, yet you felt she had the people at heart". (Queen Mary was the only royal person who, as if still alive, was chosen as a favourite "royal" in the 1960 study.)

FIFTEEN

MARGINS OF KNOWLEDGE, INTEREST, AND TASTE

Patterns of Taste

IN 1940, AT THE beginning of the Blitz, a London woman was asked to name (among other Cabinet ministers) the Prime Minister and the Secretary of State for Air. Churchill she knew, but she believed that the R.A.F. was run by somebody called Air Marshal Moering. In 1960, twenty years later, a 49-year-old widow living in the country replies to a question as to who was now the Prime Minister with:

> "It used to be Churchill, but I can't think of the one now."

Ignorance of this order is exceptional although (as we shall see later) perhaps not quite so exceptional as some might think in a modern literate society. Many responses on the lunatic fringe can be explained by deafness, misunderstanding, and perhaps by sheer cussedness and refusal to answer questions. But how educated, how intelligent, indeed how *interested*, are the less exceptional?

Few of the changes that have taken place in the quarter of a century studied by Mass-Observation can have been so dramatic as those in the education structure of the country. Before the war, there were 5½ million *children* at school: now in 1960 there are nearly 7 million, a rise of 11% even allowing for the increase in population in the relevant age groups. Those at Universities number 111,930 now against 53,420 in 1938.

Those taking extension classes, evening classes and so on number 1,973,000 in 1960 (and even more a few years back), against less than half this number before the war. Nobody now leaves school before he is fifteen; very few are hampered by purely financial reasons from becoming as "educated" as they want to and can be.

Undoubtedly assisted by this increased educational activity, although not entirely caused by it, has come a quite marked increase in what are called "cultural activities". At the time of writing, twice a month over a period of some six months the BBC are presenting on television a series of programmes covering all Shakespeare's English historical plays—good, bad and indifferent. The average audience for these programmes is 13 million per night. It would take the Old Vic over seven years playing Shakespeare continuously with never an empty seat to reach the same audience once.

Shakespeare is not the only "highbrow" to have been produced on television in fairly undiluted form and yet to have gained mass audiences of a size which would have been undreamed of even ten years ago. Ibsen, O'Neill, Shaw, Eliot, have not merely been shown at peak hours but have, on occasion, attracted large and enthusiastic audiences. Programmes on archaeology, zoology, psychology, medicine, are watched by audiences which run into seven figures even when some much "lighter" item is available on the alternative programme. And even the straightforward unadorned lecture by a historian or scientist can find a mass audience today.

In any field, the same sort of data can be adduced. Shakespeare is not merely popular on television: at Stratford an eight month season is consistently sold out now. On London, the three main musical hits are founded, in all cases with very little alteration, on Shaw's "Pygmalion", on Charles Dickens' "Oliver Twist" and on Shakespeare's "Romeo and Juliet". The longest runs of all may be Agatha Christie and the Whitehall farces, as before the war they were "Ten Minute Alibi" and the Aldwych farces. But J. B. Priestley and Somerset Maugham have been replaced by Pinter and N. F. Simpson, if not such "important" dramatists surely more "difficult", ones who would barely have been given a chance at the box-office even five years ago. And Terence Rattigan, famous in 1938 for the light comedy of "French Without Tears", has as his current success a serious study of Lawrence of Arabia, and as an immediate take-off flop (July 1960) a musical rehash of the earlier work.

Penguin Books are now twenty-five years old. Many gave them no chance of survival when they risked non-fiction and serious novelists in their "first ten". Now, with the list of their best-sellers including such works as the *Odyssey* and the *Iliad*, they have not merely published, but also commissioned, series of books on history, English literature, physics, architecture and so on. The paper-back market is now numbered in tens of millions, a great deal of it non-fiction. But, side by side with this, the market for hard covered books has continued to expand, while in the last ten years alone the issue of books from libraries has increased from 300 million a year to 430 million (though a good deal of this has increasingly gone abroad.)

The Press has shared in this expansion of interest in reading. The eight main dailies had a combined circulation in 1938 of some 9½ million, whereas in 1960 they have risen to nearly 15 million. But more marked than this general rise is the extent to which it has been concentrated in the so-called "quality" papers. In the last twenty years the circulation of the *Daily Telegraph* has doubled, the *Guardian* has more than quadrupled, while the circulations of most of the popular papers (except the *Daily Mirror* and the *Daily Express*) have altered little. The same has occurred among the Sundays, where the most marked and consistent increases have taken place with the *Sunday Times* and the *Observer*. While the weeklies with the assumed "popular" appeal, like *Illustrated* and *Picture Post*, have disappeared from the scene, the "quality" weeklies have gone from strength to strength. The *Economist* has now six times its pre-war circulation, the *Listener* three times, the *New Statesman* three times.

The medium of entertainment which has suffered most in the post-war period has been the cinema. From the post-war peak of $27\frac{1}{2}$ million entrances a week, it has now dropped to $14\frac{1}{2}$ million, and is still dropping. Much of this decline is *said* to be due to television. But one wonders how much of it is due to the fact that Hollywood and Wardour Street seem singularly unable to grasp that tastes have changed, standards have risen, and repetition bores.

Two of the films which have made money for the British film makers this year have been "Room at the Top" and "The Angry Silence". The first is a film version of an "outrageous" novel, including X and sex, but contains no *obvious* material for a box-office draw. The second is the story of a strike. Ten years ago, a previous story of a strike acclaimed by the critics ("Chance of a Lifetime") was given circuit booking only after legal action had been taken, although even then there were signs that an intelligent film was not the box-office poison it was so often said to be. Most of the films which have won recent critics' awards have also been considerable successes in cash terms. "The Bridge on the River Kwai", for example, with neither women nor aberrations, has made more money than almost any other picture ever made—although the greatest money-maker of them all looks like being the new but virile "Ben Hur". Much of the script of this epic was written by Christopher Fry, mainly known for his plays in verse, high-brow.

The Enlargement of Choice

The same presentation could be made to show the great increases which have taken place in serious music. Concerts attract more and more people; and the slide in "pops" for gramophone records has been counteracted by steady increases in the call for the classics. Art exhibitions, museums, cultural festivals prosper. Ballet is no longer only a subject for music-hall jokes or (at Blackpool) apologies and some ogling of legs.

This is quite intentionally a one-sided view of popular taste. It ignores the rise of the *Sunday Pictorial*, as well as of the *Sunday Times*; of *Woman* and *Woman's Own* as well as of the *Economist*; of "Carry on Constable" as well as of "The Angry Silence": and so on. Nor does it necessarily imply a *change* in popular taste. People can now afford to buy more books, see more films of the kind that they wanted to even before the war: and those who provide entertainment, reading matter, and so on are often more in tune than they were with what people really want. But the broad facts as they stand seem indisputable. To provide what is generally regarded as intelligent material for the public does not in 1960 court disaster. In 1937 it often did. Culture is no longer profitless. There is a sizeable and apparently growing market for those who do not seek the Lowest Common Multiple. The ability to understand does not automatically imply a *willingness* to understand; nor does it imply that understanding will be expressed in those terms that it is thought it ought to be expressed in.

Mass-Observation's books and bulletins are full of examples of this: of propaganda, for example, which failed to achieve its (often entirely meritorious) purpose because it made wrong assumptions, either that the public would do what it "ought" to do, or that the public would understand what was explained in the specialised language of government or some other group. One instance; in a report, *Language of Leadership*, we showed that what was officially released as a popular digest of a white paper defeated many people, from the very outset, by a front page illustration of a graph—a concept which, in pre-television days, was outside most people's immediate understanding.

Our files of correspondence for hundreds of market research surveys abound in similar problems of communication and understanding; particularly the need to explain to clients that because the products they offer are often better quality, or better packed or better value for money, the customer may still *not* buy: because he is not interested or does not understand. It is no use selling evening dresses which are washable, if a woman's basic ideal is to wear one twice only. It is no use advertising pencils which last for three years, if most people lose them after six months. It is no use selling a headache powder with better drugs in it, if people still prefer to select the one with the best taste (or smell).

The "muddle" and confusion which exist in people's minds is hardly less, if less at all, than it was twenty years ago. Advantages in standards of living, education and so on have been great; their effects apparent and important. In spite of this, are people really different in any measurable degree?

It must be remembered, too, in all this context of taste and knowledge change, that impact may be very small either in depth or scale (or both). But that the "Misc." of today is the possible "Mass" of tomorrow. Further, that even quite tiny shifts by statistical standards can cause major changes when measured by the standards of theatre-box-office, sales of poetry or good prints. If only 1% of the population are influenced afresh, that is enough to fill the Mermaid Theatre for years, turn any book into a best seller or make the chosen painters rich. Much of the effect discussed above is at that scale, at first, It is none the less tremendously significant now and for the future.

Puzzled People

To lead a satisfactory and full life it can well be argued that it is essential to have a clear idea of one's relationship to God and one's soul on the one hand (even if this implies a denial of the existence of either), and a relationship with one's fellow men on the other. These fields are basically covered by the concepts which we call religion and politics. Here, surely, if nowhere else, it might be thought that people might begin to show greater clarity of thought, less confusion and muddle.

Such is not, however, the case. In religion, in politics, in knowledge of what goes on around one, survey results still show how confused and how disinterested people can be. We have already seen something of this in Worktown. Let us now look more widely.

First let us consider *religion*. In August 1960 a middle-aged Londoner said that he did not believe in God, that he did not believe Jesus was more than a man, that he did not go to church and that he did not pray. Asked whether he had any other comments to make he added in all seriousness:

"I suppose you would call me a very religious man."

This interview took place in the course of a follow-up survey designed precisely to reflect, in question and in analysis, a survey which we had carried out very carefully in the same area in 1944-5.

In this interval we have learned more about the technical processes of social and market research; but it seemed best to repeat the survey as closely as possible along identical lines in order to make comparisons more valid.

The findings of our big 1945 survey were published in a book called *Puzzled People* (Gollancz, 1946). The third chapter of this book had as its title "The Great Muddle". This was the position those years ago:

"Of the Doubters, Agnostics and Atheists in this London borough over a quarter say they pray on occasions to the God whose existence they doubt. One in twelve went to church within the past six months, compared with one in three of those who say they believe in God. Over half the non-believers consider that there should be religious education in schools.

"Of those who attend Church of England services regularly or intermittently, one-quarter do not believe in an after-life; on the other hand, one-fifth of those who don't go to church at all do believe. Of those who don't believe in a Deity or are agnostic, nearly a quarter tend to think that Christ was 'something more than a man'; on the other hand, a rather larger proportion of Church of England churchgoers say he was only a man. Of those who say he was only a man, one in five also say they believe he was born of a virgin. But of those who attend Church of England services, one in four doubt the doctrine of the Virgin Birth and only one in three give quite definite assent to it."

This is a brief summary of some of the confusion of thought and attitude which exist today on the subject of religion. Taken in isolation, some of the points which we discussed then—and shall now further discuss here—may seem encouraging to the religious, some to the atheist. Interrelated, there is little which can cause much elation to either; or, for that matter, to anyone between the extremes, whose views hold any degree of "consistency". Three years ago the Gallup Poll carried out a large-scale survey. In this they found that 78% said they believed in God, nearly 50% said they believed in life after death, 82% said they thought that children should be baptised, 56% thought they should be taught to say their prayers. One in three said they believed that religion was more important than economic security. Yet despite this widespread acceptance of religious values *less than one in six* claimed that they went to church last Sunday. Again a 1960 *Daily Mail* enquiry showed that of those baptised into the Church of England, 74% said that the Church meant security to them, 67% that its continued existence is essential, 59% that it was run efficiently. But *only* 18% said that they attended a religious place regularly. (Compare here also the particular statistics of Worktown, Chapter 4, based on observation rather than interview.)

There is, to say the least, an inconsistency here in people's unwillingness to take their own medicine and readiness to find excuses for their attitude. But there is nothing in the least surprising in finding a wide difference between some attitudes of those who define themselves as Christian and the original teaching of Christ. Almost without exception, surveys carried out, not merely in the British Isles but also in many parts of Europe and America, indicate a tendency for religious people to be more "reactionary" than non-religious people. Those who go to church are more likely to approve of capital punishment, corporal punishment, anti-semitism, than those who do not; with Roman Catholics being the least progressive. There may of course be explanations of these attitudes other than religious ones.

In 1960 we quota-sampled the same area as 1944 exactly. The table below suggests how little public attitudes have changed since:

	1945 %	1960 %
Doubters, Agnostics, Atheists saying—		
that they pray	25	33
that they have been to church in the last six months	9	14
that they believe in life after death	32	18
that they believe that Christ was more than a man	25	21
Those Believing in a Deity saying—		
that they do *not* believe in life after death	25	26
that they never go to church	48	33
that they never pray or pray only in church	25	18
Those going to C. of E. Services saying—		
that they do not believe in an after life	46	42
that Christ was only a man	27	18
not giving definite consent to the Virgin Birth	56	49
Those saying Christ was only a Man also saying—		
He was born of a Virgin	19	29

This is not the place to discuss the significance (or otherwise) of the changes shown in this table. There are certainly differences between 1945 and 1960, but the basic pattern of inconsistencies remains the same. The extracts from *Puzzled People* which we have quoted could still in general terms apply today.

We would not expect to find the same unmoving picture when

we turn from religion to politics. However unruffled or stagnant the depth of the pool, ripples show temporarily on the surface; and it is only the surface which is visible in the answers to simple direct questions in public opinion polls. We would not expect to find a position of "no change" on the likelihood of war in the next twenty-five years, in surveys carried out in 1960 and on the eve of Suez and in the middle of Korean hostilities. We would not expect to find the same *admitted* lack of interest in politics immediately before an election when nobody reading or viewing could fail to be aware of what was going on, as we should find after a year of control by a party with an overwhelming majority.

Our previous consideration of increased readership of papers, increased participation in cultural activities, would lead us to believe that knowledge of politics, if not interest in politics, would be growing. There are indeed certain figures which could suggest that this is so; but these are somewhat misleading. Recent party political broadcasts, for example, have usually made the "top ten" in studies of the size of television audiences. It is extremely doubtful, however, whether this means much. They are the only programmes which appear simultaneously on both ITV and BBC, so that those who have their TV sets on continuously have no option but to "watch" them —how much they take in may be quite another matter.

In general, audience measurement of figures, however, could point to the fact that a good deal of television time is taken up by M.P.s debating Parliamentary and other issues, and undoubtedly the creation of Independent Television has brought with it the opportunity of far greater freedom on the air for discussion of political issues. Again, however, it by no means follows that an interest in programmes in which M.P.s appear is an interest in politics. It is perfectly possible to argue with just as much evidence that the continued appearance of certain Members of Parliament in programmes which contain lively debate, but in which all participants can invariably be guaranteed to take the party line, is increasing the value of Parliament as an *entertainment*, but reducing its value as a servant of democracy. It is probably all to the good that a Member of Parliament should be known to as many people as possible, and, while (as we shall show) the numbers knowing such figures are alarmingly low, television is presumably helping to push them up, or at least to keep them from going down!

We have seen (Chapter 12) already that, in lip service at any rate, most people still regard a Member of Parliament as doing a more useful job than a TV entertainer, although they may rank him well below a doctor, an atomic scientist and even a grocer. Among the two-fifths of the population who express themselves *not very interested* in politics, even this gap narrows. As many as 41% of this group believes that a TV entertainer may be doing a very useful job, against 62% who refer in this way to M.P.s.

But to believe that an M.P. is doing a useful job does not imply interest in, or active help for, what he is doing—nor for that matter a greater degree of close thinking in this field than we have already found in the fields of religion. Less than one person in ten admits at the moment that he will probably not vote at the next election he is involved with; but the same proportion are unable to give the name of the present Prime Minister, while one in four cannot name the leader of the Opposition, and two out of every three cannot name the Liberal Leader. *Only one person in four* of all those interviewed in fact correctly named all three—yet all three of these have recently appeared in programmes which have been given audience measurement figures of five million or more.

Ignorance is not only related to national personalities. Of our 2,000 quota sample, two in five were unable to name the present M.P. for their own constituency, nor could one in ten even name the party which was represented in Parliament for their constituency. Nor is this lack of knowledge related only to one section of the community. It is true that ignorance (in this sense) seems higher among those in the working classes, a fact which is to some extent reflected in the figures for political affiliation. But even among those who said that they would vote Conservative the next time, 4% could not name the Prime Minister; and the same percentage did not know which party their own M.P. represented. Conservatives, however, have the consolation that proportionately *more of their supporters (82%) know the role of Mr. Gaitskell than do members of his own party (69%).*

There is nothing *new* in this lack of knowledge. When Peter Thorneycroft was Chancellor of the Exchequer about half the population did not even know his name. The present figure of 41% knowing the name of their M.P. is, in fact, an *apparent* increase in awareness against earlier figures gathered by the Gallup Poll; in 1954 only 33% of the general public said they knew the name of their member. A year earlier a *Manchester Guardian* survey had shown less than one in five able to identify the meaning of NATO, half unable to name any Russian satellite countries, half unable to identify the party in power in America at that time. A survey in 1947, when UNO was sitting at Westminster, showed that nine in every hundred did not know what it was. Seven years later, at the time of Suez, although many other politically inconsistent answers had been ironed out, there were still six in every hundred who did not know what UNO was.

Just before election campaigns began in 1958, only one third knew the name of their political candidate (no candidate was known by much more than half). In 1950 a Mass-Observation bulletin, *Voter's Choice*, indicated that one in ten was unable to name any candidate sitting for the constituencies concerned; and only one in three knew the names of all candidates. We wrote:

"The candidate who had represented the constituency for the previous five years seems not to have reaped any particular advantage here. 79% knew the name of the Labour candidate in the 1950 General Election, but only 59% could name the Member of Parliament who had won the seat at the last Parliamentary election, and only a further 10% could say what party he stood for! In other words—and other surveys conducted on a national scale confirm this finding—an M.P. at the end of five years in office is unlikely to be even a name to one in three of his constituents. This figure rises as high as two in three among those who have themselves lived in the area less than five years.

"The number to whom their representative is more than a name is even smaller. Of Mass-Observation's entire sample only 6% had been in any form of contact with their M.P.s apart from meetings. This, it should be emphasised, applies to constituencies all of which are within half an hour's journey from the Houses of Parliament.

"With so little knowledge of their M.P., it is perhaps not surprising that constituents were, for the most part, unwilling to give an opinion about him. 61% of the entire sample when asked how they felt about their M.P., had no views to offer.

In 1954 a Gallup Poll survey similarly showed for the country as a whole, that 83% said that they had never written or talked to their M.P., 71% that they had not read anything about what he had been doing recently.

Even expression of interest does not imply any increase in participation or knowledge. It might well have been thought socially acceptable to express an *interest* in politics; but even in pre-election times rather less than half the electorate deemed it necessary to do so. In a recent M-O national survey carried out nine months after general election, only 12% said that they were *very interested* in politics, and of *this* group:

87% said that they would vote at the next election (against 81% of all respondents) and 77% said that they thought an M.P. was doing a very useful job (against 67% of all respondents)

but 13% said they did not know the name of the Prime Minister (against 8% all respondents)

25% said they did not know the name of the Leader of the Opposition (against 23% of all respondents)

74% said they did not know the name of the Leader of the Liberal Party (against 65% of all respondents)

42% said they did not know the name of their own M.P. (against 37% of all respondents)

Although we have given some perhaps discouraging examples of political attitudes, we are *not* suggesting that on all political and allied subjects attitudes continue to be unchanging and irrational; on some subjects, such as capital punishment and the effectiveness of United Nations, there have been marked changes in public opinion in the past years. But these do not seem in any way to change the *general pattern*; nor to decrease markedly the number of people not very interested —let alone those not privately really so interested as they may claim to be in public.

Nor do any of these trends in relation to politics, religion and other accepted formal institutions and establishments appear to extend with the same dulling effect to "newer" approaches to life, and to such sectors as good writing, music, theatre and "culture" in the broad sense (not necessarily excluding innovation and experiment).

SIXTEEN

WHO IS/WAS WHO?

ATTITUDES TO POLITICS and religion, it would seem, remain by no means clear-cut, and suggest that people are still puzzled, still muddled, still apathetic. But if they are more educated, if more of them are able to appreciate the classics in the theatre, books, and so on, surely they are at least more knowledgeable?

Probably the answer is that they are—up to a point. Certainly it is extremely difficult to assess differences of this kind over a period. But gaps in knowledge can still reach fairly major proportions.

In the week before Anthony Armstrong-Jones married Princess Margaret, we asked 2,000 people why certain people had been "in the news". We included his name among a number of other people's, and the form of the question was that which we had used on two previous occasions. Many people laughed at being asked if they knew why he had been in the news; many more answered in terms which in effect meant "surely *everybody* knows him".

Everybody did not. Over one person in ten failed to answer the question. Admittedly, only a few gave wrong answers (although one person thought that he was best man at the wedding rather than the groom) but many did not know, many said that they had not heard of him.

Yet the figure of 88% correctly identifying him is the highest recognition figure *ever scored on this type of question asked by M-O*. No other "famous person" whom we have listed in this way has been known by quite so many as this. Indeed, being known to even as many as three out of four of the population is an honour which he shares only with a television comedian, a rock'n' roll singer and a mass murderer.

Generally, to be an entertainer seems the best way to become known not merely widely but also intimately. Asked, shortly after their deaths, which they thought to be the greatest loss "to people generally", more than three times as many people named President Roosevelt as Tommy Handley. But asked which death upset them most personally, 34% of this same sample mentioned Handley against only 24% referring to Roosevelt.

At his peak Tommy Handley had an audience of eleven million. Tony Hancock on BBC Television can not command quite so big an audience (although he is popular on sound radio as well), but 85 in every 100 people know him—a much larger proportion than own television sets. And while there are no signs that Hancock can stir the same degree of affection as could Handley with the overtones of ITMA's wartime code, he is clearly a well liked, as well as a well known, figure.

In 1957 Tommy Steele was known to slightly fewer than Hancock; by 1960—78 in every 100 (others thought that he was a parliamentary candidate, a lawyer, "the man on the Coal Board", and "something to do with a runaway heiress"); but despite the Press agitation for and against him very few of those who identified him showed signs of any strong diaspproval.

Murder is more of a hit and miss affair in this context. Just after his Old Bailey trial John Halliday Christie, the Notting Hill mass murderer, was known to 82% of the population. Three years later, however, less than half (44%) could correctly identify him. In another case which (judged from Press comment) seemed to create just the same degree of interest, the accused was acquitted; he was known only to two-thirds of all people interviewed. Again, the name of Patrick Byrne was known to only 12%. The murder which he committed (decapitation in a Birmingham Y.W.C.A.) was headline news for days: the trial, on the other hand, with Byrne admitting his guilt and being found to have diminished responsibility was somewhat of an anti-climax.

Names from sport and politics are well behind the leaders in show business and crime. We have already seen a marked lack of interest in politics, and a marked lack of current knowledge of Party leaders and local M.P.s. This form of survey quiz confirms this disinterest: Peter Thorneycroft at the time he was Chancellor was known to less than two-thirds of the population, Senator McCarthy at the height of his power to only half, Ted Hill in the middle of a strike in which he was a key figure to only a quarter. Three sports figures—a walker, a cricketer, and an athlete—"scored" between 40% and 50%. Details are given in the table overleaf (p. 266).

But it is not only the living who suffer. A Gallup Poll in 1955 showed 8% of women in Britain unable to say who Shakespeare was, one in four of our population unable to identify Napoleon!

This form of question, of course, has severe limitations and many of the more startlingly wrong answers can be caused simply by not quite hearing the question. The woman who thought that Kinsey, of Sexual Behaviour fame, wrote the *Water Babies* was quite right if she thought the investigator said Kingsley: the many who suggested that McCarthy had a ventriloquist's dummy were probably thinking of another famous American with a different first name: and it is not too difficult to get confused between Ted Hill, of the Boilermakers' Union, Billy Hill of Soho, and Benny Hill of television. But even making due allowance for this, there remains a large area of ignorance and disinterest.

In all studies, in fact, the proportion who are really well informed is a comparatively small one. Asked in 1952 to single out from nine well-known politicians, show business personalities and others, which three were still alive, only four people in every ten were right on all counts. And one in two, even eight years ago, assumed that at least one of Gordon Richards, J. B. Priestley or Lord Montgomery was dead—although they are all still very much alive today. In 1957, although the least known name on the list (Ted Hill) was known by more than one in four, less than 20% of those asked knew all five names about which they were asked, while 5% knew none of the five.

On the whole, on issues such as these, men know more than women (perhaps because they read newspapers more). Such differences can be very marked; Ted Hill, for example, being known to more than twice as many men as women. Anthony Armstrong-Jones, however, proved an exception to this. Only 8% of women were unable to identify him fairly accurately, against 15% of men. In almost all cases, those in the middle classes are more knowledgeable than those in the working classes; and, if anything, those aged between 28–44 are likely to be better informed than other age groups. Here, however, there are more exceptions. Tommy Steele, not unexpectedly, was known to almost all (94%) of the under twenty-fives, but to only a little more than half the over forty-fives. There is little difference in knowledge according to what part of the country people live in; but those who live in towns seem somewhat better informed than those who live in the country.

One figure shown on our table has not so far been referred to at all —anthropologist, ornithologist, televison personality, founder of Mass-Observation, and author of this book. Width of interest is clearly not related to the extent to which people may become known! Our internal report on the subject is quoted verbatim:

"Tom Harrisson was known to less than 1% of all groups except men, those in Class AB, and those aged over 45. Between eight and ten times as many people in all sub-groups gave wrong answers about Tom Harrisson as gave right ones (although a small proportion of these referred to the actor of the same name). Those who did know of him seemed equally likely to refer to his Borneo activities, to Mass-Observation, and to his television films. Those who gave incorrect answers said, among other things, that he was Rex Harrison's son, a relation of Kathleen Harrison, Lord Mayor of Hull. He was also described as a new singer, a jockey, a racing motorist, a racing tipster, a mountaineer who climbed Everest with Hillary, and a pianist.

"He was said to be in charge of the Aldermaston marches, 'the man who started the balloting to expose Communism in the Trade Unions', 'the president of the Mineworkers Union who is retiring this year', and, perhaps most startling of all:

"'He was put to death in America last week.'"

But the author can take comfort from knowing that the 1% or less who make up the "Misc." group of today may contain the germs of a future; or alternatively that it is nicer to be a forgotten man of the thirties, overtaken by time, and live quietly in Borneo, than bustling in Blackpool or Bloomsbury. . . .

"IN THE NEWS" SURVEYS

Survey	Person	Correct %	Incorrect %	Don't know or Vague %
1960	Anthony Armstrong-Jones	88	1	11
1960	Tony Hancock	87	1	12
1954	John Reginald Halliday Christie	82	2	16
1957	Tommy Steele	78	6	16
1954	Sir Edmund Hillary	72	3	25
1957	John Bodkin Adams	66	5	29
1957	Peter Thorneycroft	63	9	28
1960	Wendy Lewis	54	7	39
1960	Brian Statham	53	4	43
1954	Dr. Kinsey	51	4	45
1954	Joseph McCarthy	51	8	41
1957	John Reginald Halliday Christie	44	6	50
1958	Gordon Pirie	38	6	56
1957	Ted Hill	27	17	56
1960	Patrick Byrne	12	11	77
1960	Tom Harrisson	†	9	91

† less than 1%

SEVENTEEN

PANORAMA OF PROJECTS: 1937-60

FROM 1937 TO 1940 Mass-Observation worked from two main headquarters, one in Worktown and the other at Blackheath in London. In those years the effort was deployed on major reports and manuscripts intended for eventual publication, as well as many newspaper and magazine articles, lectures, broadcast texts and general propaganda urging realistic social research. Much of this work was not published, owing to the advent of war in September 1939; all of it remains, for future revision, on M-O's files—and the present volume is in part a by-product of this period.

Soon after the outbreak of the Second World War, Mass-Observation found itself faced with a choice: to work for government in the the war effort, or close down. Through the war we continued, based on a Holland Park H.Q. (and with a country depot for valuable papers near Malvern in Worcestershire). During these years a great many studies were made for government departments (mainly the Ministry of Information and the Admiralty) and a group of advertising agents, the Advertising Service Guild, led by A. Everett Jones and J. R. Brumwell, both of whom are now directors of M-O.

T.H. was responsible for most of these war-time documents—a selection of which are listed below to indicate the range of activity—until he left England on war service in 1943; after that H.D. (Bob) Willcock ran things until after the war, when T.H. returned for a year (1946-7) from service in Borneo. Presently T.H. went back to the Far East, and then H.D.W. went to the Social Survey (government) as Principal. The running of M-O has ever since been in the effective hands of Leonard England and Mollie Tarrant, operating from 148 Cromwell Road, South Kensington, London, S.W.7.

Since 1948 most of the written-up reports prepared for "clients"—the marginal numbering in the list refers to these, starting in 1939—have been big ones based on national surveys of market research type. M-O is now a successful market research organisation, and L.E. is Vice-Chairman of the Market Research Society (the leading professional body in this field) for 1960-1. This does not mean that we have neglected non-commercial and long-term interests, though they have been kept up in a seldom (after 1950) published way: this book further indicates that facet—and we hope to continue in the "public" sphere with further activity to come. . . .

This is the last chance to thank some others who have helped a lot in the considerable work leading into the present brief and limited study. Notably Frank Singleton, in 1937 a junior reporter and now happily Managing Editor of *Worktown Evening News*. Again, up there, Roland Currier for continuing help with vital background information; and Nell Umney for skilful special field work in the zone Blackpool-Westhoughton-Worktown. Also F. R. Poskitt and other senior teachers in the area.

More widely over the years special help of various kinds has come at significant times from Ambrose Appelbe, David Archer, Brian Barefoot, Vernon Bartlett, Gerald Barry, J. D. Bernal, Dennis Chapman, Cyril Connolly, Surrey Dane, Geoffrey Gorer, Leslie Hale, Alan Hodge, Tom Hopkinson, Robert Hyde, Tangye Lean, S. C. Leslie, John Madge, Kingsley Martin, Priscilla Novy, A. D. Peters, Stephen Potter, P. Sargent Florence, Geoffrey Thomas, P. E. Vernon (before he was a professor) and Bruce Watkin (I wonder where Herbert Howarth and he are now?)—as well as others already mentioned in the text; and many more who helped in all sorts of ways, too numerous now to name.

This is also the time gladly to mention some who worked exceedingly hard to keep M-O alive and kicking in the difficult period between the relative affluence of war-time government patronage and the actual affluence of modern business understanding. To these, recognition is warmly due: Pamela Vince, Michael Lyster, Doris Hoy, Lena Bleehan, Ivan Piercy, Bernard Latham, the Pamplin-Greens, Eric Gulliver and Kay Butcher.

Since the early days described in the opening chapters of this little book, many have been intertwined within Mass-Observation. And Mass-Observation has followed many paths—being always eager to explore new ones. Its present activities carry it especially into the fields of commercial, industrial and motivation research, with the use of psychological as well as anthropological approaches. Always, though, we seek to study the specific problem in the wider context. The future, cheerfully, visualises a welding of the best of the past with the best of the present, in our own particular—and, by now you may be entitled to say, peculiar—way.

MAIN M-O PUBLICATIONS (SINCE 1937)

1937 *May 12th, 1937 (the Coronation)*. Faber and Faber
1938 *First year's Work, 1937–8*. Lindsay Drummond
1939 *Britain*. Penguin Special.
1940 *War Begins at Home*. Chatto and Windus
1940 *Politics and the Non Voter* (unpublished: in proof)
1941 *Clothes Rationing*. Advertising Service Guild
1941 *Home Propaganda*. Advertising Service Guild
1941 *A Savings Survey (Working Class)*. Privately printed for circulation
1942 *People in Production*. Advertising Service Guild (John Murray)
1943 *War Factory*. Victor Gollancz (2 editions)
1943 *The Pub and the People*. Victor Gollancz (3 editions)
1944 *The Journey Home*. Advertising Service Guild (John Murray)
1945 *Britain and her Birth-Rate*. Advertising Service Guild (John Murray)
1947 *Puzzled People*. Victor Gollancz
1947 *Brown's and Chester*. Lindsay Drummond
1947 *Exmoor Village*. Harrap (W. J. Turner)
1948 *Juvenile Delinquency*. Falcon Press
1949 *The Press and its Readers*. Art and Technics Ltd.
1949 *On Sunday*. Noldrett Press (illus. by Ronald Searle)
1949 *At the Doctor's*. Noldrett Press (illus. by Ronald Searle)
1949 *People and Paint*. (I.C.I. publication)
1950 *The Voters' Choice*. Art and Technics Ltd.

Also more than 100 M-O *Bulletins* (usually about sixteen printed pages) distributed free to voluntary observers, research contacts and friends of M-O.

Many books and other publications have discussed M-O at various levels in recent years. The following three are widely available in Britain and contain entertaining chapters on M-O's alleged pre-war methods. Some of the third's words—describing our "movement" as purely pioneer and pretty naïf—can now be taken pre-salted.

Into this Dangerous World by Woodrow Wyatt. Harrap, 1952.
Indigo Days by Julian Trevelyan, McGibbon & Kee, 1957.
The Thirties by Julian Symons, Cresset Press, 1960.

SELECTION FROM M-O REPORTS FILE, 1939-59

Year 1939
1 Channels of Publicity
2 Government Posters
3 Public Information Leaflets
4 A.R.P. Instructions
6 Sport in War-time
9 Six Railway Posters
11 Evacuation
14 Christmas Shopping

Year 1940
16 Faking of Newsreels
20 Recording the War
23 Church—Religion and the War
24 The Cinema
26 Women's Organisations
28 Fashion
30 Shop Notices
33 Music Halls
44 Astrology
45 Pantomime
47 War-time Reading
51 Work's Magazines
58 Pantomime and Music Hall
65 Lord Haw Haw
66 Films Response
71 The Lightship Leaflet
73 Norway Crisis
77 Gert and Daisy (BBC Talks)
78 Anti-Semitism in Limehouse
79 Public Feelings about Aliens
85 Budget Reactions
86 War and Learned Societies
87 What Children think about War
88 Argyll By-Election
89 Morale Now
99 Political Crisis
120 Ministry of Food Publicity Campaign
122 Duff Cooper's Broadcast
135 Mosley Internment
136 Street Literature
139 Class and Sex Differences in Morale
140 Women's Attitude to Evacuation
144 Publication of German Communiqués
150 Air Raid Fear
152 War Work and Local Authorities
170 Suffolk Village
172 A.R.P. Preparedness
177 War Jokes
197 Propaganda Ideas
210 Arrest of an Observer
225 International Use of M-O
226 French Armistice

Year 1941
234 Royal Family
238 Refugees
305 Unintelligible Words (in Official Propaganda)
311 Does Public Opinion Count?
312 Conscientious Objectors
313 Civilians in Air Raids
314 Newsreels
325 "Cooper's Snoopers"
329 Hore-Belisha
346 British Israelites
347 Hyde Park Meeting
479 Messerschmitt in Streatham
482 The Third Evacuation
489 Non-Physical Ear Plug Problems
495 Coventry
496 Wartime Politics
534 Lundy—Isle of Puffins
551 Reactions to Boothby
552 "Daily Worker"
553 Young People
563 Derby
564 Jehovah's Witnesses
566 The French
567 Carrots
568 Morale in 1941
569 Airmen
584 Wearing White in Blackout
585 Rumour at Cambridge
586 Invasion Feelings
651 Questions in the Public Mind
562 Budget
653 Leisure in R.A.F.
658 Easter Sunday
659 Sleep
661 The Small Shopkeeper
662 Poison Gas
694 Demand for Reprisals
695 Hess?
722 Social Welfare and Blitz Towns
723 Civilian and Service Morale
727 Liverpool Seamen
769 Mass Astrology
773 War in M-O Diaries
774 Clothes Rationing
776 Smoking Habits
782 Sex Differences in Overheards
807 Post-War Prospects and Demobilisation
808 Habit Changes
838 Provincial Dogs
869 Salvaging History
870 Home Propaganda
871 Government Exhibitions
293 Clyde Situation

Year 1942

- 933 Street Literature
- 934 Effect of War on Happiness
- 999 American Tinned Food
- 1005 Rumours
- 1022 How Britain Eats
- 1023 Two Blitz Occasions
- 1024 Liberalism
- 1083 Summary on A.T.S. Campaign
- 1084 Supply to Production
- 1085 Dislike of Ministers
- 1088 Expectations of 1942
- 1093 Ministry of Production
- 1094 Feelings about Australians
- 1111 Opinion on Cabinet Changes
- 1112 Closing of Small Shops
- 1149 Greyhounds and National Unity
- 1162 Propaganda for Town Planning
- 1166 Sir Stafford Cripps
- 1196 Blaina Investigation
- 1198 M. of I. Shorts
- 1207 Prestige of Government Leaders
- 1209 Ignorance
- 1210 Opposite Sex and War Difficulties
- 2111 Port of Hull
- 1225 Rubber Salvage
- 1226 Uncommon Sense
- 1266 Clogs
- 1267 Political Truce
- 1268 Traditional English Sunday
- 1269 Post-War Education
- 1301 Heated People
- 1306 Americans in Ireland
- 1309 Ulster Shipping
- 1311 Morale on Corvette
- 1314 Marginal Creative Personnel

Year 1943

- 1568 Public Reactions to the Beveridge Report
- 1569 America and The Americans
- 1593 The Sort of Home the Englishman Wants
- 1594 Food Indirects
- 1599 Public and V.D.
- 'o Watford By-Election
-   Women in Pubs
-   Religion and the Future
-   ʾtors in Home Building
-   ʾobilisation
-   ʾing Off No. 1
-   ʾestments
-   ʾs Feb.—June 1943
-   ʾ about the Dutch
-   ʾime
-   ʾ-time

Successful

Year 1944

- 1995 The Village of Luccombe (Exmoor)
- 1996 Significance of Public Opinion Surveys
- 1997 Morale in December
- 1998 "Browns of Chester"
- 1999 Demobilisation
- 2000 Vengeance
- 2018 Books and the Public
- 2019 Public Attitudes to Advertisements
- 2024 Churchill as Post-War Prime Minister
- 2035 Bury St. Edmunds By-Election
- 2036 West Derby By-Election
- 2112 Superstition
- 2121 A Survey on the Pilotless Planes
- 2133 Training for the Mines
- 2134 State Managed Pubs in Carlisle
- 2135 The Forces Vote
- 2136 A.F.B. 2626
- 2156 What is a Pin-Up Girl?
- 2157 Panel Bulletin
- 2159 Blackout to Dimout
- 2165 German Prisoners
- 2182 The Reluctant Stork
- 2188 Indirects on Royalty
- 2189 Flying Bomb Evacuation

Year 1945

- 2205 Sex Morality and the Birth Rate
- 2207 V.2—Report on South-East London
- 2220 British Legion Competition Essays
- 2221 Duke of Windsor's Resignation
- 2229 Death of Roosevelt
- 2230 R.A.F. Exhibition at Dorland Hall
- 2231 Do People Tell the Truth?
- 2233 Preliminary Figures for Domestic Science in Schools
- 2259 Attitudes to the Liberal Party
- 2260 Politicians' Prestige
- 2269 Retailers and Condition Medicines
- 2271 Russia Declares War on Japan
- 2272 Public Reactions to the Atom Bomb
- 2278 Feelings about the Peace
- 2285 Women's Reasons for having Small Families
- 2286 Prisoners of War
- 2291 Dock Strike
- 2301 Attitudes to Russia
- 2302 Trends in By-Elections

Year 1946

- 2363 Modern Homes Exhibition (Note and Counts)
- 2370 World Organisation and the Future
- 2375 Stevenage Satellite Town
- 2387 Salvation Army
- 2388 Drinking Habits
- 2394 Black Widow Posters

PANORAMA OF PROJECTS, 1937–60

Year 1946—cont.
2395 Holiday Weather
2405 People Feel: 1939–1945
2411 Anti-Semitism and Free Speech
2424 Trade Unions and Closed Shop
2425 Paratroops Mutiny
2426 Implications of Peckham
2427 Famous People
2430 The Hotel Strike
2431 The Squatters
2432 Popular Attitudes to Palestine and Arab Countries

Year 1947
2450 Coffee Drinking
2451 Biscuits
2454 Anti-Americanism
2460 People in the Co-op
2461 Southern Railway
2465 "Pseudo-personality" in Prostitution
2466 Political Parties: Oxford Undergraduates
2467 Leisure—Saturday Night
2468 Fuel Crisis—Gains and Losses
2477 Usage and Abusage
2480 Legend of Lorna Doone
2485 Atomic Weather
2491 Deserters
2492 Book Buying Habits
2494 Landlords Opinions on the Prospect of a Penny on the Pint
2495 The State of Matrimony
2496 Shopping Hours
2497 The British Household
2498 Sunday School and Church Attendance
2508 Aspects of Charities
2509 Holidays
2535 A Report on Popular Photographs
2536 Charity and the Blind
2537 Reading in Tottenham
2538 An Interim Report on Gambling
2546 The Application of Face Cream
2547 Custard Powder
2549 Anatomy of "Don't Knows"
2553 Willesden and the New Towns

Year 1948
2558 Manpower Movements
2560 Mass-Gambling
2575 Marshall Plan
2577 Football Pools
2998 Princess Margaret Rose
2999 Trade Unions
3000 Political Film Campaign
3001 Three Surveys on Capital Punishment
3002 Embarrassments
3006 Hat Wearing Habits
3008 Who are the Astrologers?

3012 Children out of School
3017 Employment of Women
3018 Opinion Forming
3027 Church Going
3030 Mantelpieces
3036 Queueing
3037 Pattern of Smoking Habits
3038 Standards of Living
3045 British Sport
3065 Home Decorating and Repairing
3066 Party Games
3073 The Middle Class

Year 1949
3085 The £.s.d. of Home Saving
3086 Loving-Making in Public
3087 Trade Marks
3091 Contemporary Churchgoing
3095 The New Look
3096 Dreams
3097 Baby Foods
3098 A Washing Machine
3105 Radio Listening and Attitudes towards Rediffusion
3106 Television Beginnings
3107 Ideal Families
3108 Chemist Shops
3109 National Health Service
3131 Paint, Colour and the Housewife
3140 The National Health Service
3142 Meet Yourself on Sundays
3143 Washing Habits
3150 Teenage Girls
3162 Radio Personalities
3180 The M.P. and his Constituency
3181 Soft Drinks
3183 New Year Resolutions
3190 Worming Medicines (Dogs)
3192 Man and his Cigarette

Year 1950
3200 Upper and Middle Class Soup Eating Habits
3201 Retailer Attitudes
3202 Sweet Pickles
3210 Toilet Preparations for Men
3211 National Lotteries
3220 Shampoos (for Dogs)
3231 Courtesy Shopping
3242 Filter Tip Cigarettes
3244 Some Attitudes to Life
3245 Cookers (electric)
3249 Four Years of Squatting
3255 "In a Plain Envelope"
3258 Music Hall Humour
3259 Army and Navy Stores
3261 Breakfast Menus
3280 Crying at the Pictures
3284 Members of Parliament
3291 Listening to Music
3295 Three Orange Squashes—a Taste Test

Year 1951
3305 Summer Holiday
3311 "Honest" Theft
3315 Stone of Scone
3316 Handmade Goods
3317 Anti-Semitism
3320 Garden Fertilisers
3322 Sport in Britain
3325 Drunkenness in Five Towns
3326 Betting and the Derby
3335 South Bank Exhibition
3336 Domestic Dislikes
3342 Three Methods of Assessing Attitude to Coloured People
3350 Bird Nesting
3357 Stout Drinking

Year 1952
3361 Baby Cereals
3371 Heaviness of Beers and Stouts
3387 Electric Clocks
3390 Going to the London Zoo
3392 Commodity Survey
3395 Laundry Customers
3399 Foundation Garments
3401 Buying at Chemists
3410 Recognition of Rayon
3424 Proprietary Medicines
3425 Glassware

Year 1953
3441 Home Sewing
3447 Nylons
3453 Shaving Market
3455 Television Set Buying
3465 Free Enterprise
3466 Cod Fillets
3475 Clarks of Retford
3480 Laundry Summary Report

Year 1954
3490 Refrigerators
3494 Oven Table Glass
3500 Knitting Habits
3503 Marks and Spencer
3505 Frozen Foods
3508 Drinking Habits of Young People
3510 Drink Advertising
3515 Sweets
3535 Habits and Tastes in Mineral Waters—II
3536 Motorists' Panel

Year 1955
3540 Design Readership
3546 365 Handkerchiefs
3555 Clarks of Retford—Customer Survey
3560 Suet
3562 Furnishing Fabrics
3570 Recruitment of Dentists
3571 Jewelry Sales
3574a Cameras
3576 Rediffusion—lost customer
3597 Water Heaters

Year 1956
3600 Capital Punishment
3610 Fish Liver Oils
3614 Drapers Chamber of Trade
3639 The Market for Furniture
3646 Baked Beans
3653 Frozen Fish
3654 Ford's—Prefect and Anglia
3660 Prestige Advertising
3366 Southern Region British Railways
3367 Dyes
3670 Attitudes to Stout
3671 Men's Shoes
3672 Peace and the Public
3674 Boys' Shirts
3675 Attitudes of Young Middle-Class Dog Owners
3681 Cosmetics
3690 Travel Sickness
3705 Design Centre
3711 Housewife's Day 1956
3713 London Hotels
3730 Circuses
3752 Branded Food Products
3753 Dry Cleaning

Year 1958
3756 Personality Types and Smoking
3762 Saturday Reading of Newspapers
3767 Coffee
3769 Glucose Products
3772 Cigarettes (Class "B")
3775 Readership of University Students
3777 Pet Ownership Attitudes
3788 Why do Wives go to Work?
3790 Tableware
3817 Photographic Display
3818 Laundry Continuous Index

Year 1959
3825 Teenage Shirts
3828 Household Soap
3830 Foot Treatment
3831 Ice Cream
3835 Attitudes to Bread
3838 Bookshops
3840 Pork Joints
3863 Attitude to Gardening and Gardening Products
3871 Cats
3882 British Typewriters
3883 Pies and Sausages
3888 Instant Coffee

POSTSCRIPT

by

Professor Charles Madge

POSTSCRIPT
by
Professor Charles Madge

WHEN TOM HARRISSON wrote to me about the project for a *Britain Revisited* volume, I was about to leave for South-East Asia. So he asked if I would write, as a postscript, some thoughts on what had happened, since 1937, to the ideas that lay behind Mass-Observation in its early form.

In our first joint pamphlet, Tom and I put on record what we then felt to be a difference in our points of view. It seems less important now, but is just worth recalling. We wrote:

"Tom Harrisson believes that Mass-Observation, by laying open to doubt all existing philosophies of life as possibly incomplete, yet by refusing to neglect the significance of any of them, may make a new synthesis. This may lead to something less fierce, more understanding and permanent, than the present miserable conflicts of dogmatic faiths in race, politics, religion. The whole study should cause us to reassess our inflated opinions of our progress and culture, altering our judgments on others accordingly. We must find the range of mass agreement and variation, the L.C.M. and H.C.F. of man, between which lies his practical potentialities.

"In the other author's opinion, Mass-Observation is an instrument for collecting facts, not a means for producing a synthetic philosophy, a superscience or super-politics.... It is not enough in itself to ensure mass-regeneration, and has no pretence to being the salvation of anybody, either spiritually or politically."

Tom was more definitely and consistently unwilling to take sides politically than were I and some others of the small initial group at that time. However we, no less than he, were motivated by the need to understand "ordinary people", in relation to the great issues of politics. All of us felt keenly the need for more, many more facts of almost any kind, about average human behaviour and belief. Our indiscriminate interest was reflected in the hotch-potch character of M-O publications. Nor were we unduly disturbed by criticism of this "natural history" approach. Let those who spend so long discussing methodology now show us what they can do with it, we were inclined to answer. In the meantime, we offered our mixed bag of observation, for what it was worth.

The Worktown programme, if it could have been pushed a bit further, might have left a precipitate of more coherent principles. As it is, M-O did indeed begin to look more closely, and make others look more closely, at what politics and religion mean in the world of "ordinary people". Though since 1937 much interesting work has been done in the sociology of religion and in political sociology, there is still room for more of the direct observation and close contact with its material which were the strength of the Worktown programme.

What we were looking for was a more imaginative and active kind of sociology than seemed available at the time. It is unfortunately true, at any rate in Britain, that academic sociology has by and large been timid, bookish and unproductive. Tom Harrisson used to proclaim this in a way which was meant to annoy the academics and which quite often succeeded. "It was a shock", he wrote after the war, "to come home in September 1946 and find sociology marking time on 1937, despite its new opportunities and responsibilities." This was in "What is Sociology?", published in *Pilot Papers* (Vol. 11, No. 1, March, 1947), a lively discussion—I think perhaps the best that Tom has written—most of which is still pertinent in 1961. I noted editorially at the time that it was more tolerant in tone than his writings of ten years earlier. I note now, in *Britain Revisited*, a further mellowing and many more references to the work of academic social scientists. This is welcome enough, especially in so far as it shows that there really is more work nowadays worth referring to.[1]

Nothing could be more futile at this stage than a fragmentation of social science and research into factions. Criticism, from inside and outside, will always be necessary, but breadth and tolerance are quite essential. Some of our most able sociologists are constantly forgetting this. It is easy enough to minimize and denigrate such small achievements as we have so far to our credit. The motives, methods and orientations of social scientists are diverse and will continue to be so. Tendencies to convergence have been claimed but divergence remains

---

[1] But there is still something constricted and infertile about the research output of University departments in the social sciences. It was left to another free-lance, Michael Young, to break new ground by promoting the Institute of Community Studies. The work which he and his colleagues have done in Bethnal Green, Woodford and elsewhere has the first-hand quality that we sought in M-O, and shows clearly what can be gained from independence.

the more obvious phenomenon. What is needed is a greater willingness to look for what is helpful in the work of others.

M-O was born in the midst of political perturbations, but it was not a political movement. It grew from the interest, that was shared by politically committed and uncommitted, in *"the objective description of human society and behaviour"* (I quote the phrase from Tom's article in *Pilot Papers*). "Objective description" can only begin from suspended intolerance; and once begun it leads in the long run to the wider tolerance that comes from wider knowledge. This was the very sound basis of the philosophy that Tom put forward in the quotation from the first M-O pamphlet cited above. Personally I soon found it impossible to combine political with sociological activity. Even as a socialist, I felt I must put sociology first. There have been many varieties, many solutions of this personal dilemma. It did not confront Tom Harrisson in quite the same way but in due course he was involved—and with notable distinction—in the fighting that replaced the political slogans of the thirties.

Across the map of world society—the total object of sociological study—a major intolerance still spreads itself today in the shape of the cold war. Whereas in the thirties uncertain rationality faced militant unrationality, in the fifties two rationalistic ideologies have been contending with each other. In this there might lie some hope for the future if enough objectivity could be kept alive on either side of the political frontiers. Sociology in all its forms could have a great potential part to play in this, provided it could be objective enough and its findings pervasive enough. In this respect the central idea of M-O has all its original meaning and force, and more.

In the thirties, poetry and politics and nascent sociology grew confusedly side by side. In the fifties, poetry and politics had lost, at any rate in Britain, the revolutionary impulse of the thirties. Sociology was slowly growing, in an institutional sense; but it was mostly something to talk about rather than an act of exploration. The fifties were in the doldrums, intellectually and aesthetically. But from the point of view of "ordinary people", in Britain and in many other countries too, it was a good decade. Industrial populations were better fed, better housed, better educated, better informed, had more money to spend, were more widely travelled than ever before. This was the "change" that was most apparent in Britain revisited. The M-O studies of the thirties, for all their shoe-string methodology, provided a base-line for comparison which by itself justifies them now. The changing colours in the streets, the changing shapes of tombstones, these visual elements caught the eye of observers for whom such observation was not just an amusing exercise in triviality. Some sort of a net had been spread to catch that fleeting, glinting apparition, the essence of the time. For this I think we may still be glad that M-O was partly literary and artistic in its origins.

As for what Tom has called the "unchange" in Worktown and elsewhere, this is a subject that needs careful, patient, penetrating study. The forays of M-O can hardly do more than draw attention to it, but this too is valuable. Traditions, institutions, cultural personalities, these are not changeless but so far as observation goes, they often are extremely slow to change. Never have they had so much battering from new stimuli, new technology, new methods of communication. How are they holding out? How long will they continue to hold out? What sort of unknown infra-structure of human need are they providing for? As the rational world unfolds, the remaining pockets, atavisms, resurgences, rephrasings of the non-rational in Britain assume a heightened significance for the observer. They have always been the concern of M-O, and M-O methods are well suited for studying them.

The ideas that lay behind M-O in its early form seem now from one point of view not to have been very clever or practical. The performance of M-O does not seem quite commensurate with those early ambitions. The ferment of those days has given way to the "cool" era of careerism, one-upmanship and cautiously qualified opinions. But the scope of M-O seems on re-appraisal to have been excellent. Compared with stodgier, if steadier, sorts of social inquiry, it assumed that a wide range of human phenomena had serious significance, and it opposed a narrowing of the spectrum of scientific concern. This in retrospect seems to have been a worth while position to establish in the thirties, a position which deserves to be re-established in the sixties. By now there may be more chance of an independent organisation, like the early M-O, remaining independent, carrying out the kind of reconnaissance for which it is so flexible an instrument, and co-existing amicably with academic sociology.

INDEX

INDEX

Asahi Evening News, 21
Addison-Wesley, 91
Allwood, Brian, 21
Armchair Science, 17
Atkin, Rayner, 13, 28, 178
Atkinson, Hindley, 107
"Atticus" 206

Baker, F., 217
Baring, Lady Rose, 153
Barker, Colonel, 12, 148-9, 151
Beaver, Sir Hugh, 168
Beaverbrook Press, 209
Bell, Graham, 21
Benney, Pear and Gray, 91
Bernstein, Sidney, 21
Bevins, Rt. Hon. R., M.P., 206
Bickerstaffe, John, 144
Birmingham Evening Dispatch, 16
Bleehan, Lena, 268
Board of Trade, 171
Bonny, John, 148
British Birds, 89
British Medical Journal, 200-2
British Railways, 197
British Trust for Ornithology, 89
Brown, Ivor, 17
Brumwell, J. R., 21, 267
Butcher, Kay, 268
Butler, D. E., and Rose, R., 89, 91, 104
Butlin, Billy, 148

Campbell, S. M., 200
Camus, 56
Carter, G., 21
Cathode, 133
Cawson, Frank, 89
Clarke, Alan, 151
Cocker, Dr., 144
Cogan, Alma, 153
Collier, John, 63
Converse, P. E., 91
Co-op., 39, 101
Council for Nature, 20
Cramp, Stanley, 20, 89
"Critic" (Kingsley Martin), 244, 268
Crossman, R. H. S., 56
Crowther Report, 35
Currier, Roland, 178, 268

Daily Express, 16, 166, 229, 249, 254
Daily Herald, 17

Daily Mail, 17, 257
Daily Mirror, 254
Daily Telegraph, 104, 133, 254
Daily Worker, 16, 234
Derby, Earls of, 186
Ditchfield, 217
Doll, R., 200
Driberg, Tom, 21, 205

Economist, 254-5
Economist Intelligence, 171
Empson, William, 15
England, Leonard, 21, 201, 267
Everett Jones, A., 21, 267
Eysenck, Prof. H. J., 201-2

Faith, Adam, 148, 153
Farnworth, 89, 91-4, 97-9, 102, 105, 117
Ferraby, John, 21
Firclough, Alderman, 164
Fisher, James, 20
Fisher, Prof. R. A., 201
Fitter, Richard, 20
Formby, George, 148
Frazer, Sir James, 216
Fremlin, Celia, 21

Galbraith, Prof. G. K., 88
Gascoyne, David, 15
Gosnell, Prof. H. F., 91
Guardian, Manchester, 233, 254, 260
Gulliver, Eric, 268
Gypsies, 152

Harris, Leonard, 21
Harrisson, Barbara, 133, 178
Harrisson, Tom, 20, 27, 29, 197, 206, 265
Heywood, Sir Reginald, 143-4
Hill, A. B., 200
Hirst, Diana, 28
H.M. Customs and Excise, 171
Hoggart, Richard, 55
Holland, Bill, 151
Hood, Walter, 69, 89
Howarth, Herbert, 89, 268

Hoy, Doris, 268
Hulton Survey, 200
Hutchinson, George, 21
Huxley, Francis, 133, 178
Huxley, T. H., 63
Huxley, Sir Julian, 17

Illustrated, 254
Institute of Psychiatry, 201

Jackson, Peter, 197
Jennings, Humphrey, 15, 109
Jones, A. Everett, 21, 267

Kirwan, Larry, 28
Kronhauser, W., 91

Lack, Dr. David, F.R.S., 21
Lancashire Daily Post, 16
Lane, Sir Allen, 17
Lane, Margaret, 229
Latham, Bernard, 268
Lazarsfeld, Berenson, McPhee, 91
Legge, Stuart, 15
Leverhulme, Viscount, 26, 28, 31, 86, 205
Lipset *et al.*, 91
Listener, 16, 254
Low, David, 233
Lyster, Michael, 268

Madge, Prof. Charles, 15, 17, 26, 28, 109, 197, 216, 275, 277
Malinowski, Prof. Bronislaw, 197
Marks and Spencer, 35
Milne, R. S., and Mackenzie, H. C., 91
Ministry of Transport, 39
Montague, F., 17
Moore, Henry, 156
Morrison, Lord, 107

National Institute of Adult Education, 40
Naughton, Bill, 109-10, 132-4, 178, 212, 215
New Statesman, 15-16, 229, 236, 244, 254
News Chronicle, 17, 333
Nicholson, Max, 20
Night and Day, 17
Nuffield Foundation, 88, 205

Oakley, Dr. Kenneth, 196
Observer, 17, 20, 88, 164, 254
Oliver & Boyd, 201

Oppenheimer, Dr. R., 21
Orwell, George, 26

Pamplin-Green, Mr. and Mrs., 268
Parker, Ralph, 148
Pease, Humphrey, 20
Penguin Books, 17, 206, 216, 253
Pepper, Charles, 21
Petulengro, 152, 158
Picasso, 132
Picton, Richard, 21
Picture Post, 254
Piercy, Ivan, 268
Poskitt, F. R., 268
Powell, Dilys, 16, 132

Raine, Kathleen, 5, 14, 15, 24, 142, 228
Rhodes, E., 91
Rowntree, Seebohm, 187-8
Royal Geographical Society, 28
Ruddock, Dr. Ralph, 40

Schwartz, George, 5
Searle, Ronald, 269
Selley, W. T., 40
Silvey, R., 247
Singleton, Frank, 268
Simon, Lord S. of Wythenshawe, 21
Sommerfield, John, 174, 179, 181, 184, 194
Spectator, 16
Spender, Humphrey, 11-13, 20, 45, 61, 133, 178
Steele, Tommy, 160, 264-6
Stiffkey, Rector of, 150
Stocks, P., 200
Stonier, G. W., 16
Summerskill, Dr. Edith, 107
Summerson, John, 236
Sunday Pictorial, 255
Sunday Times, 16, 132-3, 206, 254-5
Symons, Julian, 269

Tarrant, Mollie, 21, 201, 267
The Times, 16, 34, 133
Thornber, Rev. William, 143
Time and Tide, 16
Tingsten, Prof. H., 91, 93
Todd, Ruthven, 15
Tomlinson, Rt. Hon. George, 11, 89
Tonge, 91, 93-4, 97
Toynbee, Arnold, 56
Trevelyan, Julian, 13, 20, 27, 45, 133, 178, 205, 269
Tribune, 16
Turner, W. J., 269
Tussaud's, 158

Umney, Nell, 178, 268

Vince, Pamela, 268

Watts, Stephen, 164
Waugh, Evelyn, 17
Which?, 172
Wickham, Michael, 12, 20, 178, 222

Wiggin, Maurice, 16, 133
Willcock, H. D., 21, 267
Willesden Chronicle, 236
Woman, Woman's Own, 255
Woolf, Myra, 201
Worktown Evening News, 39, 40, 133, 268
Wyatt, Woodrow, 15-16, 197, 214, 269

Famous people exhibited in wax (p. 159), mentioned in overheards (Chapters 9, 10, etc.), seen in royal settings (Chapter 14), occurring in conversations and questionnaires (Chapters 16, etc.) or otherwise obliquely anywhere, are not indexed unless also relevant in another context. See also those thanked in the last but one paragraph on p. 268, arranged alphabetically.